THE WORLD OF NUMISMATICS

GENERAL EDITOR: PETER A. CLAYTON, F.S.A.

Byzantine Coins

by P. D. WHITTING

G.P. PUTNAM'S SONS
New York

First published in the United States of
America in 1973 by G. P. Putnam's Sons,
New York, N. Y. 10016

Copyright © 1973 by Office du Livre,
Fribourg.

Published simultaneously in Canada
by Longmans Canada Limited, Toronto.
Library of Congress Catalog Card Number:
73-76714
SBN 399-11028-3

Printed in Switzerland

CONTENTS

5

APPENDICES

FOREWORD

This book could not have been written and indeed would have had little purpose without the original contributions made to the subject by Professor Philip Grierson and Michael Hendy, with both of whom I have enjoyed the privilege of friendship. Naturally neither must be held responsible for the way in which their work has been used.

Practically all the illustrations have been taken from coins in the collection of the Barber Institute of Fine Arts at Birmingham University, and I wish to thank the Trustees for their permission to make use of them and also Timothy Boatswain and Eric Taylor for their skilful and ever ready cooperation in the work involved. I am most grateful to the Centre for Byzantine Studies at Dumbarton Oaks for permission to use their photographs, Nos. 140, 141, 293, 308, 309 and 310; to the Trustees of the British Museum for Nos. 102–104 and 454, 455; to Peter Donald for photographs of his coins, Nos. 143–145, and for his drawing of Ian Roper's coin on p. 72. Finally, this book was written at a time of great personal strain and I wish to thank our General Editor, Peter Clayton, for his considerate

and helpful attitude at all times as well as acknowledging his technical expertise.

This is a period of discovery and change in Byzantine numismatics, and while this book was in production an excellent catalogue extending over the period 491 to 1204, *Monnaies byzantines de la Bibliothèque Nationale*, by Cécile Morrisson was published and should be added to the titles recommended in Chapter II. I hope that this book will help readers both to understand what is going on and to take the subject further on their own initiative, as well as perhaps opening a window on a fascinating period in which much of enduring beauty was produced. I believe some Byzantine coins to have been amongst these objects of beauty and comparable with the better known work done in mosaic, ivory or cloisonné enamel.

Philip Whitting

BOOK I.   MAKING A START

I. WHY CHOOSE BYZANTINE COINS?

The words byzantine and Byzantine Empire are not always familiar or precisely understood amongst people generally; indeed there has been a long and inconclusive battle over the name of the Empire and as to what chronological span it should cover. Should it be called the Later Roman Empire, the Eastern Roman Empire, the Lower Empire (*le Bas-Empire* with its implications of later and less reputable than the Roman) or just the Byzantine Empire? Should it begin at A.D. 330, 395, 476, 527, 610 or even later? These are points for academics in search of precision and need not concern the collector and student of Byzantine coins, except to remind him that it is as well to know something of the background and to define his own sphere of interest—both matters to which a return will be made later in this chapter.

The growing popularity of the Byzantine series amongst coin collectors is a recent phenomenon which prompts enquiry into what may have brought it about. Undoubtedly there is an element of investment value as coins can be both works of art and antiques which, under modern conditions it seems, often prove more attractive to investors—great and small—than market stocks and shares. The Byzantine series provides a prolific gold coinage with many rarities and some outstanding works of art, although little so obviously attractive to the investor or art collector as the Greek or even the Roman Imperial and English Hammered series have done. Byzantine coins of all metals have been drawn more slowly than others into the maelstrom of fantastic price rises but are now as affected by it as any other series. By the 1960's there had been a dramatic change from the immediately post-war period when collectors were few with plenty of coins to choose from, at prices not greatly increased from 1928 when Hugh Goodacre included them in his book, or 1930 when the Ratto sale, with its immensely valuable catalogue, took place. As a rough estimate compared with 1945 a common gold solidus will fetch today some ten times as much and a mixed lot of copper in average condition about twenty times as much.

It was a growing number of collectors seriously interested in the series that began to cause scarcity, particularly of copper pieces, and so began to set prices rising. Investors, more interested in gold and silver, brought rapid price increases which have been recently reflected—often with fantastic effect—in copper. It is now difficult for the increasing body of interested collectors to find large sale lots of copper, the sorting of which is of such educational value both to collectors and students: coppers tend to appear singly or in small lots averaging high prices. This is the more surprising as Byzantine copper is being found in East Mediterranean lands in large quantities, particularly in the Lebanon, Syria and Israel, though in quality of preservation it tends to be poor, as indeed it normally is everywhere. Thus all collectors are suffering, but the way of the beginner is particularly hard. What is interesting is that new collectors are still coming in and persisting; in short, Byzantine coins are attractive in themselves.

What is it that attracts collectors? Perhaps first of all should be placed the element of exploration. This is a 'new' series without a long history of collectors and a large literature. There is still much to be discovered by anyone with a good eye and prepared to do a little studying on the background. Indeed, Byzantine studies even at the highest level have had no great following in Western Europe, except in France which took the lead in this respect in the seventeenth century and again at the end of the nineteenth century. Today much work is being done on Byzantine history and art in Britain as elsewhere and anyone interested, such as the coin collector, can get help which even a generation ago was far from easy to find. There is still much room for research and discovery —to take but one aspect—by professional scholars and amateur numismatists alike.

The collector who sees himself dealing with one of the artistic products of its day and with a circulating medium of exchange, subject to the same vicissitudes as his own, can find plenty to interest himself, and often the scholar as well. The Englishman today who has seen in succession the 1 ▸ farthing and the halfpenny demonetized 2 ▸▸ and even the long famous penny changed out of all recognition, can view the same processes at work on fractions of the Byzantine follis in the sixth and seventh centuries. The lower denominations phase themselves out in the finds at the great excavations at Corinth and Athens for instance: under Tiberius II it is the five nummia piece that is becoming scarce, under Maurice the ten nummia and under Constans II even the half-follis of twenty nummia rarely appears. Professor Philip Grierson has suggested that the folles issued at Cherson by Maurice, large pieces marked 8 (× 5) nummia, may have been part of an 95, 96 official plan to demonetize the single nummion or nummus, in favour of a 5 nummia unit.

Popular unwillingness to discard a well known coin type was well demonstrated in Britain when the 'Britannia' type, banished from the decimal coinage had to be brought 3 ▸ back to preside over the 50 new pence 4 ▸▸ piece equivalent to a ten shilling note: it was an improbable role. But people do become attached to types and the people of the Byzantine Empire did so more than most; they clung to types no longer needed which degenerated until utterly without meaning. The reverse of the follis of 5, 6 Michael II and Theophilus (described on p. 78), may be taken as an example: it is

1, 2 Marcian *(450–7)*. *Gold solidus*. Obv. *Helmeted and armoured bust with lance over right shoulder—the same type as that introduced by Constantius II a century before. The emperor is entitled Dominus Noster (DN) and Pius Felix (PF).* Rev. *Victory (a female personification) advancing to the left holding a long cross. The legend reads ' Victory of the Emperors ', the GGG representing Augustorum in the plural. The last letter H (8) is the number of the officina (diam. 19 mm.).*

3, 4 Anastasius *(491–518)*. *Gold solidus*. Obv. *The emperor's bust is the same as that of Marcian in No. 1 but the shield on the left shoulder shows more clearly its device of a horseman spearing an enemy. In the legend PF has been changed to PP for perpetuus, i.e. ' the undying Emperor '.* Rev. *A repeat of the reverse type of Marcian in No. 2. The legend lacks an officina letter and the two stars indicate the mint of Thessalonica. CONOB in the exergue here means precisely the standard (obrysum) of Constantinople gold, not the mint itself (diam. 21 mm.).*

14

what the French term a *type immobilisé* and as such can be awkward when met by an inexperienced collector. In the Byzantine series types tend to last a long time and changes therefore become important: can they be explained by a particular event or perhaps a change in official policy? Questions like these may bring home the wide field which there is to explore and the kind of awareness as to modern coinage that can help the collector in understanding it.

Wide is surely the right word to describe the field when the extent of the Byzantine Empire and of its coins in space and time is taken into account. The collector is offered a vast choice between assembling coins for a general historical outline for over a millennium or for periods, for mints or for demonstrating special problems: this is surely another of the attractions of the series. The Byzantines were the inheritors of the Roman Empire and from the coin angle, as from many others, it is difficult to discern any clear-cut dividing line. Normally that line is seen in the reign of Constantine the Great when the capital city—Rome had long since ceased to be that—was fixed in one spot again, in the 7 especially rebuilt city of Constantinople (A.D. 330). Coincidentally with this, Christianity was given a privileged status in the Empire as indeed the coins show, though with a hesitancy only to be expected in so conservative a medium. In the West the barbarian tribesmen, Franks and Anglo-Saxons amongst them, swept over the Roman frontiers and the bases for settled government had to be rebuilt from the foundations. The Eastern part was able to stave off disaster, though it was only by handing over control of the army to barbarians with all the insecurity which that entailed. Early Byzantine emperors—and notably Justinian I (527-65)—always had in view the restoration of the frontiers of the old Roman Empire, but it consistently proved beyond their powers. Geographically then the Byzantine Empire involved the Eastern Mediterranean from Italy to Dalmatia, the Balkans, Asia Minor, Syria and Palestine (where the age-old war with Persia which had lasted from the days of the Roman Republic was still being carried on), Egypt and, for short periods, the Western Mediterranean littoral. The Black Sea was important for trade and there was a settlement in the Crimea at Cherson whence a watch could be kept on the north, where Mongol tribesmen were coming in waves along the rolling steppe route as the area of their homeland dried out into the desert that it is today. Through appalling vicissitudes the imperial heartland lay in the Balkans and Asia Minor: yet throughout it is well to remember the factor of changing size—from something like the Roman Empire at its greatest, to a beleaguered capital and a few towns with their hinterlands which was all that remained in the last century of the Byzantine Empire's existence.

If the beginning of the Empire is taken as 330, then it lasted 1123 years until its fall in 1453 to the Osmanli or Ottoman Turks under Mehmet II. The Byzantine Empire therefore may be compared with other and seemingly more ephemeral multinational empires like those of the Mongols, the British (which goes back less than 400 years) or the Soviet Union. Historians do not all agree as to beginning the Byzantine Empire in 330, depending on the aspects of the Roman Empire that they are stressing: so great an institution did not disappear in a day. The famous consulship which meant so much under the Republic did not disappear indeed until the seventh century, but for centuries it had ceased to be meaningful. The date 330 is a useful one because so much that was to be the making of the Byzantine Empire occurred in that year—the refounding of Byzantium as the capital city of Constantinople and the special status given to Christianity. Numismatically speaking it does not constitute an important point except in one respect—the weight of the solidus was changed. A far better point can be found in the reign of Anastasius I (491-518) when the 'characteristic' Byzantine copper coinage was introduced as will appear later; even so the gold coinage continued with a type begun under Constantius II well into the reign of Justinian I. Great numismatists such as de Saulcy, Warwick Wroth in the British Museum Catalogue and the editors of the Dumbarton Oaks Catalogue have made their starting point with Anastasius and this book is going to follow their lead. Sabatier and Tolstoi, amongst the great names in Byzantine numismatics, made their start at the end of the fourth century. Wherever the start is made it is impossible to neglect what went on in the fourth and fifth centuries even if the coinage then appears more Roman than Byzantine. In any event the coin collector can choose as he likes. He will find that some periods, like the reign of Justinian I, have left behind them a multitude of coins, others,

8, 1*, 2*
78*, 79*

like the eighth century, have left very few— each has its obvious attractions. In some periods history is fairly well established from literary sources, in others like the seventh century there are many dark places where coins can perhaps throw light.

This has led to a third attraction of the Byzantine series which lies in the rich field of research and interest provided by the relationship of coins to history and art. In the twentieth century there has been a growing appreciation of Byzantine art made the more active by ease of travel and the magnificent modern techniques of colour reproduction. Similarly, in a more restricted and mainly academic field, the significance for the West of the complicated and often very confusing history of Byzantium has been given more attention. Coins are at all times an important manifestation of contemporary art and in the days when precious metals were the accepted form of currency, coins reflected changing economic and political circumstances. The occurrence of debasement, whether in the reign of Michael IV at Byzantium or in that of Henry VIII in England, is of obvious significance. But coins can often be related very closely indeed to political, religious, military and economic circumstances, while all the time reflecting—often rather slowly —changes in artistic standards. This will be seen obviously enough in the reigns of Justinian II and Leo III. Coins can be even more useful when literary documentation is weak, as for instance in the reign of Heraclius.

454, 455

Mention of several emperors in this way brings to the fore some initial difficulties in the study of Byzantine coins. The history is so long that many dynasties are involved, many usurpations and a succession of rulers' names such as Isaac, Basil, Andronicus or Nicephorus which are unfamiliar. It is essential to see the panorama of Byzantine history with some clear fixed points for reference. The Empire was not steady and unchanging but constantly facing crises and undergoing tumultuous variations of expansion, contraction, usurpation and civil war. Some suggestions for reading

about this in connection with numismatics will be found in the next chapter, but it may be possible to indicate here something of the ebb and flow of events over more than a millennium. At the expense of over-simplification a diagram may be of assistance with the high points of apparent success on the left represented by the names of emperors and their dates, with periods of stress and their immediate causes on the right.

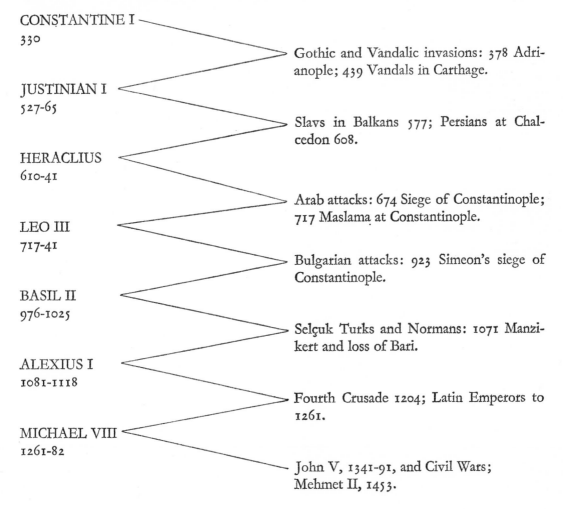

CONSTANTINE I
330

Gothic and Vandalic invasions: 378 Adrianople; 439 Vandals in Carthage.

JUSTINIAN I
527-65

Slavs in Balkans 577; Persians at Chalcedon 608.

HERACLIUS
610-41

Arab attacks: 674 Siege of Constantinople; 717 Maslama at Constantinople.

LEO III
717-41

Bulgarian attacks: 923 Simeon's siege of Constantinople.

BASIL II
976-1025

Selçuk Turks and Normans: 1071 Manzikert and loss of Bari.

ALEXIUS I
1081-1118

Fourth Crusade 1204; Latin Emperors to 1261.

MICHAEL VIII
1261-82

John V, 1341-91, and Civil Wars; Mehmet II, 1453.

In this long period of dramatic changes, however much the emperors may have wished to represent something immutable and rooted in the will of the Almighty, they found the task impossible. The student of the coins can follow many of these changes great and small in considerable detail. The ambitious programme of Justinian I for instance, and the inability to retain its momentum; the life and death crisis in Heraclius' reign and the emperor's successful—but only temporarily so—emergence in 629; or the effect of Iconoclasm under Leo III. He is for ever watching fluctuation, not 'the tedious and uniform tale of weakness and misery' as Gibbon would have us imagine. The significance of the contribution that coins can make in solving a number of outstanding problems in Byzantine history has only recently been recognized: the humblest collector, if he will master the background so as to place his pieces accurately in it, can play some part in these new discoveries. Particularly, coins can often provide significant portraits of the emperors as a useful visual aid to the understanding of the literary sources which tend to be bogged down in phraseology imitative of the ancient classical masters.

In studying both coins and the historical background the collector will at once run into another and peculiarly intransigent difficulty—the interchangeability of Greek and Latin terminology. First perhaps a word about the use of Greek on coins may be useful, for those without the language may feel that it poses an insuperable obstacle: it does not. One must know the alphabet, the numerals—in this case formed

5, 6 Michael II *(820–9). Copper follis, obverse and reverse. The emperor bearded and wearing a chlamys on the left; his son Theophilus beardless and wearing the loros on the right. The reverse is a type immobilisé with, by this date, almost everything meaningless. There was no need for the follis sign M as all copper coins were folles. On either side are relics of a date ANNO XXX from Constantine IV's time, and reversed. There was no officina Θ for copper (diam. 28 mm.).*

7 Constantine I *(324–37). Bronze medallion celebrating the dedication of Constantinople as capital of the Roman Empire in 330 after its refoundation six years before. The Constantinopolis type was adopted for small coins in ordinary currency between 336 and 340 (diam. 31 mm.).*

8 Constantius II *(337–61). Gold solidus, obverse. The three-quarter facing bust with spear over right shoulder is a new and destined to be long lived type: regularly in use until Justinian I, it was revived by Constantine IV (diam. 21 mm.).*

9, 10 Justinian I *(527–65). Copper follis, obverse and reverse. Year 12 (539) was the first year of the reformed issues with a facing bust, and the date added to the reverse. The coins were larger, heavier, more carefully designed and technically better produced. This piece is from officina 5 of the mint of Constantinople. The legend is entirely in Latin (diam. 37 mm.).*

11, 12 Leo III *(717–41). Gold solidus, obverse and reverse. On the obverse and bearded is ' Our Lord Leo, may he reign for many years '. On the reverse, is his son, beardless ' Our Lord Constantine '. This is a typical ' family coin ' of the iconoclastic period (726–843) in impressionist style. Odd letters from the Greek alphabet, like Є, appear amongst the Roman characters (diam. 21 mm.).*

5

6

7

8

9

10

11

12

13

14

15

16

17

18

19

20

21

22

23

24

13, 14 Alexius I *(1081–1118). Gold hyperper, obverse and reverse. A scyphate coin having Christ seated as the obverse where the legend begins ' May the Lord help ' and then continues on the reverse ' Alexius the Emperor of the family of Comnenus '. Alexius is viewed from close up and underneath, exaggerating the height of the body, and the decoration of his chlamys which is large on the right and much smaller when further away on the left (diam. 30 mm.).*

15, 16 Basil II *(976–1025). Copper follis, obverse and reverse. An anonymous coin (Class A(ii)) without the emperor's name and with only sacred legends—on the obverse ' Emmanuel ' and on the reverse ' Jesus Christ, the king of those who rule ' (diam. 32.5 mm.).*

17, 18 Constans II *(641–68). Copper follis of 643/4, obverse and reverse. Copper coins were token money and the size did not matter: compare this coin with Nos. 9, 10 and 15, 16 above—all are folles. This coin has Greek legends for the first time: ' By this sign [the Christogram held in the emperor's right hand] may you conquer ' on the obverse, and ' Recovery ' on the reverse. Regnal year III is on the left of the reverse and officina letter* **A** *beneath*

the **m**. *Note the casting lugs on either side of the flan (23 × 18 mm.).*

19, 20 Constantine I *(324–37). Two gold solidi, obverses. The first shows the normal right-facing profile bust of Roman emperors: mint of Ticinum dated 315. That on the right, from Nicomedia of 335, is the type referred to by Eusebius, the contemporary biographer of Constantine, as upward looking ' as though communing with God ' (diam. 19 and 21 mm.).*

21, 22 Manuel I *(1143–80). Billon trachy, obverse and reverse. Scyphate in form, the bottom die has a bust of the young Christ. The reverse shows Manuel beardless and wearing a chlamys with large tablion (see No. 449): it was part of his first issue (diam. 29 mm.).*

23, 24 Tiberius II *(578–82). Gold solidus, obverse and reverse. Until the reign of Justinian II, the emperor occupied the obverse, but when Christ was introduced as a normal coin type the emperor had to be relegated to the reverse, as in Nos. 21, 22. The cross on steps was a new type, subsequently becoming standard for a long period, introduced by Tiberius II (diam. 22.5 mm.).*

by letters—and a few titles (and their abbreviations) with some often repeated phrases. Coin legends through the ages and in all places tend to echo the same few necessary titles and facts such as the issuer's name and position, the denomination, date and place of mintage. Knowledge of the script with a vocabulary of a dozen words or so will take the coin enthusiast a very long way. A guide to this necessary minimum will be found on pages 300, 301.

What is interesting—and also confusing—in Byzantine coins is the gradual change from a purely Latin legend to a purely Greek one, beginning with changes in the letter forms. Gradually whole words are transliterated into Greek characters, others are translated and, as is the case in all series, it is the abbreviations that make matters more difficult. Take as a starting point the legend on the large folles of Justinian I, commonly found and large enough to be easily read as it is in Latin:

9, 10

D[ominus] N[oster] IVSTINIANVS P[er]P[etuus] AVG[ustus].
Our Lord Justinian for ever Emperor.

Under Justinian II (685-95) a legend reads still in Latin:

D[ominus] N[oster] IႶSTINIANႶS MႶLTႶS AN[nos].
Our Lord Justinian [may he live] many years.

The form of the V has changed and the engraver does not seem to have understood that it should read MVLTOS agreeing with ANNOS. This last phrase soon became abbreviated to MႶL and is often preceded

11

by the old P[erpetuus]A[ugustus], then reading PAMႶL. This development can be seen in the Leo III legend about thirty years later:

δ[omino] N[ostr]O LЄON P[erpetuo] A[ugusto] MႶL[tos Annos].
[May the Lord give] many years to our Lord Leo for ever Emperor.

In this, Greek letter forms δ (D) and Є (E) have been used as well as Ⴓ (V). This was a period of transition in which Greek letters and language were being used more officially. Later still in the eleventh century the legend of Alexius I is in Greek:

✝KE POHΘEI AΛEZIΩ ΔECΠOTH 13, 14 TΩ KOMNHNΩ.
May the Lord help Alexius the Emperor, of the family of Comnenus.

Things had moved a long way during the 550 years since Justinian I's time, so far as coin legends went. One may well ask what was the common language used by people in the new capital that Constantine the Great had made: it was in a Greek-speaking area—and had originally been a Greek colony in fact—but was full of Latin speaking civil servants from Italy and barbarian soldiers. At first there must have been a pretty clear-cut division, but gradually Greek (including a host of borrowed terms) became the single language. Already by Justinian I's time new laws were being promulgated in Greek 'so that they could be understood' and the coins give an interesting insight into the process of change.

For the student of coins the first thing is to transliterate accurately, and then to be on the watch for common words and abbreviations: such things as *DN* or *δN* for *Dominus Noster*, *AVTOKPATOR* used for Latin *Imperator* and referring to the emperor as commander-in-chief, later on *BACIΛEVS POMAIΩN* meaning King of the Romans and, above all:

IhSʯS	Jesus
XPISTʯS	Christ
BASIΛEʯ[S]	King
BASIΛEʯ[ΩN]	of those who rule

The first two lines are often abbreviated $\overline{IC}$ as in $\overline{IC}$ $\overline{XC}$ = May Jesus Christ $\overline{XC}$ *NI KA* Conquer.

Points like the interchangeability of *S* for *C* as of *V* for *ʯ* will soon present no difficulty and the constant repetition of these phrases and others like $\overline{MP\ \Theta V}$ *(MHTHP ΘEOʯ)* = Mother of God; or the numerals *M* (40), *K* (20), *I* (10), and *Є* (5) give the keen student plenty of easy practice.

The mixture of Greek and Latin on the coins themselves has had repercussions on the language used *about* Byzantine coins. Every author has difficulties in following with consistency the Latin or the Greek names. Some of these are virtually the same, like nummus (nummion), others quite different, like solidus (nomisma). Too great an attempt at consistency only makes for more difficulties and, unsatisfactory as it is, the terms used in this book will be inconsistent but those commonly used. One day the time will come for a generally recognized terminology and transliteration: but those who know anything of Muslim studies will appreciate how hard it is to achieve. Suffice it to say that the Byzantines had this problem themselves and often used transliterated Latin words in parallel with their own Greek ones, sometimes both together to make things clearer. What one wants to avoid is the mixing of Latin and Greek forms in a single word, *e.g.* the plural of nomisma must be nomismata, not a Latin plural like nomismae, which has been used. Equally, pieces of five nummia can be called pentanoumia or pentanummia, but not pentanummi. Thus there are pitfalls for one with no knowledge of Latin or Greek, but they need not be exaggerated; the making of plurals is one of them that needs to be watched.

Before looking at one or two other difficulties it would be as well to emphasise another great attraction of Byzantine coins. Most people, let alone coin collectors, find interest in the arts of one period or area if only because they differ so much, and one or other will, for no apparent reason, light up the imagination. This has happened on quite a large scale with Byzantine art amongst Western Europeans perhaps because of its contrast with what they normally see, especially in northern parts. Another reason may be that modern trends have been abstract, impressionistic and laying emphasis on the exploitation of the texture of materials used—all things in which Byzantine artists were also interested and in which they often excelled. For whatever reason, Byzantine art has now a wide following and a part of its artistic endeavour—too often neglected as such—lay in coin design and execution. At times coins demonstrate some of the best work being produced; in the late seventh century and particularly the Comnene period (1081-1185) coin designs can challenge the best work of even magnificently productive

382*-384*
280-283

times. The amazement of the Fourth Crusaders from the West when they saw 'the Queen of Cities' and its treasures in 1204 can still strike their successors, who have too often only heard the word 'byzantine' as an adjective of denigration or abuse.

With so much to interest and attract the collector, the difficulties involved in the Byzantine series pale into near insignificance. But there are two problems of a practical nature which need to be faced in the early stages. The coins need to be displayed in trays or cabinets and in two respects this can be awkward. First, there was at times a great difference in the size of pieces: the copper follis—a basic coin—can have a diameter of anything from 9, 10 44 mm. under Justinian I to 13 mm. under 17, 18 Constans II and wide variations within a single reign like that of Heraclius. Arranging coins in the meaningful order aimed at can be difficult, and generally needs a plentiful supply of trays. Secondly, for some three hundred and fifty years the Byzantines struck coins of all metals, but particularly gold and electrum, in concave 21, 22 'scyphate' or cup-shaped form. This naturally entails unusually deep holes in trays if scyphate coins are not to project and be damaged by rubbing. It is not always easy to assemble all the coins of one emperor in a single tray and decisions have to be made to suit the space available. Cabinets with interchangeable trays are helpful but generally do not solve all the problems.

Then of course there is the difficulty of obtaining Byzantine coins at all, to which reference has already been made. With prices high and competition for all classes

of Byzantine coins severe, the modern collector needs to be much more selective in his purchases: this in turn means that he should have more knowledge *before* buying anything. In this last he is now in a better position than a few years ago, as reprints have made older books, long out of print, available again and some new and very important publications are appearing. Even so, the difficulty of obtaining large unsorted lots of copper deprives the student of one of the best ways of mastering the series, alongside the chance of finding sometimes interesting small varieties previously unnoticed. The opportunity of studying such random collections of copper whenever they occur, should never be missed.

However surprised he may be at the thought in his early days, the collector of Byzantine coins is in the end all but forced to collect gold pieces as well as copper, simply because only so can he really see the artistry, and sometimes even the intentions, of the die engravers. Copper coinage was needed in vast quantities and was produced in haste with incredibly little attention to regularity in the flans or the placing 81, 82 of the types on them. Copper coins in *extremely fine* condition are normally scarce and often rare, commanding a price higher than many gold pieces: the latter exist in such great quantity that they are, in the general run, neither rare nor expensive, setting aside pieces in exceptional condition. Silver coins have always been difficult to obtain though some finds in recent years have considerably reduced their scarcity. The collector must realize at once that, except in gold, Byzantine coins in really good condition are hard to come by and that in copper he must never be surprised by—and often should be interested in—shockingly amorphous flans many times restruck.

From a practical point of view the coins most readily available on the market are of the sixth and seventh centuries, broadly those from the reigns of Anastasius to Constantine IV. After this, with two notable exceptions, Byzantine coins appear to be scarcer overall and in some reigns, both for silver and copper pieces, the flow appears to dry up almost completely. The 16, 109 exceptions are the copper Anonymous series issued between 969 and 1092 and the billon and copper scyphates of the later Comneni and Fourth Crusaders, both of which can be found in quantity in local museums and also in the sale room from time to time. Both series are full of interest and small varieties such as keen collectors revel in. Because of the glut of material available for the sixth and seventh centuries readers of these pages may find more emphasis on this period than on others. But these are the coins collectors are going to meet in their early days and the period was one in which the 'characteristic' Byzantine coinage took shape with the copper pieces of Anastasius and the gold of Justinian.

II. BOOKS AND BACKGROUND

It is usual for books to have their bibliographies and suggestions for further reading at the end, but for numismatists books are always so important and for Byzantine students and collectors so especially essential that a note on these topics is being introduced at an early stage. Increased knowledge means increased appreciation of the interest and relevance of coins, and for the beginner especially the ability to buy selectively. The Byzantine collector has to deal with coins struck over a millennium if the Empire is judged to have begun with Constantine the Great in the fourth century A.D., and the coins were current over the vast area of the Mediterranean and Black Sea litorals. Without some restriction and selectivity the beginner is bound to feel at sea—and more experienced collectors too. Safe anchorages in space and time are needed and can best be provided by knowledge available in books. In this series, more than most, books and maps are wanted to dispel so much that is unfamiliar: equally, the series still needs so much detailed study that background knowledge soon converts coins into active historical documents. They are documents not only illustrating what is known, but helping also

to lighten the many dark places in so long a period.

Professor G. Ostrogorsky's *History of the Byzantine State* (2nd edition 1963: Blackwell, pp. 514 and 8 maps) provides that rare treasure, a textbook of great authority covering the whole ground in a reasonable compass: it is invaluable. But as a start something shorter like Professor Joan Hussey's *The Byzantine World* (2nd edition 1961; Hutchinson, pp. 191 and 2 maps) may be found easier. Both books at their different levels of detail are easy to refer to for basic historical and geographical detail.

A handy general book with maps and illustrations is *Byzantium—An Introduction* (ed. Philip Whitting; Blackwell, 1971, pp. 178, 6 maps and 8 plates). The numismatist will find that he needs detail, often of the most minute kind, but these books should give him a command of the historical background sufficient to enable him to find his own way forward.

Fortunately there are now many excellent publications on Byzantine art, with a wealth of illustration making them immensely valuable to the numismatist seeking comparisons between coins and other media. Perhaps John Beckwith's *Art of Constanti-*

19, 20

nople (Phaidon, 1961, pp. 184, including 203 illustrations) and D. Talbot Rice's *Art of Byzantium* (Thames and Hudson, 1959, pp. 348, including 240 illustrations) may be singled out as admirable starting points. Numismatists are fortunate in this respect as Dr Henri Longuet's *Introduction à la Numismatique byzantine* (Spink, 1961, pp. 158, with 24 illustrations) provides a convenient bridge between coins and art generally with the emphasis firmly on coins: this is a thought provoking work based on subjects rather than chronology and of exactly the kind to challenge the collector too apt to rate his coins in date order to the exclusion of so much else. Though entitled an 'introduction' Dr Longuet's book is perhaps best considered as an introduction to second stage reading.

For a long time it was virtually impossible to purchase books specifically on Byzantine numismatics: they were few in number, old, out of print and, if found, immensely expensive. This is no longer the case owing to a number of recent reprints, though these can still be expensive. The classic books on the Byzantine series are:

F. de Saulcy: *Essai de Classification des Suites monétaires byzantines* (Metz, 1836: 2 volumes).

J. Sabatier: *Description générale des Monnaies byzantines* (Paris, 1862: 2 volumes). Reprint 1955.

W. Wroth: *Catalogue of Imperial Byzantine Coins in the British Museum* (London, 1908: 2 volumes). Reprint (in one volume) 1966.

——: *Coins of the Vandals, Ostrogoths and Lombards* (London, 1911). Reprint 1966.

J. Tolstoi: *Monnaies byzantines* (St Petersburg, 1912-14: unfinished, stopping at Basil I: in Russian). Reprint 1968.

All these books are well illustrated but that by Wroth (1908) used photographic illustrations for the first time with Tolstoi following suit. This was an important departure as line drawings are not always a satisfactory guide, whereas technical progress in photography and in reproduction have made photographs a fairly satisfactory substitute for the coins themselves, for purposes of study. But these excellent works in their day have been cast somewhat suddenly into the shade by the publication of the massive *Catalogue of the Byzantine Coins in the Dumbarton Oaks and Whittemore Collections* (Washington, vol. I, 1966, vol. II in two parts, 1969). There are at least three, probably four, more volumes to come and two of these are already well advanced: indeed what is virtually the introduction to one of them—M. F. Hendy's *Coinage and Money in the Byzantine Empire 1081–1261* (Washington, 1969)—is already in print. The passage of fifty years, including two world wars, since Tolstoi's publication began, in some sense accounts for the dramatic progress achieved in the Dumbarton Oaks Catalogue with its massive photographic backing: but this would be to underrate the dozen years of work and planning that went into it before the publication of volume I, and the impressive scholarship of its editors A. R. Bellinger and Philip Grierson and their many assistants.

Though their work is now becoming outdated Sabatier, Wroth and Tolstoi are still great names whose writings must be mentioned with enduring respect. All the books so far mentioned as specifically on coins are of an advanced type and there is not much to suggest for the collector wanting a briefer outline. Hugh Goodacre, in 1928–33, provided just this in his *Coinage of the Byzantine Empire* (Spink, pp. 361: 2nd edition with some additions, 1957) and though the historical introductions are of a lurid and romantic kind (and the values attributed to the coins now read like a joke in bad taste), the book is what it set out to be—simple, comprehensive and short. J. F. Lhotka's *Introduction to East Roman Coinage* (pp. 112: reprinted from the American magazine *The Numismatist*) is another highly practical beginner's book, crammed with information and deserving of a more attractive format.

Auction sale catalogues when carefully prepared and well illustrated often form an important part of the literature of any coin series. One of the earliest of these ' classic ' catalogues was that of a sale in 1930 at Lugano by Rudolpho Ratto with its 68 excellent plates: it is one of the most valuable books on Byzantine coins for everyone interested in the series, with or without experience. It has rightly had the honour, rare for a sale catalogue, of being reprinted (Amsterdam, 1959). Ratto in this sale was making a considered effort to put Byzantine coins more prominently on the map with collectors. At the time he did not seem to have achieved his aim, but he had sown good seed.

These are the basic books, but the keen collector will soon find himself looking for articles in the growing periodical literature of numismatics. In addition to names already mentioned, scholars and enthusiasts such as H. L. Adelson, T. Bertelè, T. Gerassimov, J. P. C. Kent, D. M. Metcalf, A. Veglery and G. Zacos, to quote but a few, are continually bringing new aspects of Byzantine coinage to the collector and student.

On the periphery of the Empire lay states with coinages influencing the Byzantines and also influenced by them—Cilician Armenia, the Sassanians in Persia and their Arab successors, the Turkish tribes such as the Artukids, Zangids and Osmanli, the Crusader states in Palestine, the Normans in Sicily and South Italy and Venice in the North, besides Lombards, Ostrogoths and Vandals. Here lies a fruitful and legitimate extension of the Byzantine interest, of fascinating variety and complexity. To all of them Dr Longuet, in his book mentioned above, provides a minuscule introduction precisely documented by illustration. In more detail G. Schlumberger's *Numismatique de l'Orient latin* (1878: reprinted Graz, 1954) is invaluable over a wide area of the field. R. Göbl's *Sasanidische Numismatik* (Brunswick, 1968; English edition, 1971) is expertly compact and P. Z. Bedoukian's *Armenian Coinage* (New York, 1962) is magnificently exhaustive but for the difficulty of tieing up inadequate reproductions in the plates with the text. Unfortunately the fascinating medieval Turkish issues of the eleventh to the fourteenth centuries have no books available for easy reference now that B. Butak's *Resimli Türk Paraları* (Istanbul, 1947) is out of print. The most easily obtainable book, and one very well illustrated for its time, seems to be Ghalib Edhem's *Catalogue des Monnaies turcomanes* (Ottoman Museum, Constantinople, 1894). For coins of the Normans in Sicily and much more of importance to the Byzantinist in medieval coinage, reference must be made to Giulio Sambon's *Repertorio Generale... 476–1266* (Paris, 1912); it is a book, like Ratto's Sale Catalogue of 1930, that one always needs to have handy. Lastly, the impact of the Arabs on the Byzantine Empire and the very difficult coinage resulting therefrom is dealt with by John Walker in his pioneering *Catalogue of the Arab-Byzantine and Post-Reform Umaiyad Coins* (British Museum, 1956).

The change in the popularity of Byzantine coins, involving both collectors and investors, with its effect upon the availability of coins and on prices is great enough to be termed revolutionary: but it only matches what has been going on in other series. The student of Byzantine coins is today faced with other changes so fundamental as to render well tried guides like Sabatier or Wroth in the British Museum Catalogue out of date on small details as well as bigger issues. For these changes alter the allocation of obverse and reverse for many pieces and also the names by which several pieces have been customarily known. The two points must be taken separately:

1) All collectors know the custom of accepting the royal or issuer's bust or figure as the obverse: they mostly know too that the bottom die (the 'anvil' or 'pile') lasted much longer than the upper ('trussel') die which was actually struck by the hammer. The die requiring the best workmanship was normally therefore the bottom 'anvil' one and it was generally used for the changing royal bust. So the royal bust was the obverse. But when coins were struck in the curious cup-shaped or 'scyphate' form widely used in the Middle Ages the bottom die, to retain the metal, must necessarily be the concave one and the 'trussel' consequently convex. Tens of thousands of Byzantine scyphates witness that the figure of Jesus or the Virgin, or occasionally a saint, occupies the convex side (pressed into the concave die)—that is the obverse—while the emperor takes his place on the concave side impressed by the upper convex die struck by the hammer—that is the reverse. Take a fairly common scyphate coin of Manuel I (1143-80) as described in the *British Museum Catalogue* II, p. 574, No. 38 (Pl. LXX, No. 3) under the general heading *Nomisma Type 9 (Bronze)*:

Obv: MANЧHΛ ΔЄCΠ. Bust of Manuel, bearded facing, holding in r. labarum, in l. globus cr.; wears crown with cross and jewelled dress with star in centre. Two borders of dots.

Rev: Bust of Christ, beardless facing, wearing tunic, mantle and nimbus cr. with ∴ in cross: in l. *volumen*; r. hand in benediction. In field $\overline{IC}$ and $\overline{XC}$. Two borders of dots.

The editor has slipped in describing Manuel as bearded which he clearly is not, nor is he on the similar coin illustrated here. Both illustrations make it clear that the bust of Christ is the convex side taken from the concave ' anvil ' die. Thus what is above described as the *reverse* should be the *obverse* and this is how the latest book covering these coins has it. The same type is thus described by M. F. Hendy in 1969 as:

Obv: $\overline{IC}$ – $\overline{XC}$ in field. Bust of Christ beardless and nimbate wearing tunic and colobion, holds scroll in left hand.

Rev: *MANYHA ΔЄCΠ* or var. Bust of emperor beardless, wearing stemma (crown), divitision and chlamys; holds in right hand labarum-headed sceptre and in left globus cruciger.

After this the two main varieties are detailed, based on jewels in the emperor's collar and pellets on the labarum shaft.

This coin has been taken as an example only, of the revolution that has recently taken place in coin descriptions. The process began much earlier with the dramatic change of obverse type from the bust of Justinian II (685–92) to the bust of Jesus (692–5), of which some detail must be given.

Up to and including the early years of the reign of Justinian II the Byzantine gold solidus, which was the keystone of the imperial monetary system, bore on its obverse the emperor's bust and on the reverse a design tending to remain unchanged over long periods, as did the

legend reading ' Victory of the Emperors ', followed by an officina mark denoting the precise part of the mint responsible for making the coin. First the design was a figure of Victory carrying a long cross, then in 578 a change was made to a cross on steps and this became standard from the reign of Heraclius beginning in 610. Both designs included *CONOB*—' of Constantinopolitan standard '. Occasionally co-emperors appeared on either side of the cross, but the basic cross on steps with *CONOB* beneath had remained unchanged for three-quarters of a century when Justinian II began his reign by using it once more. But in 692–5 Justinian made a second issue of solidi which are thus generally described in *British Museum Catalogue* II, p. 331 (Pl. XXXVII, No. 16):

Obv: *DIYSTINIANYS SERY CHRIST.* Justinian II standing facing bearded; wears crown with cross and long robes of lozenge pattern: holding in right hand a cross potent on 2 steps and in l., mappa; beneath *CONOP (sic).*

Rev: *IhSCRISTO REX REGNANTIYM.* Bust of Christ facing, with cross behind head; hair and beard flowing; wears tunic and mantle; r. hand in act of benediction; l. holds book of Gospels.

A glance at the illustration will show that what is described as the obverse has in fact many characteristics of the customary reverse, *e. g.* the cross on steps is there with *CONOB* beneath and the officina letter at

25, 26 Justinian II *(685–95). Gold solidus, obverse and reverse. This is the emperor's second issue (692–5) when Christ was given the obverse and the emperor shared the reverse with the old cross on steps type. The reverse legend reads 'The Lord Justinian Servant of Christ' and is followed by the officina number Δ: below the cross, CONOP (diam. 19 mm.).*

27, 28 Michael VI *(1056–7). Gold tetarteron, obverse and reverse. On the reverse the emperor, wearing the loros, uses the title 'Autocrator' which is unusual on coins. Weight 4.05 g. (diam. 19 mm.).*

29, 30 Michael VI *(1056–7). Gold histamenon, obverse and reverse. The reverse shows Michael wearing a chlamys crowned by the Virgin and again the title 'Autocrator': it is associated with military command and the emperor had been a general. Weight 4.39 g. The difference in types, both obverse and reverse, from those of the tetarteron (Nos. 27, 28) was probably an intentional underlining of the distinction in value (diam. 24 mm.).*

31, 32 Manuel I *(1143–80). Electrum trachy, obverse and reverse. A scyphate coin which Hendy ascribes to the fifth issue from Constantinople: its value was 1/3 of a gold hyperper (diam. 32 mm.).*

33, 34 Heraclius *(610–41). Gold solidus, obverse and reverse. The emperor, bearded on the left, with his son Heraclius Constantine, beardless on the right: each wears a chlamys fastened by a fibula on the right shoulder. The reverse has the cross on steps design which from this reign became standardized until that of Justinian II, but the old 'Victory of the Emperor' legend remains in spite of Victory herself having long disappeared from the type. The officina is 8 (diam. 21 mm.).*

35, 36 Heraclius *(610–41). Gold semissis, obverse and reverse. The profile bust was retained for fractions of the solidus in spite of the change to facing busts on solidi from the reign of Justinian I. The cross potent on globus becomes the normal indication of the semissis or half-solidus instead of the earlier Victory type (diam. 19 mm.).*

31   32

33   34

35   36

37

38

39

40

41

42

43

44

45

46

47

48

49

37, 38 Heraclius *(610–41). Tremissis, obverse and reverse. The rather squat cross potent becomes the usual indication of the tremissis or one third of a solidus, along with the continuous legend, instead of the earlier 'Victory advancing right' type (diam. 16.5 mm.).*

39, 40 Heraclius *(610–41). One-sixth of a solidus, obverse and reverse. These coins were exactly like tremisses except in weight, being in fact much thinner. This specimen weighs .72 g. They are rarely found today and perhaps suffered much damage in use and so had to be melted down (12.5 × 14 mm.).*

41, 42 Nicephorus III *(1078–81). Debased gold tetarteron, obverse and reverse. The legend includes his family name Botaneiates. Weight 4.01 g. should be compared with that of the histamenon Nos. 43, 44 (diam. 17 mm.).*

43, 44 Nicephorus III *(1078–81). Debased gold histamenon, obverse and reverse. This coin contains rather less than 8 carats gold and was struck shortly before the reforms of Alexius I. Its difference from the tetarteron is emphasized by its broad thin fabric and scyphate form, in addition to its weight 4.37 g. (diam. 29 mm.).*

45-47 *Lightweight solidi, reverses.* 45 *Justinian I (527–65), has in the exergue OBXX, i.e. 20 siliquae (weight 3.75 g.);* 46 *Maurice (582–602) OB+*, i.e. 22 siliquae (weight 4.06 g.);* 47 *Constans II (641–68), BOΓK, i.e. 23 siliquae (weight 4.28 g.) (diam. 18, 19.5 and 20 mm.).*

48, 49 Maurice *(582–602). Lightweight solidus, obverse and reverse. One of a series of lightweights of 23 siliquae distinguished by a star on both obverse and reverse: weight 4.27 g. This type in contrast with the others is not so obviously marked as being substandard in gold content (diam. 20.5 mm.).*

the end of the new type legend in which 'The Lord Justinian' is described as the 'servant of Christ'. But, additionally, the emperor at full-length is shown on the right holding the cross. The so-called reverse has the emphatic legend 'Jesus Christ the King of those who rule' round 25 the bust. Taking the two together, there can be no doubt that it is the reverse that shows the emperor and that the bust of Christ is intended as the obverse. The coin is not scyphate and so the dies do not help in this case, as with the coin of Manuel I.

It has been thought wise to go into some detail over this piece of Justinian II because *from this time forward the figures of Jesus, the Virgin or the saints are considered as the obverse today and pictures of the Emperors as the reverse.* Further confirmation that this is correct can be seen for instance on the gold coins of Alexius I (1081–1118) 13, 14 where the legend begins round the seated figure of Jesus, 'may the Lord help', and continues on the other side where the emperor (referred to correctly as 'emperor of the Comnenos family' in the dative case) stands frontally in his magnificence, touched above by the hand of God. Thus the Justinian II coin turns out to be important for all collectors of the series— as it is for historians too—and it can be studied in detail by those who wish in Professor Breckenridge's informative little book *The Numismatic Iconography of Justinian II* (New York, 1959). Today one often needs to be very careful in deciding which type of a given coin is the obverse, and even more careful in describing it to others, as what has been said above is not yet common ground. Although used in

Dumbarton Oaks publications, it is obviously not to be expected in earlier standard works such as Ratto, Tolstoi, the British Museum Catalogue or Sabatier, all books still used much in cataloguing.

2) Coin collectors do not normally reckon on having to look carefully at a coin before deciding on which is its obverse, nor would they normally hesitate over pronouncing on its name or denomination. But more detailed study in recent times, particularly by Philip Grierson and Michael Hendy has thrown the whole question of the names of Byzantine coins and the denominations of some of them, into the melting pot. Contemporaries in Constantinople and in the West did not always use the same terms and the custom of collectors has brought a strange and illogical mixture into currency. The complicated issues involved have not yet led to agreement but on some points at least a clear pattern has emerged and one quite different from previous usage. On so fundamental a matter it is once more essential to take up a little space in clarification.

The reader may well think that once the term solidus is abandoned for the key gold coin, the whole system becomes impossibly complicated. Nor is he far wrong as the Byzantines themselves came down to qualifying the single word used, in order to make sure: the nomisma was 'the most esteemed', 'the old', 'the new', 'the three-headed', 'the hyperper type', etc. But recent scholarship has done much to distinguish references to coins of different value and metal amongst these many names and the following notes may be found useful both in reading this book and for

general reference until something more complete is possible.

a) The solidus was the standard gold [1*, 2*] coin of the later Roman Empire and the name means 'whole', 'complete' or 'pure' (gold). This Latin term was often used by Greek writers—in the early centuries of the Byzantine Empire especially—for what they normally called a 'nomisma' (= coin) and sometimes more specifically a 'gold nomisma'. When, in 1966, Philip Grierson made an attempt to bring order into the jungle of names, he suggested that the term 'solidus' was a good one to use down to the reign of Nicephorus Phocas (963–9), although by [438*, 4] this time writers were regularly using 'nomisma'. The point is that a *new* gold coin lighter than the solidus was introduced at this time and it has to be distinguished. The distinction was by no means obvious at first but appears in the British Museum [305] Catalogue as one between coins of 'thick' (actually the new coin, though it looks more [303, 3] like the old solidus) and 'spread' fabric.

b) The new and lighter coin was called [27, 28] the nomisma tetarteron. These tetartera cannot be distinguished by eye until the later part of Basil II's reign—about fifty [300, 3] years after their introduction—and they continue through a series of debasements until the coinage reforms by Alexius I in 1092. The name means 'a fourth part', *i. e.* a piece of standard weight diminished by a quarter of a tremissis equivalent to 1/12 of the whole. After Alexius' reform the name 'tetarteron' continues but only for a copper coin taking the place of the old follis. [341, 3]

c) The term nomisma histamenon

(= standard) grew up after the introduction of the tetarteron, for a gold coin of standard weight though of progressively reduced fineness, the pieces referred to as of 'spread fabric' above. These pieces are the old solidi in a different form and the name histamena or stamena should be used for them until the reform of Alexius I introduced a new standard and a new name. It is at this stage that Greek names begin to multiply because of the changing fineness of metal. After the reform of Alexius the word—generally stamena—is loosely used for billon coins which should be called 'trachea'.

d) The hyperper (hyperperon) is a name found in many forms and describing many different coins; but it is specifically related to the basic gold coin of Alexius I's 1092 reforms—in British Museum Catalogue terms, a spread fabric nomisma. Many derivations have been suggested of which the most convincing is 'highly tried in the fire' or refined (gold). The name was retained for the large silver pieces of John V onwards until the end of the Empire when there was virtually no gold minted. In the intervening period the name should also be used for the gold (with silver and copper alloy) scyphates issued from the mints of the Empire of Nicaea and the early Palaeologan emperors after the recapture of Constantinople from the Latins in 1261. Thus the hyperper completes the series of standard Byzantine gold coins beginning with the solidus and followed by the nomisma histamenon.

e) One other name must be added to the list—the trachy—although it appears more commonly in other metals than gold,

especially electrum, billon and copper. The Greek word means 'rough' and is usually applied to scyphate coins in electrum or billon after the reforms of Alexius I had established the gold hyperper of 21 carats as the standard coin. Both electrum and billon trachea were referred to as 'white' so that they have to be distinguished by context or qualifying adjectives. Hendy refers to normal issues as 'electrum trachea' or 'billon trachea' being respectively 1/3 and 1/48 of the hyperper. It was Hendy who, from a maze of different names for trachea, established the essential relationship of the hyperper with its 1/3 and 1/48 pieces as the backbone of the reformed coinage, justified on metal content. He was thus able to reduce to order the mass of so-called 'bronze scyphates' so many of which were too badly struck to have legends that were legible or types that were precisely recognizable.

Other changes in the present day approach to Byzantine coinage are less obvious than the two just considered but no less important—on treatment of hoards, the emphasis on mints and periods of currency reform and the now universal acceptance of millimeters and grammes for measurement. All collectors must have noticed the emphasis currently placed upon hoards and the importance of their interpretation, but few are in a position to purchase a complete hoard or the available portion of it which they have been shown. What they can sometimes do is to make a rough analysis of its content as good and detailed as available time allows, and they can at least always make sure that any pieces they buy from it are related to the hoard on their own tickets or catalogue. It is often difficult for dealers themselves to find out where and when hoards they are purchasing were discovered, but any scraps of information that can be picked up are worth noting: they may fit into what may later transpire. Collectors make an important contribution to the study of coins by picking and taking care of good specimens, but they should also remember Michael Hendy's recent remark that a hoard 'gives a far more reliable picture of the circulating medium than the trays of a collection'. This is true of course, but notes on the provenance of pieces in a collection can make them much more important than they were without any.

There are new views too about mints. When the British Museum Catalogue was published over sixty years ago, the tendency was to ascribe everything to Constantinople unless it was specifically marked as minted elsewhere. In that catalogue W. Wroth began to ascribe gold coins on the basis of style and fabric, and in spite of *CONOB* appearing on them, to Carthage and Italy especially. Modern writers have carried the process much further, indeed to an extent that occasionally appears far-fetched. But all coins need looking at from the angle of style and details of the crown and its pendilia, the number of jewels on the emperor's collar, or on the hem of his chlamys or on his sceptre and many such detailed points, which can differentiate mints besides officina within them. On the other hand differences can come from the vagaries of individual die sinkers and there is here a wide field of study for a collector with an eye for detail, a sense of logical arrangement and, perhaps above all, perseverance.

As scientists are coming increasingly to the aid of numismatists in metal analysis especially, it may be time to review the normal symbols used for coins. It has recently been shown for instance that Byzantine 'bronze' is usually copper (Cu), but the symbol Æ for bronze remains in the Dumbarton Oaks Catalogue. Equally, numismatists always refer to silver as Æ but scientists as *Ag*. Much that has been long described as Byzantine 'bronze' can be shown (by scientific analysis) to be billon: the eye simply cannot be relied upon to make the distinction but, as has been recently shown, the difference between those that are billon and those that are copper, can be of crucial importance as, for instance, around the year 1200.

The Byzantine collector brought up in the old ways has a great deal to assimilate if he is to bring himself up-to-date.

50 ▶
51 ▶▶
52 ▶
53 ▶▶

50, 51 Anastasius *(491–518). Gold solidus.* Obv. *This is the first issue of the reign, and the change to PERP subsequently abbreviated to PP has been noted in No. 3. Contrast the style of this Constantinople piece with that of Thessalonica (No. 4).* Rev. *The type is still the same as in No. 4 but with an officina letter Γ (3) at the end of the legend and only one star, on the right (diam. 19 mm.).*

52, 53 Justin I *(518–27). Gold solidus.* Obv. *The titles are the same as on the last Anastasius's coins with PP for PERP. The deep engraving of the die contrasts with that on the Anastasius's pieces above.* Rev. *The Victory type is repeated with small changes (diam. 20 mm.).*

IV. METALS AND DENOMINATIONS

In this chapter metals will be taken as the controlling factor and denominations considered under these headings. This can lead to confusion as the same words were used for coins of different metals at different times, and it is necessary to range over a millennium. If a simpler view be wanted, a given point should be selected such as the reign of Justinian I, from whose times such a wealth of coinage has been preserved. Since the work of Michael Hendy on the reforms of Alexius I that reign, which shows a very different system in operation, is another good point to select. There was another fundamental change in the mid-fourteenth century and these are all dealt with in the chronological section of this book. Equally there are periods which are as yet confusing, when old systems were breaking down and new had not been worked out such as, for instance, the eighth and ninth centuries and in the thirteenth and fourteenth centuries.

Gold

1*-4* The coinage was based on the gold solidus of which seventy-two were struck from a pound weight of metal. They in fact weigh 4.5 g. each or a little less. The 83 Roman pound is traditionally considered to weigh 327.45 g., and the balance of 3.45 g. may have been the seigniorage deduction for minting expenses. The solidus weighed 24 siliquae or keratia (carats) and was theoretically pure gold, so that the carat, originally a weight, has come to be regarded as a standard of purity or fineness.

A few examples of the aureus are known, notably of Anastasius and Justinian I. This coin was struck on the pre-Constantinian standard of sixty to the pound weight and surviving examples are so rare as to allow it to be placed outside the normal currency system as a medallic or ceremonial piece.

The fractions of the solidus issued as coins were the 1/2 or semissis and the 35, 36 1/3 or tremissis. But ephemerally there 37, 38 appeared other fractions in the sixth and seventh centuries and particularly the 1/6 of a solidus is important in Heraclius' reign as it linked the gold with the silver coinage. Two silver hexagrams were, in theory and in practice, equal in value to 1/6 solidus. Fractions lower than the tremissis are very rare indeed, but semisses and tremisses are common and generally

show more wear than solidi. The fractions
20-22 retained as obverse type the old imperial
profile bust facing right long after the
typically Byzantine facing bust had been
adopted for the solidus.

Although ' solidus ' is the usual term for
the complete coin from Constantine the
Great to Nicephorus II in the tenth century,
the Byzantines usually called them nomismata (plural of nomisma). Up to this time
the weight, fineness and size of the coin had
remained virtually unchanged and even the
types were rarely altered. But Nicephorus II
introduced a new gold coin—the tetarteron
—lighter by a 1/12 than the solidus and in
appearance virtually indistinguishable from
it. The reason for introducing the tetarteron is still debated: Byzantine chroniclers
blamed the avarice of the emperor and his
wish to extort more in taxation, but
possibly it was the result of Nicephorus'
eastern conquests and the need for a coin
more or less on a par with the Fatimid dinar
of c. 4.10 g. In the reign of Basil II the coin
300, 301 was made more easily recognizable by
making the standard heavier coin—the
nomisma histamenon—at once larger and
thinner than the tetarteron.

It was only in the reign of Michael IV
(1034–41) that the standard nomisma histamenon began to be debased in metal
fineness, and the process went on until
Alexius I's reforms in 1092. By this time
it was only 6.5 carats fine, that is containing
some 26 % of gold. The shape of the coin
had by then undergone a spectacular
change, as it was minted in a cup-shaped
325, 326 (scyphate) form, a practice which appears
to have begun in the reign of Constantine IX
(1042–55).

Alexius I's reform brought in the new
standard coin—the hyperper—of 21 carats, 13, 14
though theoretically of pure gold. Like
its predecessor it was a large thin piece and
scyphate in form. The hyperper continued
to be issued up to the Latin conquest and
indeed after it at Nicaea. Debasement
began and the coin became smaller and
thicker but remained scyphate. After the
restoration of the emperors in Constantinople the hyperper still continued although
by the mid-fourteenth century it had been
debased to 11 parts gold, 6 silver and 7 377, 3
copper. Some specimens still appear cop-
pery to the eye but by this time the hyperper
was no longer a normal commercial medium
of exchange and had to be quoted in
Venetian ducats: 2 hyperpers = 1 ducat.
Within a few years Constantinople ceased
to mint gold and the name hyperper was
transferred to the silver coin which became 63, 64
the new standard piece.

Lightweight gold coins. From the reign of
Justinian I to that of Constantine IV gold
coins were issued marked clearly and
specifically as light in weight. In this
respect there was no deception at all but
analysis has shown that some at least
were not up to standard fineness either,
and that could not be seen. The marks
usually found are:

> *OBXX* or *BOXX*, *i.e.* 20 siliquae, 45
> and thus light by 4 siliquae.
> *OB+** or *OB*+**, *i.e.* 22 siliquae, 46
> and thus light by 2 siliquae.
> *BOΓK* or with * on obv. and rev., 47-49
> *i.e.* 23 siliquae, and thus light by 1
> siliqua.

Their exact purpose is not clear and in
particular more analyses of fineness are

46

needed before the facts necessary in making a judgment are available. A case has been made for their being manufactured within the Empire for use only outside it, and some large hoards have been found in South Russia. Alternatively they might be the tail end of a batch made lighter to make up the required number of coins to the weight of metal. Besides, the alteration of *CONOB* (' standard of Constantinople ') to *OBXX*, etc. the reverse type almost always has the cross removed from the orb carried by the winged angel in his left hand, or by the seated personification of Constantinople in the reign of Justin II. The meaning of *ΘS* at the end of the reverse legend on many pieces is another mystery in this series. A number of coins show an

⁵⁴ alteration of *CONOB* to *OB*+** on the die and a 22 siliquae piece from Ravenna clearly shows the alteration to *C+N+B*

^{8*, 204*} by obliterating the *O*'s.

Silver

In Justinian I's time twelve miliaresia went to a solidus but it is difficult to see a logical pattern in the surviving silver coins of the Byzantine Empire. An early problem lies in the name—the commonest in use for silver coins—miliaresion: of what is it the 1/1000th part? The hexagram *(ἡ ἑξάγραμμα)*, a heavier coin, was first minted by Heraclius and continued until the early eighth century: this can be tied

^{55, 56} into the system of gold fractions (2 hexagrams = 1/6 solidus) and, with its often crudely cut flans, it looks like the product of a crisis in Heraclius' reign. There was one

such when the silver vessels of the Church were sent in vast quantities to the mints in an effort to persuade Heraclius not to leave the capital. Unfortunately, in a reign unusually bare in literary evidence, there is a date for the introduction of the hexagram which is too early to fit this particular crisis at any rate. It was a coin of real value —not a token—equal to 1/12 of a solidus, which brings it into line with the miliaresion of Justinian I: but the latter has not yet been positively identified as a coin and may have been only money of account. Heraclius and other seventh-century rulers issued what appear to be miliaresia and half-miliaresia, roughly one half and one quarter of the hexagram, but, as yet, the number of specimens available is too small to establish a firm relationship.

From the eighth century the miliaresion was normally a token coin much thinner than the earlier hexagram and miliaresion, and weighing about two grammes, but rising to three grammes in the mid-ninth ^{57, 58} century. The weights can be misleading as miliaresia were issued with a wide edge around the types, which invited the attention of clippers: those of John Zimisces for instance—one of the few common silver pieces today—are seldom seen in any condition other than clipped down to the type with only a trace of the three surrounding rings left. Miliaresia of Basil II (976–1025) vary in diameter from 3 cm. as issued, through 2.25 as frequently ³⁰² found in good condition to 1.65, clipped down to the central cross and busts, an example of which was once handed to the author in Greece amongst some small change nickels. The weight difference between these two extremes is nearly one and a half grammes.

These eighth-century miliaresia began by being aniconic and derived from the Arabic dirham: some are actually struck over dirhams especially in the reign of Constantine VI. Romanus I in the tenth _{295, 296} century was the first to include his portrait in the type. In the later eleventh century surviving silver pieces are scarce and often in bad condition too, but they broadly divide themselves into larger pieces sometimes scyphate of about 2.6 g. weight and small flat pieces of half the weight or less: _{317, 318} these coins seem to continue the miliaresion and half-miliaresion series. Some of them have representations of the emperor in _{59, 60} full armour on the reverse, and the obverse is often occupied by a type of the Virgin. A world shortage of silver may have been one reason for the changes, but silver coins seem to have been used in a different way from the time of Basil II to that of Alexius I, as yet unexplained.

In the reformed coinage of Alexius I and his successors till the Latin conquest, silver plays a small part only in the currency and seems not to be significant until the last centuries of the Empire. Andronicus II _{61, 62} and his son, Michael IX (1295–1320), adopted the Venetian grosso or matapan as a model for what appears to have been a large issue: it was symptomatic of Byzantine trade falling very largely into Italian hands. When the issue of gold coins ceased altogether in the reign of John V (1341–91) silver pieces, which _{63, 64} combined traditional features like the bust of Jesus obverse with others from the western gros tournois (the current silver

54 Justin II *(565–78). Exergue of a lightweight solidus enlarged to show that OB *+* (22 siliquae) has been recut on a die originally reading CONOB for a full-weight coin. Note particularly NO under *+.*

55, 56 Heraclius *(610–41). Silver hexagram, obverse and reverse. Byzantine silver coins are usually tokens but these were designed to be worth their denomination, 1/12 of a solidus. The reverse type with its legend ' May God help the Romans' (in Latin) continued into the reign of Constantine IV. After this the coin itself was little struck and ceased to be used in the early years of the eighth century (diam. 21.5 mm.).*

57, 58 Basil I *(867–86). Silver miliaresion, obverse and reverse. Leo III issued no hexagrams and introduced a new type of miliaresion which continued in use until the reign of Basil II. The coin here is of Basil I and his son Constantine. The new miliaresion was a token coin, lighter and thinner than earlier silver pieces and its epigraphic reverse, following the design of arabic dirhams, made the most of the decorative value of Greek letters (diam. 25.5 mm.).*

59, 60 Constantine IX *(1042–55). Silver miliaresion, obverse and reverse. After the reign of Basil II the silver coinage underwent changes in form and types. Miliaresia are large, thin and becoming scyphate in form and the piece illustrated shows the change in both obverse and reverse types. On the latter Constantine appears at full-length in military dress and his family name ' Monomachus' can be seen on the right. Half-miliaresia, small and flat with an epigraphic reverse, become increasingly used as silver currency, but are rare today (diam. 30 mm.).*

61, 62 Andronicus II *(1295–1320). Silver miliaresion, obverse and reverse. This type based in weight, form and types on the Venetian grosso was introduced with other western-looking billon and copper pieces in this reign. Andronicus on the left stands with his son Michael IX holding a labarum. From the number of varieties surviving, a large issue seems likely (diam. 20 mm.).*

54

55

56

57

58

59

60

61

62

63

64

65

66

67

68

69

70

71

72

73

74

75

76

63, 64 John V *(1341–91)*. *Silver hyperper, obverse and reverse. This large silver piece took the place of the gold hyperper when the minting of gold ceased in this reign. The legend normally begins on the outside circle but here it begins on the inside just above and to the right of the emperor's crown (diam. 29 mm.).*

65, 66 Justinian I *(527–65)*. *Silver 250 nummia, obverse and reverse. The numerals C (200) and N (50) fill the reverse of this neatly designed piece from Ravenna where a large number of silver denominations were minted: others were 125 and 120 nummia and some were without any denomination numeral included in the type (diam. 14 mm.).*

Greek numerals on Byzantine copper coins. Justinian I's follis has been illustrated above, Nos. 9, 10. Others are:

67 Justinian I *(527–65)*. *Copper half-follis of Constantinople, officina 5 and year 13 (539/40) (diam. 27 mm.).*

68 Justinian I *(527–65)*. *Copper quarter-follis of Antioch, year 21 (diam. 20.5 mm.).*

69 Justinian I *(527–65)*. *Copper five nummia of Constantinople, officina 4. The obverse has a profile bust (14×16.5 mm.).*

70 Heraclius *(610–41)*. *Copper three-quarter-follis (30 nummia) of Constantinople, first officina, year 20. This is the first time Greek numerals were used for this denomination (diam. 24 mm.).*

71 Justinian I *(527–65)*. *Copper nummion, reverse. This is the last reign in which single nummion pieces were struck in any numbers; inflation had rendered new issues unnecessary. The piece illustrated is of uncertain mint, perhaps Carthage. It has a Christogram with alpha and omega below; others have ' A ' for ' one ', or a lion (diam. 6 mm.).*

Roman numerals on Byzantine copper coins. Some emperors, like Phocas, show a preference for Roman over Greek numerals.

72 Phocas *(602–10)*. *Copper follis of Thessalonica, year 4 (diam. 30 mm.).*

73 Phocas *(602–10)*. *Copper half-follis of Nicomedia, officina A, year 3 (diam. 24 mm.).*

74 Phocas *(602–10)*. *Copper quarter-follis of Constantinople (diam. 16 mm.).*

75 Justin I *(518–27)*. *Copper five nummia of Rome struck by the Ostrogoths in the emperor's name (diam. 12 mm.).*

76 Phocas *(602–10)*. *Copper five nummia of Constantinople with a Byzantine version of the Roman V. The Greek numeral 5 was the letter epsilon (diam. 14 mm.).*

coin), took their place. A large silver coin, weighing about 9 g., was called an hyperper after the gold coin it replaced: it was of good silver and equal to four Venetian grossi in value. There were fractional issues of a 1/2 and 1/8 hyperper as well. John V, Andronicus IV, Manuel II and John VIII all issued these silver hyperpers with slightly diminishing purity and weight and a much more obvious deterioration both in imitating the design and in technique of striking the coins. The last emperor, Constantine XI—brother of John VIII—issued no coins.

Until the last stages of the Empire it will be clear that the part played by silver in the currency has proved very difficult to assess. Grierson wrote, in 1961, 'a silver coinage did not form an essential part of the Byzantine monetary system' and he regards many of the later miliaresia as ceremonial issues—like Maundy Money in Britain—rather than true currency. No attempt has been made here to put into perspective the issues of small silver pieces, often referred to as 'siliquae', which were produced in considerable numbers at Ravenna and Carthage in the sixth and seventh centuries. The numbers of these that survive and the worn state in which they are often found, would appear to show that they at any rate were used for currency. Some of those from Ravenna have a denomination marked upon them—250, 125 and 120 nummia—but even so, in relation to their weights, this has not served to define their place securely in the currency. The collector is bound to come across some of these types, though some of them are of extreme rarity. In studying the silver coinage the major

difficulty lies in the word *miliaresion* which seems to be used of almost any silver piece; also it was, for the most part, a token coinage so that weight relationships need not necessarily be meaningful.

Copper

Recent analyses have shown that Byzantine 'bronzes' are in fact copper, though still referred to by the symbol *Æ*. The basic copper coin from the time of Anastasius onwards was the follis and in Justinian I's reign 15 of these went to a silver miliaresion or 180 to a solidus: in the ninth century it was a matter of 24 folles to the miliaresion. The follis represented forty nummia and its normally minted fractions were 1/2, 1/4 and 1/8 with others occasionally found. The denomination was usually expressed in Greek numeral letters but sometimes Roman numerals were employed:

1 Follis = 40 nummia or (Greek) *M* (Roman) XXXX
1/2 Follis = 20 nummia or (Greek) *K* (Roman) XX
1/4 Follis = 10 nummia or (Greek) *I* (Roman) X
1/8 Follis = 5 nummia or (Greek) *Є* (Roman) V
3/4 Follis = 30 nummia or (Greek) *Λ* (Roman) XXX
1/40 Follis = 1 nummion or (Greek) *A* (Roman—I nummus)

At *Thessalonica* 16 nummia = *IS*
8 nummia = *H*
4 nummia = *Λ*
2 nummia = *B*

54

At *Alexandria* 33 nummia = $\Lambda\Gamma$
12 nummia = IB
6 nummia = S
3 nummia = Γ

At Cherson issues seem to have been in multiples of five nummia, so that a follis-sized piece is marked H, *i.e.* 8 ($\times 5$) and the half-follis $\varDelta$ or 4 ($\times 5$).

The process of inflation quickly eliminated the lesser fractions, just as the farthing and halfpenny have been recently demonetized in Britain. The nummion was going out in Justinian I's day: under Heraclius the five and ten nummia were fast disappearing too. In spite of attempts to restore the follis to its old size and to bring back the fractions under Constantine IV and again under Leo III, by Theophilus' reign (829–42) any copper piece was a follis: even the M denomination mark was dropped, and not used again as it was unnecessary. This was a token coinage and it was the denominational mark on it, not its size, that mattered, as can be seen by comparing a follis of Justinian I with one of Constans II. Pieces often circulated with two clearly visible marks of value, as when in 630 Heraclius tried to introduce a heavier copper follis and previous folles were overstruck with a K to circulate at half their former value.

John Zimisces introduced a copper coin of a new type, still without its follis denomination mark but also without its issuer's name. This began a long series of issues, usually referred to as ' Anonymous $Æ$ ', which lasted for some 120 years with a dozen different types. Shortly after its introduction, Basil II re-established a much

heavier follis of this anonymous type and, with varying weights, they continue until the reforms of Alexius I. One curious feature is that anonymous issues (perhaps designed for certain provinces) were produced alongside others bearing the emperor's name from Constantine X onwards. After 1092 the normal copper small change became the tetarteron, not to be confused with the gold tetarteron which petered out in a greatly debased form in Alexius' pre-reform years.

The debasement of the billon trachy (see under Billon below) from 1/48 of a gold hyperper to 1/184th made an additional copper coinage unnecessary for the billon had virtually become copper from the late twelfth century. When the Palaeologus dynasty was restored on the expulsion of the Latins, a flat copper coinage as well as a scyphate one was in use, and was much in evidence in the reign of Andronicus II, being similar in style to his western type silver issues. But from the last stages of the dynasty—and of the Empire—very few copper coins have survived: they are small flat pieces and as yet no collection and analysis of material, similar to those made by Hendy for pre-1261 issues, has been made.

Billon

This became an important official alloy for minting at the reform of Alexius I when the billon (Greek ' aspron ' = white) trachy was valued at 1/48 of a gold hyperper and contained between 4 % and 7 % silver. Most of these scyphate pieces appear in the

British Museum Catalogue as 'bronze nomismata', but a few survive to show that they could in fact look 'white' like silver with only a little copper showing on the surface. This seems to have been a matter of surface enrichment of the metal in the process of striking rather than any form of silver 'washing'. The most unlikely looking coins can, on analysis, turn out to have their 4 % + of silver in them. The billon trachy was devalued to 1/120 of a gold hyperper before 1190, probably at the third issue of Manuel I as Hendy argues, and again in 1199 to 1/184. Under the Latin emperors there is no silver in the now copper trachea.

349, 350

Electrum

Gold issues had become so debased by the time of Nicephorus III that both the 'gold' stamena and tetartera were, in effect, electrum. Under the re-organization of Alexius I, electrum was given an official position in the coinage for a scyphate piece representing 1/3 of the new gold hyperper: it had a fineness of 5–7 carats as was to be expected from its position in the coinage. This was the electrum trachy unfortunately often called 'aspron' by those using it and so making confusion with the billon trachy possible. The collector today will, however, never make any mistake between the fine looking electrum trachea and the usually unattractive, dark coloured billon ones. The electrum trachy was an important coin from 1092 until the Fourth Crusade, but does not seem to have played so large a part in the succession states or after the

332, 337
31, 32

restoration of the Byzantine emperors in Constantinople in 1261.

It may be useful to say a further word about the use of some of the terms mentioned above. The word stamenon appears in the early eleventh century referring to the debased gold coin of standard weight issued by Michael IV; but soon after, when the coin was made in scyphate shape, it is generally called 'trachy'. Once Alexius I had made the standard gold coin the hyperper, both stamenon and trachy were usually applied to billon scyphates worth 1/48 of the hyperper. The word trachy implies, in Hendy's words, 'simply scyphate in opposition to the smooth flat fabric of the tetarteron'. In the short period between Nicephorus II and Basil II gold stamena and tetartera can only be distinguished effectively by weight. The former soon became the 'spread fabric' scyphate to distinguish them from the lighter gold tetartera of lower value.

77 ▶

78 ▶

Weights

The coin collector will sooner or later come across examples of Byzantine weights, some of which are marked *N* for nomismata or solidi, with a division into 24 keratia each—for example, *NB* = 2 nomismata or 9 g. More usually they are marked *Γ* for gounkia or ounces with divisions into 24 scruples (1.13 g. each)—for example, *ΓA* = 1 ounce (27.3 g.). Pound weights, marked *Λ* for litra, are not common, but the others, whether marked with an N or *Γ* or simply with numeral letters are con-

79 ▶
83
84

85

77 Justin I *(518–27). Gold solidus.* Rev. *A new type of reverse was introduced during the reign in which the female ' Victory advancing left ' was changed into a male figure (an angel or St Michael) facing. The legend referring to Victory however goes on unchanged (diam. 21 mm.).*

78, 79 Justinian I *(527–65). Gold solidus.* Obv. *This is the first of Justinian's issues, using the same type of bust as his uncle Justin I used.* Rev. *Justinian repeats his ' angel facing ' type. The officina is A (1) (diam. 20 mm.).*

tinually found. Usually the letters are surrounded by a wreath and divided by a cross, and sometimes are inlaid with silver or copper on the normal brass base. Weights of glass were commonly used in Egypt and some of these bearing the monograms of Byzantine emperors or officials are known: they appear to be rare and have been little studied, as against the important series of Arab glass weights.

V. MINTS

It is not always easy to attribute Byzantine coins to their mints, especially after the second half of the seventh century. Up to then copper coins in particular were generally given a recognizable mint mark unless too small to include it. But silver coins were seldom so marked and gold coins after Anastasius very seldom. Much therefore depends on stylistic differences and the interpretation of sigla, or secret marks. The vast majority of gold solidi after Anastasius are marked in the exergue of the reverse, where the mint name is normally to be sought, *CONOB*, a shortened form of τὸ ὄβρυςον Κωνσταντινουπολεῶς—the pure standard of Constantinople. It is therefore not exactly a mint mark but an indication of the quality of the gold. Rare pieces are known with *ROMOB* for Justinian I and one example with *ΑΛϤOB* (Alexandria) for Justin II without any differing quality of fineness, so that *CONOB* can, like the others, be normally taken as a mint mark. Prior to Anastasius *TESOB* or *THSOB* (Thessalonica) is often found with many other mints also striking gold.

The mint of Carthage produced solidi of visibly different character from those of the capital and yet still marked them *CONOB*: they were smaller, thicker and often have a date which those of the capital did not. Others also marked *CONOB* have so consistently a different style and technique in die cutting that they have long been attributed to Ravenna; this mint produced copper pieces bearing its name, and so stylistic comparison is made possible. Clearly there could be a bigger breakdown of *CONOB* pieces than this, especially in Italy, as stylistic differences are sometimes marked and the letters and other marks on the coins need explanation. It is on these lines that scholars are working today and as an example of a clear-cut group the solidi of the reign of Heraclius now firmly attributed to Alexandria may be instanced: there are unusual letters at the end of the reverse legend as well as an individual style of die cutting. Less acceptable is the identification in the Dumbarton Oaks Catalogue of a type of Maurice with a broad-faced bust as being of Antioch; this is tied up with the interpretation of ΘS in the legend of many lightweight solidi as Θεόυπολις ('the city of God'), a name given to Antioch after the destructive earthquake of 528.

86, 87

88, 89

90, 91

181

The problems over *CONOB* do not arise in the early years of the Empire when solidi have a large variety of mint marks, but later they are complicated by added letters and symbols. Especially in the seventh century *CONOB +*, *CONOBA*, *CONOBC*, *CONOBS*, *CONOBΘ*, *CONOBI* and *CONOBT* are used and under Heraclius there are symbols in the field as well as his monogram. Many suggestions of dating, mint practice over what the Royal Mint call a 'journey' or batch of coins, and special marks for a particular office of state have been put forward. These may provide clues but as yet no comprehensive solution to the problems has been found.

In short there are well authenticated identifications of gold issued from Sicilian and Italian mints (especially Ravenna) and from Thessalonica, Carthage and Alexandria. Others—and Antioch must be amongst these still—are less certain, so that Constantinople with its ten officinae organized for the issue of gold must be assumed as responsible for the rest until sufficient proofs to the contrary can be supported, as they undoubtedly will be shortly.

The Build-up of Mints

Anastasius—Constantinople, Thessalonica (gold only), Nicomedia (copper only: to 627), Antioch (copper only: to 610).

Justin I—Cyzicus (copper only: to 629), Alexandria (to 646), Thessalonica (to 630).

Justinian I—Carthage (to 698), Rome, Ravenna (to 751), Cherson (sixth to seventh centuries and ninth to tenth centuries), Constantine-in-Numidia (to 602) [and for this reign only, Perugia and Salona], Cartagena (gold only to 620).

Maurice—Catania and Syracuse.

Heraclius—Seleucia-in-Isaura and Isaura (615-18 only), Cyprus (Constantia; to 629).

Constans II—Naples (to 717).

Justinian II—Sardinia (to 716).

From stylistic differences and varying alloys alone it is clear that there were more mints in Italy than Rome and Ravenna, and one day a new pattern will be devised fitting into the turbulent history of the country and the swiftly moving political realities. Under Justinian I mints appear to be well spaced over the Empire to provide for local needs though some, like Perugia, are supported by very few surviving coins which *could* be from Ravenna or Constantinople. The bulk of the coinage came from Constantinople, Nicomedia and Cyzicus at the centre and seems to have been sent into the provinces in consignments as required. The quality of the flans and striking show clear signs of overwork at these central mints, consistent with their having an overall Imperial responsibility. The conquests of the Persians and the Arabs forcibly brought about the closure of some mints and brought into prominence others for the supply of the troops.

61

80 Tiberius II *(578–82). Copper 30 nummia, reverse. This was the Roman numeral counterpart of No. 70, for a 3/4 of a follis piece, preferred by certain emperors. Tiberius II introduced this denomination for the first time (diam. 30 mm.).*

81, 82 Heraclius *(610–41). Copper half-follis struck over an earlier follis of the same reign, obverse and reverse. In Heraclius' 20th and 21st year an attempt was made to increase the weight of the follis and this overstriking of old folles as new half-folles was part of it (diam. 20 mm.).*

83 *Brass weight with silver inlay for two nomismata (or solidi), equal to 1/3 of an ounce. Actual weight now 8.68 g.: found in Alexandria. Many weights are found reckoning by the weight of the solidus such as NΓ, NE or (as here) NB. One solidus = 24 carats or siliquae (diam. 18 mm.).*

84 *Brass weight of one ounce. The Γ stands for ' ounce ' and A is the numeral 1. This would be the equivalent of six nomismata in the other reckoning (diam. 26 mm.).*

85 *Brass weight of one pound with silver and copper inlay. The nimbate bust of an emperor in a paludamentum can be seen in the centre. Actual weight 321.77 g.: found in Istanbul. One pound = 12 ounces, each of 24 scruples : one scruple equalled six carats (56.5 × 51 mm.).*

86, 87 Heraclius *(610–41). Gold solidus of Carthage, obverse and reverse. The emperor with his son Heraclius Constantine. The last letter of the reverse legend Θ gives the date—the ninth year of the Indiction beginning 627/8, i.e. 635/6. Heraclius's reign spans two Indictions but these small thick coins of Carthage tend to become smaller and thicker as the years advance and there is generally little difficulty in telling which Indiction is involved (diam. 11 mm.).*

88, 89 Heraclius *(610–41). Gold solidus of Ravenna, obverse and reverse. The distinctive high raised ring surrounding the types is particularly clear on the reverse of this piece. The style marks it off plainly from Constantinople issues (see Nos. 33, 34) and from others attributed to Alexandria, like Nos. 90, 91 (diam. 20 mm.).*

90, 91 Heraclius *(610–41). Gold solidus of Alexandria, obverse and reverse. In spite of CONOB being present on all the three coins on this plate their different styles are clearly marked when depicting the same emperor and his son. The reverse legend here ends III which, with IX and I, is a mark associated with this style, and Egypt is the provenance of many of the coins (diam. 21 mm.).*

80

81

83

82

84

85

86

87

88

89

90

91

92

93

94

95

96

97

98

99

100

101

92-94 Justinian I *(527–65). Copper follis and half-follis of distinctive style now attributed to the mint of Salona. The follis has a facing bust and is much smaller than the other folles of this type elsewhere. Both obverse and reverse of the half-follis are illustrated (diam. 24 and 16 mm.).*

95, 96 Maurice *(582–602). Copper follis of Cherson, obverse and reverse. Maurice and his wife, Constantia, occupy the obverse which has the mint name as its legend (others have a normal Maurice legend), while their son Theodosius is on the reverse. The figure H, or 8, must result from counting by multiples of five nummia, as the size and weight of the coin leave no doubt as to its being a follis. Grierson has suggested that it may have been part of an official scheme to demonetize all denominations below five nummia, which was later cancelled. There are half-folles of this mint marked Δ or 4 (diam. 32 mm.).*

97, 98 Maurice *(582–602). Copper follis, obverse and reverse. The CON on the reverse can hardly be Constantinople in view of the style of the obverse. The straight barred A's and the well made Roman numerals are other features. Constantine-in-Numidia has been suggested as the mint producing this quite substantial group of coins, many of which have been found in North Africa (diam. 27 mm.).*

99 Justinian I *(527–65). Gold solidus, obverse. The left-hand-side has been enlarged to show the beginning of the Anastasius legend (DNANA) of the original striking. Overstriking of gold pieces is very rare indeed until the ninth century and was never common (diam. 21 mm.).*

100, 101 Heraclius *(610–41). Gold solidus, obverse and reverse. One wonders how and why this brockage has been preserved, and has survived virtually without wear. The N in the field of the reverse (quite different from the N of CONOB) has probably been added to the original die. The coin was not properly cleared from the bottom die and then a new flan was placed over it and struck with the reverse die. Note the cracks in the obverse die on the right, in both impressions (max. diam. 22 mm.).*

67

From the seventh century onwards the old system and the situation of its mints fades out with Constantinople, and to a lesser extent Thessalonica, remaining: there were probably more ad hoc mints of the kind represented by Seleucia-in-Isaura under Heraclius. The tendency today is to look for more mints, as for instance amongst the many detailed variations and styles of the Anonymous coinage of the tenth century, but so far no clear pattern has emerged until the whole coinage was reformed under Alexius I. It will no longer do to accept a number of major mints with a miscellany labelled 'Provincial Coinage', as had to be done in the British Museum Catalogue in spite of Wroth's heroic efforts to separate out certain groups. The editors of the Dumbarton Oaks Catalogue have courageously added mints like Perugia and Salona to account for clearly marked groups of copper coins under Justinian I, which they feel could not possibly be accounted for by the vagaries of individual die-sinkers within well-established mints. The tendency towards identifying new mints is likely to continue and has indeed already shown signs of running wild. Michael Hendy, in presenting his entirely original account of the coinage of the Comneni, has found a happier solution. He uses minute observation of differences in detail to group coins into main types each with a number of officinae, even identifying individuals working with some of them. This still does not exclude the possibility of ad hoc mints being set up where necessary. As always, coin collectors must be on the look-out for new stylistic groupings and for small differences in the

92-94

technique and execution of both the engraving and the usage of dies. There is much work still to be done on these lines in the Byzantine series. It can be slow and laborious, but worth while as coins can suddenly fall into place in a pattern, even without the touch of genius that can occasionally bring illumination to a whole period.

Mints and Signatures

CONSTANTINOPLE *(CON, CONOS, CONOB)* with ten officinae for gold numbered $A, B, \Gamma, \Delta, \epsilon, S, Z, H, \Theta, I$, and five for copper $A, B, \Gamma, \Delta, \epsilon$.

NICOMEDIA *(NIKO, NIK, NIKM, NI, NIC, NIKOM, NIKOMI)*. Copper only from two officinae A and B: closed 627.

CYZICVS *(KYZ, KY)*. Copper only from two officinae A and B: closed 629.

ANTIOCH *(ANTIX, ANTX, AN)*. After an earthquake in 528 the city's name was changed to 'The City of God' hence mint marks representing Θεόυπολις, *ΘVΠΟΛS* (Greek) and *THEЧP' THEЧPO* (Latin) with other abbreviations such as and . Normally one officina *(Γ)* was at work for copper but five are found and in Maurice's reign there is a sixth *(S)*, perhaps due to heavy demands stemming from military and political considerations relating to Persia. The possibility of gold issues, marked *ΘS* and in other ways, has been discussed earlier. Closed in 610.

68

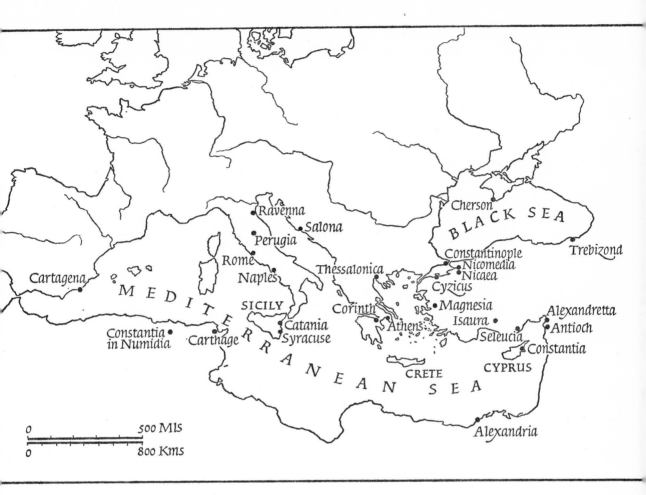

Fig. 1. *Mints of the Byzantine Empire.*

ALEXANDRIA *(ΑΛΕΖ)* normally only copper with denominations peculiar to itself—33, 12, 6, 3 nummia—and no officina mark. Occasional issues of gold notably in the seventh century when they were marked *CONOB*, with reverse legend ending IX, *III* or *I* and a distinctive style of die engraving. The Arabs conquered Alexandria in 642, with a temporary Byzantine re-occupation in 645–6.

CARTHAGE *(KART, KAR, CAR, KRTG, CRTG, KTG, CT)*. A mint of great importance issuing gold (marked *CONOB*), silver and copper. Gold coins were generally dated (*e.g. ANS= ANNO 6* = sixth year of the Indiction) but without officina letter. Copper coins of Justinian I, however, appear to show two officinae, *S* and *SO*. The final Arab conquest took place in 698 but the mint closed in 695 and probably moved to *SARDINIA* which issued gold and copper 695–715: the gold solidi were of the small diameter, dumpy type which became characteristic of Carthage issues.

SICILY *(SCL^s, SC^s)* and specifically *CATANIA (CAT)* with copper dated 582–629 and SYRACUSE *(CUPA-KOVCI)* also probably issuing copper, as under Maurice some copper is marked *SECILIA* besides *CAT*, and some is specifically marked Syracuse under Justinian II. Syracuse seems to have displaced Catania as the principal mint under Constans II when gold was issued in important quantities until Basil I—Syracuse was occupied by the Arabs in 875—recognizable by the use of the ⋀ for *A* and the ·.· mark. Wroth realized that this last sign indicated a mint but attributed it to Carthage.

RAVENNA *(RAV, RA)*. Important for gold and silver but copper issues appear to be rarer. Gold is characterized by a high ring surrounding the reverse type and distinctive style and lettering. The Lombards captured the city in 751 and there is copper of Leo III bearing the mint mark.

THESSALONICA *(TES, ΘEC, THSOB, THESSOB)*. An important mint issuing gold, though it is often marked *CONOB*, and an individual type of small copper of 16, 8, 4 and 2 nummia as well as 20 nummia, but few folles after Justin I.

Other mints

ROME *(ROMOB, ROM, RM)*: issuing gold, silver and copper, often but not always using roman numerals for denominations. Apparently not of great importance from Justinian I onwards, with poor technical standards in its copper production. But more gold coins are being attributed to it from *CONOB* marked pieces and a re-appraisal of its position may soon be necessary.

SELEUCIA-IN-ISAURA *(SELIS4, SEL)* and *ISAURA (ISAVR)* issued folles and, in the case of Seleucia, half-folles under Heraclius.

CHERSON *(Ĥ, Ĥ X)* cast fabric: copper only with denominations 8(×5) = follis and 4(×5) = half-follis. Active in the sixth century and outstandingly so in ninth and tenth centuries.

CYPRUS *(KVΠP')*: folles only, under Heraclius and one rare follis with *KVΠPOV*, year III, issued during the rebellion of Heraclius and his father against Phocas.

SPAIN *(CONOB)*. Grierson has identified a rare series of tremisses of Visigothic standard and distinctive style in reigns from Justinian I to Heraclius. Southern Spain was lost to the Byzantines in 620.

ALEXANDRETTA *(AΛEZANΔ)*: another mint during the revolt of Heraclius and his father, open 609–10.

CONSTANTINE-IN-NUMIDIA *(CON)*: a good case on the basis of style, overstriking and provenances is being made for copper folles, half-folles and dekanummia from this mint which was first identified in the Dumbarton Oaks Catalogue, for reigns from Justinian I to Maurice.

SALONA (no mint mark). Attributions made with reservations for the first time in the Dumbarton Oaks Catalogue of folles, half-folles and dekanummia for an undated group that has long mystified students of Justinian I's coinage.

PERUGIA *(P)*: another uncertain attribution in the Dumbarton Oaks Catalogue for a rare group of Justinian's dated half-folles and dekanummia, possibly issued from Ravenna or Constantinople.

NAPLES *(NϵϹ)*: issuing half-folles from Constans II to Justinian II and probably some gold, marked *CONOB*, similar in style to that of the Dukes of Beneventum for the reigns Tiberius III to Theodosius III.

This list of mints should give the collector of Byzantine coins a firm basis from which to start, in spite of some uncertainties, especially in Italy, where a much more complicated pattern is beginning to emerge. But it only takes him to the eighth century and under the Macedonians the position is far from clear. Hendy's work on the Comneni and Latin conquest enables some new mints to be added to the major ones in Constantinople and Thessalonica.

MAGNESIA NICAEA	minting gold, silver and billon 1208–61 for the Byzantine succession state of Nicaea.
CORINTH	or some other Greek centre, for copper tetartera under Manuel I and Andronicus I.
PHILIPOPOLIS	possible mint after the reform of Alexius I for gold and billon.

From 1204 to 1461 TREBIZOND was an independent Empire with rich silver mines. It issued silver aspers and a few silver trachea of distinctive style influenced by Selçuk Turkish and Byzantine types. Copper pieces widely differing in size and often scyphate were also issued, but have as yet been little studied.

VI. MINT PRACTICE

Little is known of Byzantine mint practice except what can be deduced from the coins themselves. There are no surviving dies nor is there any literary source describing activities at the mints. Even literary references are few and casual in character as Byzantine authors only mentioned money with reluctance. But the most casual handling of Byzantine coins soon shows one clear difference from those, for instance, used in Britain. The normal Byzantine die axis was ↑↓ as against the Royal Mint's ↑↑, which was the setting also used at the Alexandria mint issuing the long series of billon tetradrachms from Tiberius to Diocletian. The dies do not appear to have been mechanically adjusted or 'pegged' by projecting lugs as Venetian dies sometimes were: but the uniformity of Byzantine coins is such that there must have been some guide—quite easy to devise—for the striker or whoever held the free-moving trussel over the fixed anvil die. There are many examples of dies not meeting exactly, including an extreme case of a dekanummia of Justinian I year 30 from Nicomedia where the dies only coincide over about one third of the surface of the flan. At the Carthage mint a die adjustment of ↑→ (as

Fig. 2. *Justinian I, dekanummia of year 30, mint of Nicomedia (actual size; dies* ↑→*).*

practised by the contemporary Sassanian rulers of Persia) was often but not always used: however, when coins with such a die setting are found, it is fair to consider Carthage as the likely mint.

Anyone looking at an unsorted pile of Byzantine copper will be immediately struck by the very odd shape of many flans and by the damage caused to many of the types by overstriking. It is fair to say that whereas gold coins are only rarely found overstruck, copper coins are normally in that condition, except for those struck immediately after a reform of the coinage when the sizes of flans were also changed. This is the reason for Byzantine copper in really good condition always commanding a high price in the markets. The study of these overstrikings can be most revealing in establishing the correct order of types, as is explained later in the chapter dealing with the Anonymous

99

81, 82

series in the tenth and eleventh centuries. Two, three and even four strikings can sometimes be identified on a single copper flan, but it is not always easy to establish which is the last of them. Important issues can hang upon the point as Grierson shows in dealing with the coins attributed to Heraclonas in the Dumbarton Oaks Catalogue, vol. II, p. 392. In any event the practice of overstriking plays havoc with any artistic effect the coin may have been designed to have.

It is almost inconceivable that a regular mint could have issued some of the roughly hacked flans that are occasionally found: many could not have passed the most casual official inspection. The technical processes of making copper flans appear to have been much more difficult to the Byzantines than to the Romans whose techniques and organization they had inherited, had they wished to use them. Many coins—especially common in the reign of Constans II—show the casting 'lugs' on either side where metal has been run into a connected series of circular depressions to produce blanks for striking. The overstriking of flans meant also hammering them out of shape, while well-shaped large flans, like those of Justinian I's folles, would sometimes be sheared into quarters, or less, to produce flans for smaller folles and lesser denominations, without anyone worrying to file or smooth off the sheared edges. On some coins the traces remain of a broad, toothed instrument which appears to have been used to break off the flan from a larger mass or sheet. All these subterfuges would seem to indicate—as was to be expected—that the mints were working

17, 18

under great pressure to produce copper coin quickly: this pressure especially affected the three central mints at Constantinople, Nicomedia and Cyzicus.

On the matter of die axis mints seem to have been careful and were certainly successful in maintaining a norm of ↑↓ obverse to reverse relationship, with occasional lapses into ↑↑. Their accuracy was equal to that of the Sassanian mints—the only rival coinage so long as that Empire lasted—with their ↑→ setting. One mint—that of Carthage—appears at times to have leaned officially to this right-angular setting, exceptionally. Though Byzantine flans were often badly prepared the dies were applied in an organized way. There is another hint of organized planning in the existence of some Cyzicus and Antioch folles of Phocas dated year 9, when in fact his reign ended all but two months before the end of year 8. The dies were ready and, it seems, some pieces struck before the new year began and—as in the case of Edward VIII threepenny pieces in Britain—a few got into circulation.

The copper coinage was a token one as the contrast between a follis of Justinian I and one of Constans II—an interval of just over a century—will testify: diameters of over 40 mm. for the former and under 18 mm. for the latter are frequent, but both bear the denomination *M*. The weights of two specimens with these diameters were respectively 22.1 g. and 2.5, and are by no means extreme cases. By contrast, gold coins were carefully executed as regards shape, weight and fineness, though they occasionally passed into circulation double-struck and some were restruck brockages

10

18

still retaining clear traces of an incuse impression. Overstrikes were most unusual and one such of Justinian I overstriking Anastasius is illustrated. A freak from the reign of Heraclius has survived as twice struck from a cracked obverse die with another flan overlapping, but the author has never seen another. The mint could be proud of its gold coinage which had an international reputation to maintain and which often reflects the best artistic standards of the day. Gold coinage brought to the mint seems to have been reduced to bullion and re-issued by the reigning sovereign as necessary. It may have been a matter of sheer demand that made this impossible when dealing with copper, for new or usurping emperors must have often wished to put their names and portraits before the public: at any rate the answers were found in overstriking. In the early years of Heraclius the number of overstrikes on coins of Phocas makes it appear a matter of policy, though the critical times could have been responsible for it: in any event the reign is a happy hunting ground for the student of overstrikes.

The mint of Constantinople was organized in sections or officinae (singular officina, of which the Greek form *OΦ[IKKÍN]A* occurs on an early follis of Constans II), as had been the practice in the later Roman Empire. Ten such officinae numbered *A, B, Γ, Δ, Є, S, Z, H, Θ, I* produced gold coins and enabled a strict control to be maintained over their weight and fineness. Five officinae, *A, B, Γ, Δ, Є,* produced the vast quantities of token copper needed but, as will already be obvious, with a great deal less care. Other mints had fewer officinae— two each for instance at Nicomedia and Cyzicus—but what their relationship was to the central mint, if any, is as yet unknown. Clearly Carthage and to a lesser extent Antioch, Ravenna and Sicily had a good deal of autonomy in types produced, and Alexandria, Cherson and Thessalonica had denominational series of their own. The strange irregularity over the years of copper coinage from Ravenna might indicate local needs being met as required and without co-ordination (even of type) with Constantinople. Both Ravenna and Carthage were, of course, centres of provincial government with powerful Exarchs in charge. Official policy and the shrinkage of the Empire in the face of external attacks brought about a decline in the number of mints and the officina system declined too: it became ossified in the ninth century and was revived again, clearly but less obviously on the coins, under the Comneni. The system had certainly once meant something in practical terms as a great number of sixth- and seventh-century gold solidi have had the original number of the officina at the end of the reverse legend changed, either by obliteration or, more usually, by having a new number engraved over the earlier one.

Dies appear to have been used to the utmost as flaws and developing cracks can often be traced on gold coins. A solidus of Heraclius, where a new flan was placed on the die before the previously struck coin had been completely removed, has already been mentioned as retaining two impressions of a long crack. Occasionally flans unsuitably large for the types were

102, 103 Justinian I *(527–65)*. *Gold solidus.*
Obv. *This is Justinian's second type with an*
important change to a facing bust which was to
become a characteristic feature of Byzantine
coinage and indeed of Byzantine art. The
emperor wears a helmet with crest and a diadem
with pendilia. Rev. *The ' angel facing ' type*
is unchanged and the officina is B (2) (diam.
20 mm.).

104, 105 Justinian I *(527–65)*. *Gold solidus.*
Obv. *Justinian's third type has the obverse*
unchanged though the engraving is often thin and
lifeless. Rev. *The angel's cross has been turned*
into a Christogram. The weakness of the engrav-
ing can be seen by comparing it with No. 103
above. Officina Δ (4) (diam. 20 mm.).

used, one solidus of correct weight of Justin II has a diameter of 24 mm. and types including the annular border of only 18 mm. These things happened with copper coins too: an extreme case of a flan too large for the types struck on it, is an eleventh-century follis of Anonymous Class B with types of 23 mm. (obverse) diameter and 25 mm. (reverse). The flan used was that of a follis of Nicomedia struck by Justinian I five hundred years before and cleaned down so that few traces of the original type survived: it was 38 mm. in diameter. In this case the complete circular die face was 4 mm. wider than the engraved type. The assiduous collector will run into many examples less obvious than this as well as of the opposite, and less forgivable fault, of using obverse dies of a larger denomination on flans of a smaller one. This results in a bust with little if any legend and the mint of Antioch in the reign of Justinian I provides many examples, particularly of a follis die used for the obverse of a neat-fitting twenty nummia reverse.

The engraving of legends on the dies must have sometimes been done by illiterate craftsmen without skilled supervision. At the end of Justinian I's reign (years 36 to 38) at Antioch again, a meaningless jumble of symbols was substituted for the legend on folles. These blundered legends seem to have become traditional at the mint as they continue through the reigns of Justin II and Tiberius II into that of Maurice. This blundering is a quite different matter from the intermixture of Latin with Greek letters and their joint use in a single legend.

Some gold solidi are without an officina number and space seems to have been left for one to be inserted on the die later. Sometimes too little space was left with an effect of considerable overcrowding. Thus some dies at least were made before officina numbers were engraved and perhaps before some of the marks in the field were put on too—this particularly applies to the N in the right field of many solidi of Heraclius. It has been suggested that this N might refer to a Department of State using these solidi for a particular purpose and this would fit in with it's being later engraved on a standard die, but as yet there can be no certainty as to its meaning.

Officina numbers are only one of many markings found on Byzantine coins, particularly on the gold. Some of the others have been shown to be dates and some are likely to be privy marks within the mint. There is no firm knowledge on the matter and indeed until some new literary source is discovered progress, where there are so many unknowns, is likely to be limited.

After Leo III and Constantine V fractions of the copper follis were no longer struck, so that a copper piece of whatever size was a follis: it was a sign of the inflation which is obvious enough in Britain today where the farthing and halfpenny are no longer struck or legal tender and the penny has been revalued. In the reign of Alexius I the follis itself was abolished but its form had remained long after much of the information it carried had become nugatory. It became a *type immobilisé* in a form copied without understanding of its meaning. Thus the reverse of a follis of Justinian I which had borne the date, mint, officina and denomination as for instance:

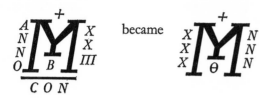

became

under Michael II. On the second piece the Θ ($= 9$) apparently represents an officina, but one never used for copper however great the pressure. The date seems to be a vestigial *ANNO XXX* reversed and the denominational *M* had long been redundant: curiously enough the one thing that could have been of importance—the name of the mint—was left off. There is a general tendency for coin design to be conservative and for types to become ossified or immobilized, like the heraldic designs on British silver and cupro-nickel pieces: this is evident on Byzantine solidi in the Victory with the long cross reverse and in the bust of Jesus on the obverse of the later gold histamena.

If one is to judge from copper issues, mint discipline cannot have been strict over flans or over passing ineffectively overstruck coins. But all are not defective: it is only in the crisis periods such as the reigns of Maurice, Phocas and Heraclius that clumsy flans become a regular feature and even then the Antioch folles of Maurice and Phocas continue with good flans, well struck with efficiently (if unimaginatively) designed dies. It could easily be a matter of too few men overwhelmed by pressure of work in the three central mints. There could also be wide variations in weight between coins of any one issue from the

same mint, though presumably a pound of copper had to be turned into a given number of coins even if they were only tokens.

Countermarks occur frequently on coins during the seventh century but generally in connection with the islands of Sicily and Cyprus. The two islands account for four out of eleven known marks, but the other seven are all uncommon, and only where there has been plentiful material has it been possible to suggest plausible reasons for them. The mark associated with Cyprus —$\mathcal{K}$—is found commonly on the folles of Constans II, placed there in the view of Grierson by Constantine IV, to indicate the devaluation of the piece from follis to half-follis. It occurs also on some pieces of Constantine IV himself, who was introducing a heavier follis (and fractions) with the old and the new values marked on each, as in MK+ or +IK for the half- and quarter-follis respectively. 235

The Sicilian series with three different marks is at once more complicated and more interesting: all are of the reign of Heraclius and all have obverse and reverse dies kept so accurately in a fixed relationship that they may have been used in a pincer mechanism. One object of the first of the countermarks, dated to *c.* 620, was to obliterate the old mint mark with a new Sicilian one. In this series coins of Anastasius, Justin I and early Justinian I were used, 114, but only very exceptionally any of the facing bust type of Justinian. Normally the countermarks are on the emperor's head and on the mint mark but one of Justinian I was originally struck ↑↑ instead of ↑↓. 116, On this the old mint mark was obliterated and the head of Heraclius is upside down at the bottom of Justinian's bust. It is an open question why the coins were countermarked at all as they are all heavy pieces— that is heavier than Heraclius's current folles—and in remarkably good preservation, considering that they were about a hundred years old. The fact of Sicily being the base from which Justinian's conquest of Italy was conducted, and a secure refuge during the many sudden reversals of fortune on the mainland, would account for a large accumulation of copper coins of these earlier emperors. The second of the Sicilian marks bearing—like the first mentioned— an out-of-date representation of the emperor and his son, is impressed on coins of the twentieth and twenty-first years of the reign (629-31), in the main freshly minted; still accurately placed, they do *not*, however, obliterate the mint mark. The third mark represents Sicily by $\overline{SC^s}$, not as in the earlier ones by $\overline{SCL^s}$, and is not accurately placed on a particular part of the coin. The $\overline{SC^s}$ brings it into line with a later Sicilian coin which certainly was struck at Constantinople and Grierson thinks that the third of the countermarks was imposed in the capital before the coins were consigned in bulk to Sicily. More recently Hendy has emphasized that Sicily was in neither the prefecture of Italy nor the diocese of Africa but was administered from the capital, so that the third countermark (and perhaps the second too) was another way of providing coin for the area, after closing the mint at Catania.

It will be convenient here to deal with the 'later Sicilian coin' referred to in the last paragraph. In considering the coinage of Constans II and the possibility of transferring some of it to Heraclonas, Grierson noted that a series of folles of year 3 mint-marked $\overline{SC^s}$ bore officina numbers normally only found in Constantinople itself: at the same time coins similar in style and type (a bust instead of the usual standing figure of the emperor) were being issued with mint mark *CON* from all five officinae. Grierson's attribution of both these issues to Heraclonas has not won general approval owing to the evidence of overstrikes, but that coins for Sicily, and even marked Sicily, were produced in the capital, seems now to be clear; indeed there are other groups both of copper and gold that may be placed in the same category as Grierson has suggested with regard to Thessalonica. This concentration of work in the mint of Constantinople Hendy regards as a matter of administrative policy undertaken before Arab attacks necessitated a reappraisal and, in fact, just when victory over the Persians would have enabled the old system to be restored. In the next centuries local mint activity can be detected occasionally on grounds of stylistic changes, as Dr Metcalf has proposed in the reign of Michael II, but it seems the exception and probably for particular purposes, rather than the rule.

Thus the mints reflect the great administrative changes which were in progress in the seventh century. The central control of money had been in the hands of the Comes Sacrarum Largitionum and it was the Prefects who struck gold issues for the dioceses under them. This system was coming to an end and instead centralized bureaux under logothetes were taking over. The

106 Constans II *(641–68). Follis of 642/3,
reverse: enlargement of left-hand-side to show
ОФА for 'officina' with Є in the exergue.
Rare appearance of the word (21 × 24 mm.).*

107 Maurice *(582–602). Solidus, reverse: enlargement of right-hand-side to show the officina
mark Θ superimposed on Δ or A. Note
also the symbol T in the field, the meaning of
which is unknown.*

108 Justin II *(565–78). Solidus, obverse. A
large flan measuring 24.5 mm. in diameter but
the 'type' is only 18 mm.: the solidus is
however of correct weight (diam. 24 mm.).*

109 Romanus III *(1028–34). Follis (Anonymous B), reverse. The cross on steps type is
struck over a cleaned flan of Justinian I (527–
65) of which part of the obverse legend can be
seen on the left (diam. 39 mm.).*

110, 111 Justinian I *(527–65). Copper half-follis,
obverse and reverse. Mint of Antioch 557/8.*

*The obverse is struck from a follis die too
large for the flan which is correctly designed for
the half-follis die of the reverse (diam. 25.5
mm.).*

112, 113 Phocas *(602–10). Copper follis, obverse
and reverse. This is typical of the crude overstrikes the Constantinople mint was prepared
to issue in the seventh century. The obverse
shows Phocas in consular robes with the date of
the earlier Maurice striking (8 = 589–90)
cutting the cross of his crown. On the reverse
the Phocas date (4 = 605–6) follows XXXX
and CON can be read underneath. The beginning of the Maurice obverse legend can be
clearly seen beneath this, with parts of his
armoured bust above (diam. 32 mm.).*

114, 115 Heraclius *(610–41). Copper follis with
first type of Sicilian countermark designed to
obliterate the earlier mint mark. It is struck on
an unusually late follis of Justinian with facing
bust and the date 33, or 559–60 (diam.
33 mm.).*

106

107

109

108

110

111

112

113

114

115

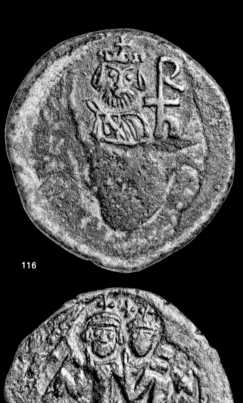

116

117

118

119

120

121

122

123

124

125

116, 117 Heraclius *(610–41). Copper follis with first type of Sicilian countermark. The original flan had been struck early in the reign of Justinian I (profile bust) but, exceptionally, with dies placed ↑↑. Thus the properly placed (↑↓) Sicilian dies of the countermark obliterate the old mint mark as intended but place Heraclius's bust over Justinian's chest instead of his head. Clearly it was the obliteration of the mint mark that was the primary consideration (diam. 32 mm.).*

118, 119 Heraclius *(610–41). Copper follis with second type of Sicilian countermark. The flans generally used for this countermark are of the 20th or, as here, the 21st year of Heraclius himself and there seems to have been no intention of obliterating the original mint mark, which can be clearly seen. Out-of-date busts of Heraclius and Heraclius Constantine in civilian robes were used (diam. 32 mm.).*

120, 121 Heraclius *(610–41). Copper follis with third type of Sicilian countermark. The busts on the countermark have been brought up to date and Heraclius's monogram put alongside the now further abbreviated Sicilian mint mark. The flans are not easy to attribute as they are generally cut down, as here, close to the edge of the countermark itself (diam. 22 mm.).*

122 Justin I and Justinian I *(527). Gold solidus, obverse. The joint reign lasted from April 1st to August 1st 527 but there are a large number of dies used for solidi alone. Many of them show signs of hasty design and workmanship and in particular CONOB appears on the obverse (as here) and reverse (diam. 20 mm.).*

123 Justin I and Justinian I *(527). Copper follis, obverse. The Antioch mint which issued this piece produced a full range of copper denominations with two busts, down to five nummia. The legend begins to the right of the cross between the heads with ' DN DN ', one ' Our Lord ' for each emperor (diam. 32 mm.).*

124, 125 Tiberius II and Maurice *(582). Gold solidus, obverse and reverse. Maurice was created Caesar on August 5th, and crowned emperor on the 13th on the same day on which he married Tiberius II's daughter. Tiberius died the next day. This coin, of which two obverse dies are known and reverse dies from the 3rd and 10th officina, has a bust similar, except for the helmet, to that of Tiberius and a reverse of Maurice type. Only immense pressure to produce dies would explain certain features of the obverse legend (diam. 21 mm.).*

Empire was taking on a new physical and administrative division into *themes*, a process of which much still remains to be discovered.

A surprising feature of the mints in the sixth century is the speed with which they could produce coins for a new emperor. When Justin I created his nephew co-emperor in 527, a joint reign of four months followed. In this period solidi, folles and fractions survive from Constantinople in fairly large numbers, folles from Nicomedia and Cyzicus, and folles with a complete range of fractions from Antioch, some of them now very rare. In 578 Justin II and Tiberius II reigned together for ten days only, but solidi—now very rare—were issued. Again, in 582 Tiberius II made Maurice Caesar a matter of eight days before he died and emperor only a day before but solidi combining a Tiberius II obverse

122, 123

124, 125

with a typical Maurice reverse appear to come from this brief interlude.

Such promptitude argues an efficiency which must be set against the crudely made and overstruck copper flans of the seventh century, and indeed the scyphate gold pieces of the fourteenth century. Gold had been much more carefully produced as it represented bullion value, but already in Justinian II's reign standards were falling and gold dies were used for silver issues. In the last centuries of the Empire roughly sheared flans of debased gold with deep striking cracks and types disfigured by double striking became commonplace. The alloy containing 7 parts copper in 24 may have been partly responsible but there was every reason for such pieces being ousted in international trade by the new gold currencies of Italy.

377,

BOOK II.   CHRONOLOGY, COMMENT AND DESCRIPTION

The Emperor Anastasius with his Count of the Sacred Largess, John the Paphlagonian, introduced the system of copper currency which was to be the pattern of Byzantine coinage for the best part of three hundred and fifty years. The reform started in 498 but went on through the reign. It was overdue in the East, as the West had already begun to take steps to remedy the crazy situation where there was virtually nothing to use for money between the third part of a gold solidus (tremissis) and a single copper nummion of which between 2,400 and 4,800 were equivalent to the tremissis. The reform was based on introducing the follis *(M)* of 40 nummia and its fractions of one half *(K)*, one quarter *(I)* and one eighth *(Є)*. The follis with its reverse type formed from its denomination *(M)* was still appearing in the early part of the ninth century but by then the system with its fractions had been completely undermined by inflation.

It was inflation in the fifth century that had necessitated the change in 498: the copper nummia in their thousands were too small to have any recognizable value in themselves and could only circulate on a basis of public confidence. The need for the coins whenever a shortage developed was quickly supplied by forgeries little different from genuine nummia rather as tokens (and forgeries) entered the English currency in the seventeenth and eighteenth centuries. Only gold pieces had real value and from a remark of a contemporary chronicler it appears that a process of bargaining took place during business transactions, over how many nummia should be reckoned to the gold solidus or tremissis.

Early in the reign of Zeno, about 475, the city of Rome produced a large copper follis of forty nummia with the head and name of Zeno on the obverse and at roughly the same time others with a head of Roma obverse, and an eagle or wolf and 126, 127 twins reverse. They were all marked *XL* and there were also half-pieces marked *XX*, showing on the reverse a palm tree and two eagles, and a wolf and twins respectively. Following these the city of Carthage in Vandal Africa issued two series of copper pieces of 42, 21 and 12 nummia, the earlier with a standing figure personifying 128, 129 the city and the other, lighter, with the city's horse's head emblem. Some rare Roman sestertii survive from Africa overstamped 83. There is fortunately no need here to explain the apparently anomalous Vandalic denominations 83, 42, 21 and 12: the point is that civilized centres like Rome and Carthage were taking steps to check inflation and to establish stable trading on the basis of the copper follis. Anastasius was to work on the same foundation.

Zeno's Dowager Empress was left with the responsibility of choosing the next emperor and at first sight Anastasius was a curious choice. He was sixty years old and —this must have weighed heavily against him—a Monophysite heretic. Nevertheless, he had a reputation for honest administration and it could be that the urgent need for currency reform was a strong influence in his selection. A chronicler says that ' he converted all the small copper into folles which circulated thenceforward in the Roman world ', and this put clearly the major change and most obvious result of the reform of 498. From there having been 7,200 small nummia to the solidus in 445, double this number—or even more—was needed fifty years later:

the real danger lay in uncertainty as to the number and which of the nummia would be accepted. Hoards of these small nummia have been found in various parts of the Empire and not only in Africa as the British Museum's Catalogue indicates in grouping them all as ' Vandalic '. They were a normal feature of trading and Anastasius appears to have stabilized the relationship of solidus to nummion at the actual current rate of 16,800, or perhaps 14,400. The reform was carried out in two stages as the surviving coins clearly indicate and in the second stage folles double the weight of earlier ones and double the value (8,400 to the solidus) were minted. It was an unpopular measure but the fine large coins of this second issue must have given confidence. Justinian I carried the reform a stage further when again with fine, heavy and well-designed coins he brought the solidus/nummion ratio back to what it had been a century before under Valentinian III, 1:7,200—once more an unpopular move as Procopius makes clear. Thus the changes may be summarized:

130, 13

134, 13

		Nummia	*Folles*	
Valentinian III, 445	Gold solidus =	7,200	= 180	(but no such coin at the time)
Vandal Africa, *c.* 490	Gold solidus =	14,400	= 360	
Anastasius, 498	Gold solidus =	16,800	= 420	
Anastasius, 2nd stage	Gold solidus =	8,400	= 210	
Justinian I, 539	Gold solidus =	7,200	= 180	(20 lbs of copper to a solidus)

The solidus was pure gold and valuable as such; what was needed was confidence in the stability of the token copper coinage. For this the coins needed to be (1) larger than the small nummia, (2) more regular in

shape so that they looked like official pieces with a value backed by the state and (3) clearly marked in value, so that there could be no debate about it. Anastasius's coins achieved these objects admirably.

90

To start with he made the innovation of making the statement of the denomination the actual type of the reverse: care was taken with the flans and the designing of obverse and reverse types was effective. The old nummia had been of roughly 9 mm. diameter and of widely varying weight from 0.4 to 1.4 g. It was difficult with coins of this size to make much of the design: a monogram—which was frequently chosen—was a wise decision, but long wear, the infiltration of forgeries and rough flans had steadily reduced such confidence as there ever had been in them. It could hardly be otherwise when parts of the types, including the mint marks and the emperor's name, were often missing on the original striking.

The first stage of Anastasius's reform 130-133 brought the issues of folles, half-folles and quarters but no eighths or nummia. The latter were probably provided by the old currency and the absence of new coins would tend to strengthen the idea that the new denominations were designed merely to stabilize current rates, not to change them. An early issue of the 'small' new follis has nothing on the reverse but the denomination and the mint; later, officina marks and stars in the field were added. Only the dekanummia had a legend *CONCORDI(A)* and at Constantinople it had no mint mark perhaps because it *(CON)* was included in the legend. The die-axis was carefully maintained at ↑↓ and all the coins were neatly produced.

Stage I		
Nummia	Diameter in mm.	Weight in g.
40 *M*	± 24	± 8.5
20 *K*	± 20	± 4.5
10 *I*	± 16	± 2.0
5		

Stage II		
Nummia	Diameter in mm.	Weight in g.
M	32–40	± 17.5
K	24–28	± 8.5
I	21	± 4.3
Є	12–15	± 2.3

134-138 The second stage doubled the weights of the coins and the comparative scarcity of the fractional denominations as against plentiful folles, makes it probable that the old lighter issues could be used at half their stated values. Every collector will know the large flans of these second stage folles of Anastasius's reform, making their message immediately clear on the essential matters of issuer, denomination, mint and officina. Already in Persia the regnal year had been added to the traditional Sassanian design and it is a little surprising that

Anastasius did not incorporate this, as Justinian I was soon to do; it may be that concentration on basic elements in the simplest possible terms had been decided on as the better policy. For better or worse the larger flans do appear rather empty and Justinian's designs are better balanced, with the regnal year added.

The heyday of the nummion was over and it was clearly and increasingly less wanted. Justinian I and Justin II were the last 71 sovereigns to issue any at all and then in very small quantity to judge from their

126, 127 City of Rome. *Bronze follis, obverse and reverse. An early effort to provide some coins bridging the vast gap between a gold tremissis and single nummion pieces of token value. This was one of two 40 nummia pieces—the XL is above the Wolf and Twins design—issued in the last quarter of the fifth century to facilitate trade. There were also pieces of 20 nummia (diam. 29 mm.).*

128, 129 City of Carthage. *Bronze piece of 42 nummia, obverse and reverse. Carthage in Vandal-occupied Africa appears to have followed the example of Rome with similar pieces of slightly different denominations, i.e. 42, 21 and 12 nummia. Both Rome and Carthage were thus forerunners of the imperial reform of Anastasius. The obverse of this piece has a personification of Carthage, and others have a horse's head (diam. 28 mm.).*

130, 131 Anastasius *(491–518). Copper follis, obverse and reverse. A typical 'small' follis of the first stage of Anastasius reform in 498*

with the denomination firmly proclaimed on the reverse type. A gold solidus was rated at 420 of these folles each of 40 nummia (diam. 25 mm.).*

132, 133 Anastasius *(491–518). Half- and quarter-follis, reverses. Both pieces are of the first stage series and should be compared with Nos. 136 and 137 which are similar pieces of the second stage. The emphasis on the precise value of the pieces in all the reverse types on this page brings out the major purpose of the reform (diam. 19 and 15 mm.).*

134, 135 Anastasius *(491–518). Copper follis, reverse and obverse. This is a second stage follis, twice the weight of one of the earlier ones and of twice the value, i.e. 210 to the solidus (diam. 37 mm.).*

136, 137 Anastasius *(491–518). Half- and quarter-follis, reverses. Both are of the second stage, double value series, of which there was also a five nummia piece (No. 138) (diam. 29 and 22 mm.).*

126

127

128

129

130

131

132

133

134

135

136

137

138

139

140

141

142

143

144

145

146

147

148

149

138 Anastasius *(491–518)*. *Copper five nummia piece, reverse. Part of the second stage series of denominations of which the higher ones are Nos. 134–137 above (diam. 12 mm.).*

139 Anastasius *(491–518)*. *Copper quarter-follis, reverse. At the end of the reign a new design for the reverses of all denominations was contemplated, but the weights of the second stage reform were adhered to. The seated figure of Constantinopolis facing left, with the denomination less obviously emphasized on the left, were the new features of this series, but up to date only a handful of pieces have been found from it (diam. 20 mm.).*

140,141 Anastasius *(491–518)*. *Gold solidus, obverse and reverse. This coin celebrating the marriage of the emperor with the Dowager Empress Ariadne in 491 has been enclosed in a mount. The obverse legend reads PERP and shows this to be a form earlier than PP. See also Nos. 3, 4, 50 and 51. The reverse shows Christ joining the hands of Anastasius and Ariadne before him (diam. 25 mm.).*

142 Justin I *(518–27)*. *Copper follis, reverse. The mint of Cyzicus is indicated by K-Y on either side of the follis mark M. Below is the date INSΔ (Indictionis 4) or 525–6 (diam. 30 mm.).*

143-145 Justin I and Justinian I *(527)*. *Follis, quarter-follis and half-follis, obverses. All are of the mint of Constantinople and retain the Justin profile bust but include the two names on the legend. Smaller denominations are very rare. Copper for the joint reign is known also from Antioch, Nicomedia and (very recently noted) Cyzicus (diam. 31, 20 and 23 mm.).*

146,147 Justinian I *(527–65)*. *Copper follis, obverse and reverse. These pieces with a profile bust were struck prior to the reform of 539 when a facing bust was introduced and the date added to the reverse (diam. 29 mm.).*

148 Justinian I *(527–65)*. *Copper follis, reverse. A late issue of the Constantinople mint (562/3) which may be compared with the first issue of 539 (Nos. 9 and 10). The strains of the reign had been great and the coinage, like much else, shewed the fact (diam. 29 mm.).*

149 Justinian I *(527–65)*. *Gold solidus, reverse. Justinian struck lightweight solidi of 20, 21 and 22 siliquae and this coin has two features normally connected with these—the angel's orb has no cross and the legend ends ΘS. But the exergue has CONOB and the coin is full weight. Quite a number of these anomalous pieces have been found, most of them without the ΘS, the meaning of which is not yet clear (diam. 19 mm.).*

rarity. But there can be many reasons for a coin being rare including sheer chance. There exists for Anastasius a series of copper *M*, *K* and *I* pieces with a completely different type of reverse from those under discussion, yet with weights corresponding to the second stage normal issue. The reverse type shows on the right a seated figure of Constantinople facing left with *CON* in the exergue and the denomination in comparatively small size on the left. Only fifteen years ago the type was unknown (it is not mentioned in the Dumbarton Oaks Catalogue) and today there are probably less than a dozen of all the three known denominations taken together. It looks like a full scale 'issue' in the last years of the reign and on new lines but as to exactly when it was struck, why it was undertaken at all and why it is so rare, are questions that cannot yet be answered.

In all his copper and silver issues Anastasius retained the traditional Roman profile bust right for his obverses and his normal legend was *DNANASTA/SIVSPPAVG*. There were no wide differences between Constantinople and the provincial mints of Nicomedia and Antioch, but it may be worth mentioning here that when Thessalonica and Alexandria issue copper in subsequent reigns they do not follow the capital's lead as to denominations.

The issue of gold had no need for reform and was still governed by longstanding laws of the fourth century. In 366 it had been decreed that taxes from the provinces should be paid to the capital in the form of gold ingots and Anastasius commuted to gold a few payments still made in kind; when he died the Treasury had 320,000 lbs of gold or the equivalent of nearly two and a half million solidi in store. In 369 regional mints had been forbidden to coin gold though Thessalonica continued to do so. Under Anastasius these solidi no longer have *TES* or *THS* as mint marks but are differentiated by a star to left and right of the Victory reverse type with the usual *CONOB* below. This type, with Victory walking to left holding a long cross in her right hand, had been used for nearly seventy years on solidi and the legend 'Victory of the Emperors' *VICTORI/AAVGGG* longer still. The obverse type continues the three-quarters right armoured bust type with a lance over the right shoulder and a shield on the left. This had been initiated by Constantius II and it was to go on until the early years of Justinian I. Equally for semisses and tremisses the old fashioned profile bust right was continued.

There were three main classes of solidi of which the first is the least common, characterized by the extension of *PP* to *PERP* in the obverse legend which is divided at *ANASTAS* instead of the usual *DNANASTA / SIVSPPAVG*. That this is the first issue is decided by one of the two really rare and exceptional coins in this reign, the solidus celebrating Anastasius's marriage with the Dowager Empress Ariadne in 491 which has the same obverse legend. It is of traditional character with earlier examples issued by Marcian and by Theodosius II for the marriage of Valentinian III with Eudoxia, all with the same congratulatory reverse

98

legend *FELICITER NUBTIIS*. The type shows Jesus standing in the centre between Anastasius on the left and Ariadne who join their hands in front of him.

The other two classes of solidi are different only in the type of cross carried by Victory on the reverse. The first has the usual heavy looking 'voided cross' and the second a thin shaft surmounted by a simple Christogram ⳨. Both were issued by all ten officinae as was probably the other class also, but only half of them have so far been identified. For this reign, as for those of Justin I and Justinian I, there are solidi and tremisses struck by the Ostrogoths to the same standard as Constantinopolitan pieces and bearing the imperial names. Their style is generally distinctive and the reverse legend usually ends with officina Λ or none at all: *COMOB* is normally in the exergue and unbarred 'A's are a feature of the series.

Two rare types of gold have been mentioned, of which the second is not a solidus but an aureus, a piece heavier than the solidus and struck on the pre-Constantinian standard of 60 to the pound of gold, instead of 72. It retains the profile bust right type for obverse and so is distinctive amongst Anastasius's gold pieces, but extremely rare, and forgeries of it have to be borne in mind. Another aureus, also with profile bust right, is known for Justinian I. These out-of-date but valuable pieces must have been distributed in a very limited way on special occasions like medallions and as such they were not currency.

To round off the coins of Anastasius mention needs to be made of a silver coin and its half, both with a reverse type of the emperor standing, the legend *GLORIA ROMANORVM* and *COB* (almost certainly for *Constantinopolis obrysum*) in the exergue. These substantial coins weighing some 4 g. and 2 g. respectively continue with the same reverse into the reign of Justin I and Justinian I, and are referred to, somewhat unsatisfactorily, as a double siliqua and siliqua. Another silver siliqua has a corrupt *VOT MVLT* legend with *CONOS* in the exergue.

JUSTIN I (518–27). The types and weight standards of Anastasius were continued in his successor's reign though the coinage appears to lack care over detail both in the engraving of the imperial bust and legend, and in production. Many copper pieces have the emperor's name wrongly spelt and some of the lighter ones amongst these are probably contemporary forgeries. For solidi the obverse was a rather coarsely conceived bust but similar to that of Anastasius, and with the legend—in this reign normally applicable to all metals— *DNIVSTI/NVSPPAVG*. In his first issue Justin followed Anastasius' last type of reverse with Victory advancing left holding a long cross terminating in ⳨. In his second issue however the Victory has become a male figure standing frontally with a plain cross in his right hand and an orb cruciger in his left, and is normally referred to as an angel, or St Michael. The legend remained unchanged *VICTORI/ AAVGGG*. Semisses had Victory seated to right and tremisses Victory advancing right, both with an obverse of a profile bust to right, just like those of Anastasius.

99

The minor differentiations on the copper coinage become more complicated in this reign, besides the addition of new mints producing it at Cyzicus, Thessalonica, and Alexandria—the two last with their non-standard fractional denominations of 3 and 2 nummia at Thessalonica and 12 at Alexandria. Constantinople folles have varied combinations of crosses, stars and crescents in the reverse field while Cyzicus adds the Christogram form ⫟ and even the mint signature *K-Y*, the last using the exergue for an indictional dating *INSΔ* (INdictioniS 4). The indiction was a fifteen year cycle beginning on 1st September and the one here involved began in 522, so that the coin is dated 525–6. An easy indiction date to remember from which to calculate others is 582–97 as it begins in the first regnal year of Maurice. When dates occur on coins it is a fair assumption that they are regnal unless, as in this case, otherwise stated. If there is any doubt over a plain dating figure it is as well to work out an indictional date to see if it makes more sense: for example, gold coins of Carthage from the reign of Tiberius II are dated indictionally with the simple *AN [NO]* before the number.

Antioch copper pieces tend to have a continuous legend or to divide the emperor's name at an unusual place; the mint also retained (even into Justinian I's reign) the *CONCORDIA* legend for dekanummia which had been dropped elsewhere, with the exception of one rare and in many ways anomalous type at Constantinople. In silver Anastasius types with *GLORIA ROMANORVM* and *VOT MVLT* are continued.

142

150, 151 Justinian I *(527–65)*. *Copper follis, obverse and reverse. Mint of Antioch— ANTIX. First issue of the reign before the destructive earthquake of November 528 when the name of the city was changed to ΘΕΥΠΟΛΙΣ, 'City of God' (diam. 28 mm.).*

152, 153 Justinian I *(527–65)*. *Copper follis, obverse and reverse. Second issue at Antioch, with the new name in Roman characters, and a completely new obverse of the emperor enthroned—found nowhere else. Antioch mint was to prove very independent in its coin designs (diam. 31 mm.).*

154 Justinian I *(527–65)*. *Copper follis, reverse. The last of four pre-reform types at Antioch, with the city's new name in Greek letters. This form was carried on into the new reformed coinage (diam. 30 mm.).*

155, 156 Justinian I *(527–65)*. *Copper folles of Antioch, reverses. The obverses have the usual facing bust as in the Constantinople coin above (Nos. 9, 10). Year 13 (539–40) was the first in which this facing bust type was used at Antioch: after this there are no further dated folles until the year 16, shown in No. 156. The reason for the interruption was the Persian invasion and occupation of the city by Khusru I (diam. both 39 mm.).*

157, 158 Justin II *(565–78)*. *Copper follis, obverse and reverse. The obverse shows Justin II on the left enthroned beside his wife Sophia. The reverse shows clearly the mint, Constantinople, its officina, A, and the regnal year, 1. These pieces were less in weight and size than those of Justinian and later in the reign two series of folles were issued in parallel: the heavier one distinguished on the reverse by ✱ and the lighter by a cross, as in this specimen (diam. 32 mm.).*

150

151

152

153

154

155

156

157

158

159

160

161

162

163

164

165

166

167

168

169

159 Justin II *(565–78). Copper follis, reverse. A coin of Nicomedia of year 4 (568–9) (diam. 32 mm.).*

160 Justin II *(565–78). Copper half-follis, reverse. A coin of Cyzicus of year 9 (573–4) (diam. 23 mm.).*

161, 162 Justin II *(565–78). Copper follis, obverse and reverse. A variation of the standard obverse (No. 157) typical of Antioch, as is also the meaningless legend at this period. The reverse shows it to come from the usual officina for this mint, the third; the date is year 6 (570–1) (diam. 34 mm.).*

163, 164 Justin II *(565–78). Copper five nummia, obverse and reverse. The obverse monogram of 'Justin and Sophia' has been read as of 'Justinian' and the coins so attributed by earlier authors. The casting lugs on each side of this flan can be seen (diam. 15 mm.).*

165, 166 Tiberius II *(578–82). Gold solidus, obverse and reverse. From Ravenna mint showing the typically high raised border associated with that mint, and the CONOB on the reverse (diam. 22 mm.).*

167 Tiberius II *(578–82). Silver piece of Carthage, reverse. The inscription reads LVX MVNDI (diam. 13 mm.).*

168, 169 Tiberius II *(578–82). Copper follis, obverse and reverse. From the Antioch mint and dated year 7 from his becoming co-emperor in 574, and so 580–1. The emperor is shown in consular robes and regalia as is normal at this mint and with a cross on his crown. Compare the bust of Maurice below, No. 176 (diam. 30 mm.).*

The reign ends with a numismatic *tour de force* after the old and illiterate emperor had associated his very differently educated nephew, Justinian I, with him in April 527, only four months before he died. In that period a remarkable coinage was produced. 122 The capital issued gold solidi showing the two emperors seated side by side, with Justin I in the senior position on the left, and for reverse the angel standing facing, adopted earlier in the reign. The mint signature *CONOB* appears most unusually in the exergue of both obverse and reverse, and only *A* of the ten officinae has not yet been published. The number of varieties in the obverse dies—especially in the representation of the throne—is remarkable, in addition to the distinction between the emperors with hands crossed on the breast, or with each holding an orb in the left hand. The legend *DNIVSTIN-ЄT IVSTINIANPPAVG* is the commonest, but again there are many varieties. As Dr Bellinger has written, 'we can only conclude that a number of engravers working in a hurry, produced dies which conformed in general but which were not strictly controlled as to details'. Constantinople also produced folles and fractions with the profile bust of Justin but with the new legend generally with Є instead of 143-145 ЄT; these are to be found in worn condition amongst groups of sixth century folles, as are those from Nicomedia, the latter having much less accurate legends. It must have been a big coinage but, most remarkable of all, distant Antioch produced a follis and all its fractions down to Є with a new obverse of two facing busts and mint signature of *ANTIX* or *ANTX*, 123 the legend beginning *DNDN* for the two emperors. These Antioch pieces are rarer than the folles from the other mints, the commonest (and worst preserved) being the pentanummia, and the rarest preserved only in one specimen, the dekanummia piece. The half-follis and dekanummia of Constantinople are also extremely rare, and no pentanummia has yet been found.

JUSTINIAN I (527–65). A mass of coinage has survived from this reign of nearly 39 years and more is continually being found in Jordan, Israel, the Lebanon and Syria where prolonged wars against Persia (the Everlasting Peace in 532 only survived eight years!) brought both military need for money, and with changes of fortune in the field, an equal need to conceal it. The collector soon becomes so accustomed to *DNIVSTINI|ANVSPPAVG* as to risk not noticing any changes in the obverse formula or types. Besides perennial difficulties over silver issues, there are many problems both in the gold and copper coinage, into which the volume of material brings the possibility of further insight, as well as its own difficulties. For this reign samples, if realistic results are to be obtained, have to be sizable and the material is there. In 539 when Peter Barzymes was Count of the Sacred Largess the copper coinage was reformed, and the work of Anastasius completed by decreasing the number of folles to 180 to the solidus. As before, much popular outcry resulted but the weight of copper in the follis was increased so that 15 instead of 20 were struck from a pound. In the previous year a decree had been pro-

mulgated on the dating of documents and in accordance with this from 539 the regnal year was added on the reverse of copper coin large enough to include it. The larger denominations of both gold and copper were given a helmeted and armoured facing bust for the first time but silver with smaller gold and copper continued with the profile bust to right. The new coins dated from the year XII were certainly of a character to inspire confidence in their users, even if the original weight standard only lasted for three years. The increasing strains of the reign with its expensive expansionist policies, the impact of the plague in 542–3 and the death of Theodora in 548 can be seen perhaps reflected in the falling off of standards in die engraving, technical production, as well as weight in the copper folles of the later years.

Fifteen mints are now distinguished in the Dumbarton Oaks Catalogue as against ten plus an uncertain group of coins by Wroth sixty years before. One of the new attributions is Constantine-in-Numidia for some remarkably western looking coins in reigns from Justinian I to Maurice, mint-marked *CON* and often with a North African provenance; distinctive A's and Roman numerals are only two of their peculiarities along with obverse die engraving which is often, but not always, equally distinctive. Salona is also introduced on a provenance basis to account for a more tightly integrated group. Justinian's reconquests in Africa, Italy and Spain meant that more mints were needed, and only in Heraclius's reign, and for very different reasons, was their number to be rivalled: Carthage was one mint to embark on what was to prove an impressive career at this time, and Ravenna another.

Solidi with the helmeted and armoured bust three-quarters right cease in 539 and are replaced by those with a similar bust but facing and with an orb cruciger in the right hand. It has two reverses, first the angel facing with a long cross and then, for a much longer period beginning in 545 it has been suggested, the plain cross is replaced by one terminating in a simplified Chi-Rho monogram ⳨. The style of this last group is less satisfactory, partly because the engraving is too light to be effective. There are three other gold pieces of this reign, two excessively rare and the other now non-existent. The last is the well-known piece of thirty-six solidi (half a pound of gold) possibly a presentation piece to Belisarius, with a fine three-quarters right armoured bust and on the reverse Victory leading the mounted emperor. It was found in 1751 and presented to Louis XV, but was stolen with much else from the French Royal Collection in 1831: fortunately moulds had been taken and it can now be seen in electrotype. Of the two others, one is an aureus with the standard profile bust right of its day, when sixty solidi were struck from a pound of gold; and the other (known from a single specimen) shows on the obverse Justinian seated facing in consular regalia with a reverse of two Victories facing each other with a cross between them. Both these pieces were probably struck early in the reign for ceremonial presentation purposes, but consular pieces had a long history before and after the reign until,

after Phocas, the emperor ceased to hold the office.

An anomalous type of solidus occasionally met is one with a normal facing bust, but the angel facing with plain cross on the reverse has no cross on the orb in the left hand and the legend ends *ΘS*, like many others marked as lightweight. The absence of a cross on the orb is a sure sign later that the solidus is officially lightweight but these pieces are of correct weight and struck from a large number of obverse dies. Their origin remains a mystery but Constantinople did strike lightweight pieces of 20 *(OBXX)*, 22 *(OB*+*)* and, unusually, 21 *(OB+*)* siliquae. Rome and Ravenna both struck solidi—one of the former has *ROMOB* in the exergue—and also Carthage from a large number of officinae including, apparently, new ones numbered *IA* and *IB*. Carthage pieces, like the others, are identifiable by style and the mint seems not yet to have settled down, as it was to do with a regular series of dated issues. One mint with an unmistakable style and using types too small for the flans, produced a rare series of tremisses from Justinian I up to Heraclius (except for Tiberius II) in Spain, and was probably located at Cartagena. Tremisses poured from the mint of Constantinople and semisses too, both using the old types of profile bust right and, for the reverses, Victory advancing right, and seated to right respectively.

A small group of silver issued from Constantinople and Carthage retains the *GLORIA ROMANORVM* and *VOT MVLT* types substantially unchanged but a series of neatly struck pieces from Ravenna sheds a little light in this dark corner of Byzantine numismatics. These last sometimes bear their denomination *CN* (250 nummia), *PKЄ* (125 nummia) and *PK* (120 nummia) and some half-dozen types do not. They must be tokens as some 120 nummia pieces weigh substantially more than those of 125 nummia, while those without denomination cover the whole weight range of marked coins and go lower.

For copper coinage the Constantinople mint before the 539 reform produced many varieties involving different combinations of stars, crosses and crescents in the reverse field. Recently attention has been drawn to the *-ρ* mark in the obverse field on coins from officina Є of which the majority of those published are from the Syrian area. Officina Є often produced copper coins of anomalous type and may have been assigned work slightly out of the ordinary run: in the case of the *-ρ* coins Dr M. Metcalf's theory of coin consignments from the capital (more usually without marks such as these have) seems to cover the limited area of provenance. The post-reform folles and half-folles speak clearly for themselves with an immediate message of mint, date and denomination, but pentanummia have no date and both these and dekanummia have the pre-reform profile bust on the obverse. The most interesting mint of which to follow the fortunes in copper issues is that of Antioch which, owing to an earthquake in 528 officially changed its name to the City of God (Theoupolis). Then, immediately after the reformed coinage was issued in year XIII, the Persians occupied the city and disrupted the coinage again. Thus the reign starts with a complete series of denominations with mint marks *ANTIX* from four officinae which seem to operate throughout the reign with occasional help from a fifth. This series is followed by three more unreformed issues with the new name, of which one, breaking away from tradition as Antioch always seemed prepared to do, represents an emperor enthroned facing and a mint mark in broadly Roman lettering *+THЄУP*.

The others had a normal profile bust right and a mint mark either similar with an addition showing it to be abbreviated or in Greek, *ΘVΠOΛS*. As this mint signature is taken up in the reformed coins of year XIII in the form *ΘVΠO*, the Greek mint name may indicate the last of the three earlier series. The order of these types needs to be decided if only to throw some light on why the 'enthroned' type was adopted and though the Dumbarton Oaks editor says that this can be done by overstrikes and mules, he has unfortunately not included the details. Even the dated series does not run smoothly. After the Persian interlude the mint signature changes five times (years 16, 20, 23, 30 and 35) in conveying Theoupolis and in year 26 an officina *Z* (= 7) is apparently added to the five previously used. The mint ends the reign with another piece of singularity: the officinae are reduced to one—*Γ*, the one normally associated with the mint—and for three years the obverse legends are for the most part complete balderdash, and this curious practice is continued as though purposefully throughout the next reign. Antioch is also exceptional in issuing dated dekanummia with a facing bust obverse.

Fractions of the solidus

170 Justinian I *(527–65)*. *Gold semissis*. Rev. *Victory is shown seated to the right inscribing the date on a shield with a formalized trophy behind and a Christogram in the field right. The obverse is similar to that in No. 171 below (diam. 19 mm.).*

171, 172 Justinian I *(527–65)*. *Gold tremissis*. Obv. *A right-facing profile bust of the emperor continues unchanged as the obverse of fractions of the solidus until the reign of Justinian II (685–95) in spite of the change to a facing bust on the solidi.* Rev. *Victory moves to the right looking back and carrying in her right hand a laurel wreath and in her left an orb cruciger. The legend VICTORIA AVGVSTORVM simply expands the VICTORIA AVGGG on the semissis, No. 170 above (diam. 15 mm.).*

In conclusion a few notes are added on mints associated with abnormal denominations. Thessalonica issued a full range of its unusual fractions 16, 8, 4 and 2 nummia pieces all with a profile bust until at the end of the reign it adopted the facing bust obverse and the normal 20 and 10 nummia denominations. The mint continues with the latter in subsequent reigns. Alexandria also had a full range of 12, 6 and 3 nummia pieces with profile bust, but added an undated piece of 33 nummia with facing bust. The mint of Cherson in the Crimea is associated with the need of the imperial government to know what was going on along the steppe route from Mongolia, especially at this time details about the advance of the Avars. Later reigns show the follis marked *H* (8) and the half-follis *Δ* as though reckoning in pieces of five nummia. The Justinian issue has a profile bust and for reverse a monogram of the town itself, and in view of the above it is listed as a pentanummia. The mint is not known to have operated again until the reign of Maurice.

JUSTIN II (565–78). Justinian was childless and succeeded by a nephew who had the misfortune to become insane. It was a time when statesmanship of an high order was needed to protect the over-extended frontiers against Avars, Persians, Lombards and Berbers, and in 574 Justin made a good choice in picking Tiberius Constantine as his deputy, and appointing him Caesar. The coinage of the reign is undistinguished but prolific especially since the discovery of the Hama and Akkah hoards of solidi in the 1950's. Solidi in virtually mint state

have been easily available ever since and amongst them a previously unnoticed type showing Justin II with a close beard from all ten officinae and with at least one lightweight issue. The obverse is an armoured and helmeted bust similar to that of Justinian but instead of the cross on the orb in his right hand there is a Victoriola crowning the emperor with a garland. The reverse was new and showed the personification of Constantinople seated facing but looking right, a figure thought by the populace, a chronicler says, to be Venus. The reverses are diversified by symbols in the field—*, +, *C*, *I* and *Ч*—and one has the letter *Z* added to *CONOB* in the exergue. One unique piece has *ΑΛZOB* in the exergue, though there is nothing else that would distinguish it as being from Alexandria. A scarce series with the legend divided *DNIVSTI|NVSPPAVI* instead of the usual *DNI|VSTI|NVSPPAVG* has been somewhat doubtfully attributed to Carthage; it is perhaps not from Constantinople or from Ravenna, which also issued solidi, semisses and tremisses separable on stylistic grounds, and repeats an unusual *A* form along with other small divergences. The reign sees the appearance of a new gold coin representing one sixth part of a solidus, using the same size and types as the tremissis but paper thin and half the weight. No other is known until the reign of Phocas but coins so fragile may well have broken in use and been disposed of as bullion. All are of great rarity and their position in the currency will be discussed under Heraclius later.

The copper follis comes down sharply in weight and size during the reign though it

95, 96

173*-175*

173*
175*

157, 158

remains substantial with an average weight of 13.5 g. There was, however, at Constantinople from the fifth regnal year onwards, a heavier issue (by a gramme) in parallel, distinguished by a ✗ above the *M* on the reverse, as against the usual ✠. The seated figures of the emperor and his wife Sophia on the right do not make an attractive design though, as usual the Antioch mint puts its own gloss upon it, and with some success. Antioch also demonstrates a short transition period from Justinian's armoured bust type to the two seated figures which did not affect the big metropolitan mints. For two years Antioch issued a copper series with a facing bust of Justin II crowned by a Victoriola as on his normal gold coinage, and the two seated figure series does not get under way there until the fifth year. At Thessalonica too the highest denomination, a half-follis, was issued with a single bust (exactly like Justinian's) for four years, while Carthage indulged in a variety of experiments. Carthage obverses have two facing busts as well as a single armoured bust, while both Greek and Roman numerals were used; the acclamation *VITA*—'Long life to our rulers'—appears on many pieces. It still needs remarking that a common type of pentanummia with a monogram for obverse, dubiously attributed by Wroth to Justinian I (Nos. 414–30), has for some time been re-attributed with confidence to Justin II at Constantinople (Dumbarton Oaks Catalogue, I, p. 218).

In silver the *GLORIA ROMANORVM* series continues at Constantinople with an additional half-siliqua reading *SALVS (AVG)* and Carthage issued a piece of about the same weight as the latter with *FELIX RES/PVBL*. But at Ravenna the fine range of issues begun by Justinian both with and without denominations is continued and, as before, their token character is underlined by the overlapping of their weights.

Tiberius II (578–82). The emperor had been made Caesar in 574 and his regnal years are reckoned from that date. He was in fact co-emperor for a matter of ten days before the death of Justin and even in that period the Constantinople mint managed to produce a now very rare coinage in gold: only three solidi are known of which one is a lightweight and the others from two different officinae. The obverse has two facing busts and the reverse reverts to the angel facing type used by Justinian at the end of his reign. The subsequent sole reign is an interesting one numismatically with many specimens surviving in spite of its short duration. A new copper denomination, the three-quarter follis was introduced at Constantinople, Nicomedia, Cyzicus and Antioch, firmly marked in Roman numerals as against the Greek *M* for the follis, though this was normally engraved in Lombardic form *Ⅲ* during this reign. For lower copper denominations coins using Greek and Roman numerals were issued in parallel—*K* and *XX*; *I* and *X*; *Є* and *Ч*. An attempt, in years 5 and 6, was made to introduce a heavier standard for the follis and one piece of Cyzicus has a diameter of 41 mm. and a weight of 17.35 g. But the follis fell back to weights around 11–12 g., a good deal lower than the average under Justin II.

80

Tiberius Constantine—and on semisses and tremisses he appears as plain Constantine—made much of his consulship in January 579. He issued a solidus with a bust crowned and in consular regalia and this was thereafter adopted as the normal obverse for his copper coins. There was, however, a period of three months before this (year 4) when some gold and copper coins were struck which have the obverse type of an armoured bust facing, wearing a crown instead of the usual helmet. These folles of year 4 retain the *M* form for the denomination and are of the old weight while in year 5 the consular bust, the Lombardic *ɯ* and a heavier standard weight were adopted. In year 7 the weight had gone down to 11-12 g.

The normal solidi of the reign show the emperor's armoured bust facing, but wearing a crown instead of helmet as described for year 4. The reverse legend is changed from *VICTORTI/ЬƐRIΛVC*, which was also used on the consular solidus, to the time honoured *VICTORI/ΛΛVGG*, all the coins having the new cross potent on four steps design, which represented a monument in Constantinople erected by Theodosius II. It is occasionally made up of pellets as though constructed of jewels. This same reverse design of a basic cross potent is also used for semisses and tremisses, although the profile bust right continues. There are lightweight solidi marked *OB+** (22 siliquae judging from their weight) and from Ravenna there is a rare group in this reign and the next reading *C + N + B*, also of 22 siliquae. On one example of two known for Tiberius II, the die originally reading *CONOB* has been re-engraved with crosses over the 'O's. Ravenna issued normal weight solidi and tremisses distinguishable by style, and from the last year of the reign Carthage began the issue of a characteristic and uninterrupted series of dated solidi. These pieces for Tiberius II are dated on the obverse with the regnal year 8 *(H)* and on the reverse with the indictional year 15 *(IƐ)* or 582. Later emperors were to content themselves with the indictional date on both obverse and reverse, besides progressively reducing the diameter and thickening the fabric of the coins; by the end of Heraclius's reign it was still of full weight and purity but only 11 mm. in diameter. Carthage also produced a new type in silver reading *LUX MVNDI* on its reverse, Constantinople another with a Chi-Rho monogram and Ravenna a minute piece weighing. 45 g. with a cross potent; all are rare and their weights, along with the small number of pieces available for study, make assessment of their role in the currency exceptionally difficult.

The bronze issues of Antioch need a short note to themselves as circumstances have combined to confuse them with those of Maurice, especially the folles which over the two reigns turn up in great numbers. The confusion stems from the very corrupt version of Tiberius' legend soon current at Antioch and continued there into the reign of Maurice. There is however a simple practical distinction between coins having a consular bust and a crown with a cross in the centre and those with a similar bust but having a crown with a trefoil ornament in the centre. Those with a cross belong to Tiberius II and must be between years 5-8:

205*
204*
165, 166
201*, 202*
167
168, 169
176, 177

the others belong to Maurice and will be referred to later.

MAURICE (582–602). A twenty-year-reign and one whose dates it is useful to remember; the beginning of it happens to coincide almost exactly with a new indiction (582–97) which started on 1 September, less than three weeks after Maurice's accession. He was a successful general, picked by Tiberius II as his successor and married to his daughter Constantina. Maurice was given the name Tiberius and at the beginning of the reign used this name alone or with his own. Three solidi have been published which may well date to the period of ten days before Tiberius' death (14 August) when Maurice was made Caesar (5 August) and then emperor (13 August). Two have the same obverse die which is a modified Tiberius one with a more rounded crown with cross and the legend re-engraved *DNNЬTIЬ/ЄRI* over a normal one. The reverse has a typically Maurice facing angel with officinae *Γ* and *I*. This looks like another example of a joint reign issue produced as speedily, but not quite as skilfully, as that of Justin II and Tiberius II. The great military and diplomatic activity of the reign against Slavs in the Balkans, in Persia, Italy and Africa is reflected in the thirteen or more mints operating: one of them, as was to be expected in a time of tribal movement, at Cherson. After the type changes of Tiberius, Maurice reverted to earlier types like the armoured and helmeted bust and the facing angel on solidi and on copper the old *M* and Greek denominations, though there were a few exceptions. The coinage in gold and copper is prolific but the latter is generally in poor condition often with poorly made flans at the start. As usual very few silver coins survive: Tiberius' Chi-Rho type continues at Constantinople, and at Carthage an early issue has the legend *SALVS MVNDI* while at the end of the reign two rare types bear the name of Maurice's eldest son, Theodosius.

There are two consular gold pieces and both most probably of the second consulate in 602 as Maurice only took up his normal consulate for a week instead of a year in 583 as a means, it is thought, of lightening the burden on an empty Treasury. Of the two, the commoner is a solidus showing Maurice seated enthroned and facing in consular regalia with the usual reverse for this reign of an angel facing with a long cross terminating with a *ꝑ*. The second, a piece of six solidi, survives in four examples all from the same pair of dies and made up with other solidi into a girdle which was part of a large treasure found in Cyprus at Kyrenia. The obverse is formed of a consular bust obviously designed from that on Tiberius II's folles and consular solidi and the reverse shows the emperor in a four-horsed chariot, a much older type associated with the representation of Sol and used by Julian amongst others. The legends are curious in that the reverse virtually repeats that of the obverse. These were not currency but medallions struck for special distribution to particular persons or officials and they are, in fact, the last issue made of gold pieces heavier than a solidus.

The enormous output of solidi during the reign provides problems in deciding in

124, 125

174 ▶
178, ?

180

173 ▶

175 ▶

173, 174 Justin II *(565–78). Gold solidus.* Obv.
This is varied from that of his uncle Justinian by
the orb being surmounted by a Victoriola. This
piece has two unusual features in the emperor's
beard and the unbroken first half of the legend.
The latter is often taken as an indication of
Carthage mint but the officina H is unlikely
there and the style is very similar to that of
Constantinople (see No. 175 below). Rev.
A new type, the personification of Constan-
tinopolis, is introduced and is said to have been
compared by contemporaries with Venus. The
legend still invoking Victory for the emperors
is unchanged (diam. 20 mm.).

175 Justin II *(565–78). Gold solidus.* Obv.
This has the usual divided legend of this reign
but a specimen of Constantinople mint with the
short beard has been chosen to make comparison
with No. 173 above easier. The reverse has
Constantinopolis as in No. 174 above (diam.
21 mm.).

what order they were issued. There is no doubt about the earliest ones which show Maurice wearing a crown with cross and the legend *DNTIЬЄRM/AVRIC...* changing to *DNMAVRIC/TIBER...*, after which the bust has a crested helmet and legend *DNMAVRC/TIЬ...* and so remains. Many attempts have been made to group this last material which also shows a change in the armoured bust from a shield covering the left shoulder to a paludamentum, but no satisfactory solution as to the order of issues and of their immense variety has emerged. On the obverses anyone can see a vast difference between a broad-faced, rather jolly, bust and a more compact, thinner and serious one—they cannot have been engraved from the same model, though the former merges into a group with the same broad bust reproduced on a smaller scale which does look as though the same model had been followed. When all these are subtracted there remain a host of types that do not fit in: some students look for guidance at the helmet, some at the angel, some postulate different mints... and there remain letters in the field *(I* and *T)* and an intrusive *K* at the end of some reverse legends to be taken into account. There is a new and fairly common lightweight issue of 23 siliquae only distinguished from ordinary solidi by a star in both the obverse and reverse fields: it joins the group containing those marked *OB+** (several of which have been found from dies with this re-engraved over *CONOB*) and *OBXX*, respectively of 22 and 20 siliquae. Ravenna has a unique *C+N+B* lightweight as well as ordinary solidi and

tremisses, while Carthage has a virtually unbroken series of dated solidi (two years only not yet published) with semisses and tremisses. Two solidi with the same obverse die, one a lightweight marked *CONXX*, are now credited to Constantine-in-Numidia. The cross potent type for semisses and tremisses introduced by Tiberius II is retained at Constantinople though a new semissis type with Victory advancing is produced both there and at Carthage and the same type is used for tremisses at Ravenna.

An immense amount of Maurice's copper survives and generally maintains the low weight standard at the end of Tiberius II's reign, but it shows a decline in care over flans which becomes even more pronounced under Phocas. The standards of die engraving at Nicomedia in particular, where the reign starts with a Tiberius legend, and at Cyzicus take a plunge downwards and the half-folles were carelessly produced—and this includes Constantinople—sometimes with dies too small for the flans. Of the five officinae producing half-folles, *Γ*, *Δ*, and *Є* can only be of Constantinople, so that those marked *A* and *B* can be distributed to Nicomedia and Cyzicus as well, some quite confidently so, on grounds of style. As with arranging the solidi the difficulty comes over where the line is to be drawn, but as both folles and half-folles are dated a closer comparison is possible with copper pieces. At both Nicomedia and Cyzicus lower denominations are mint-marked, so that half-folles represent an exceptional problem. The obverse is normally an armoured and helmeted bust except at Antioch where the

consular bust and blundered Tiberius
legend were continued. In years 20 and 21
187, 188 Constantinople, Thessalonica, Nicomedia
and Cyzicus all issued folles with a consular
bust of above average weight standard, to
celebrate the second consulship of 602.
Antioch was, of course, already using the
consular bust and had no change to make,
but in year 20 a sixth officina *(S)* appears
to be operating although not all the others
are yet accounted for, just as in year 10,
C and *Z* appear but ϵ is missing. Maurice's
Antioch coins are distinguishable from
those of Tiberius II by the trefoil ornament
in the crown until in year 9 the reverse
type is changed to *M* with the officina
beneath and a reasonably intelligible obverse legend begins *DNMAЧГI*, co-
inciding with the establishment of more
orderly relations on the frontier with Persia.
It is the legends just before this change that
are interesting as in years 8 and 9 a serious
effort was made to improve the blundered
legend, aiming at *DNTIЬCONSTANT*
—that is, not a Maurice legend at all! With

all this it is curious to find Antioch coins
more neatly struck on better flans than any
other copper and the series of dated half-
folles and dekanummia are especially com-
mendable.

Carthage continued the practice of the
mint under Justin II in issuing a wide range
of copper, interestingly designed, in this
case, to include *N M* (for nummia), the
denominational figure and the mint and
producing one series from *M* to ϵ with
the indictional date *IND III* (584–5) in
the exergue instead of the mint name.
Thessalonica, for one year, issued a type
for half-follis showing an emperor and
empress seated as it had done in the two
previous reigns; the cramped legends need
careful watching on these coins. After
this the obverse type varies between an
armoured bust with a crown and one with
a helmet, a variation that can occur at any
mint in this detail when there is not a great
deal of difference between the two: the
presence of a cross generally betrays the
crown, and a crest or plume the helmet.

The seventh century is characterized by a steady maintenance of the fineness of gold coins despite all the vicissitudes of the Empire, and by a more varied series of types, including many portraits and bewildering privy markings. The lightweight solidi, with all their problem features, reach a peak in the reign of Heraclius only to fall away and finish altogether under Constantine IV. In copper the standards of production collapse, overstriking becomes a general rule and weights slip downwards in spite of heroic efforts to re-establish them by Heraclius in years 20 to 21 and, even more spectacularly, by Constantine IV. Inflation tends to destroy lower denominations altogether, though pieces of five and ten nummia have a noticeably longer life in African and Italian issues than in eastern ones. It is a time too when, quite exceptionally, countermarks abound. The silver coinage takes a larger place than before, particularly with the prolific issues of hexagrams. Old established mints disappear through enemy action or administrative change, their places taken by ephemeral ad hoc creations. The pace quickens in the change from Latin to Greek letter forms and in the adoption of the Greek language itself. It was an age of Avar and Arab invaders who imitated imperial coin types, and veritably a 'dark age' for the people living in it who were perforce often driven to bury their little hoards of coins, many of which they were in no position to find again. Scholars today find it a dark age too for it lacks literary sources and it is the buried hoards and the story told by the coins themselves that can occasionally remedy the lack of literary evidence.

PHOCAS (602–10). There can be no doubt that the bust with a distinctive pointed beard which appears on all of Phocas's solidi and all but a few of his other pieces which carry on with the traditional profile bust right, is a portrait of the emperor himself. It is sharply differentiated from the representation of his predecessor Maurice, the many variations of which make portraiture unlikely, and from that of his successor: Phocas can be recognized at once. His solidi fall into four classes of which the two earlier are scarce and the two later, very common. His normal bust shows him wearing a crown with a cross and sometimes also with pendilia (pendants) hanging from either side, a cuirass and a

176, 177 Maurice *(582–602).* *Copper* *follis,* *obverse and reverse. Mint of Antioch year 1 (582). The obverse bust has a trefoil ornament on the crown, characteristic of this emperor who, like his predecessor, appears at Antioch in consular robes and regalia. The legend is a debased form of Tiberius Constantine as seen above in No. 168 (diam. 30 mm.).*

178, 179 Theodosius, son of Maurice. *Silver piece of Carthage, obverse and reverse. Issued in 602 perhaps when Maurice celebrated his second consulship and made much of his son's association with him as emperor. More likely— as noted in the Dumbarton Oaks Catalogue— issued later in the year before it was known that Theodosius had been killed along with Maurice and his family. The two figures on the reverse are termed A[ugu]CTI (diam. 13 mm.).*

180 Maurice *(582–602). Gold solidus, obverse. A consular commemorative piece of 602 (diam. 20 mm.).*

181, 182 Maurice *(582–602). Gold solidi, obverses. Two contrasting busts of Maurice. Do they come from different mints? No. 181 has* been attributed to Antioch, but for unconvincing reasons (diam. both 21.5 mm.).

183, 184 Maurice *(582–602). Gold solidus, obverse and reverse. A typical small thick solidus of the Carthage mint dated on the obverse ANT and on the reverse simply Γ, i.e. 599–600, the third year of the Indiction beginning in September 597–8 (diam. 16 mm.).*

185, 186 Maurice *(582–602). Gold semissis, obverse and reverse. The 'Victory walking to the right' type had been, up to Justin II's time, associated with the tremissis and indeed was so used at Ravenna in Maurice's reign. The type was not quite the same but can be confusing (diam. 19 mm.).*

187, 188 Maurice *(582–602). Copper follis, obverse and reverse. The obverse has a bust with consular robes and regalia, normally only used at Antioch, but the date, regnal year 20 (601–2) gives the clue as Maurice assumed the consulship for the second time in 602. Hence consular copper coins from Constantinople, Nicomedia, Cyzicus and Thessalonica in regnal years 20 and 21. This follis is from Nicomedia (diam. 31 mm.).*

176

177

178

179

180

181

182

183

184

185

186

187

188

189

190

191

192

193

194

195   196

197   198

199   200

189, 190 Phocas *(602–10). Gold consular solidus, obverse and reverse. The pendilia on the crown connect it with the first issue of ordinary solidi. Phocas assumed the consulship in December 603. The second consular type of the same year is illustrated, No. 236 (diam. 23 mm.).*

191, 192 Phocas *(602–10). Gold solidus, obverse and reverse. The emperor's last issue with the revised reverse legend (compare No. 190), which refers to a single emperor only (diam. 20 mm.).*

193, 194 Phocas *(602–10). Copper follis of Antioch, obverse and reverse. The major mints began by issuing copper showing Phocas with his wife Leontia standing facing. Only at Antioch was this carried on, as this specimen dated year 7, demonstrates. The others used a consular bust of the emperor alone, which Antioch also adopted in year 8 (diam. 21 mm.).*

195, 196 Revolt of the Exarch Heraclius. *Copper follis, obverse and reverse. Struck at Alexandretta in 610–11, year 14, i.e. of the Indiction beginning 597–8. The Exarch is shown on the right and his son, subsequently the Emperor Heraclius, on the left, both crowned (diam. 29 mm.).*

197 Heraclius *(610–41). Copper follis, obverse. The type shows Heraclius in military uniform on the left holding the cross which he had just recaptured from the Persians. This issue, in years 20 and 21 of the reign, attempted to re-establish the weight of the follis, but this had to be halved in the very next year (diam. 29 mm.).*

198 Heraclius *(610–41). Copper follis of Seleucia-in-Isaura, obverse. This follows the type normal at old-established mints for its year of issue which was 6 (615–16) (diam. 30 mm.).*

199, 200 Heraclius *(610–41). Copper follis of Seleucia-in-Isaura, obverse and reverse. The other follis type adopted by this 'military' mint copies the solidi of the time with busts of the emperor and his son. The reverse shows the mint, date (year 7) and officina (B) (diam. 27 mm.).*

paludamentum covering his left shoulder such as appeared on all but the earliest issues of his predecessor. Although favouring the consular bust for his copper issues, for his solidi Phocas continued with this armoured type except for the actual consular issues of December 603. These last fall into a very small and a much larger group. The first has a crown with pendilia and the name spelt *FOCAϵ*, the few known specimens are all from the tenth officina and the same reverse die; the second has a crown without pendilia and comes from several officinae. All Phocas solidi have the angel facing with long cross reverse but the legend changes. The order of issues can be established as:

189, 190

236*

first — Crown with pendilia, and armoured bust: a scarce issue though probably all officinae were involved (only *A*, *H* and *Θ* are not yet accounted for).

second — The consular *FOCAϵ* issue (crown with pendilia) closely followed by the consular type having a crown without pendilia.

third — The common issue, involving all officinae, of the armoured bust and crown without pendilia.

fourth — The obverse type is continued but with a changed legend on the reverse from the plural *VICTORI AVGG* [*Augustorum*] to the singular *VICTORI AVGЧ*[*STI*]

191, 192

Grierson has placed the change of legend in 607 when Phocas wished to make clear that he was not associating his son-in-law Priscus with him as co-emperor. The fourth

issue is as common as its predecessor and comes from all ten officinae; it begins however to be noticeable that coins from the fifth and tenth officinae are much more abundant than others, and this trend was to continue.

All these issues except the consular ones have a type with *N* in the field and the last has many examples in which the legend begins *δNN* instead of the regular *δNFOCAS*/*PERPAVG*. In neither case can the intrusive *N* be satisfactorily explained. All the issues too, again excepting the consular ones, have a full compliment of lightweight denominations of 23 siliquae (star in obverse and reverse field), 22 siliquae *(OB+ *)* and 20 siliquae *(OBXX)* instead of the standard 24. There are semisses and tremisses for both the common series, with profile busts and one type of tremisses has a bearded profile, a significant change that was not developed. There is also a very rare (and confusing) one sixth of a solidus piece struck with tremissis dies but of half the weight; this will be discussed with a similar piece in Heraclius's reign. Gold solidi were also struck at Carthage where the dated series continues, and at Ravenna which also issued some bearded profile tremisses, and possibly at Thessalonica. The distinctions concerning pendilia and consular and armoured busts can be followed in provincial mints: at Carthage, for instance, Indiction 6 (602–3) has a solidus with armoured bust, but Indiction 7 both one with a consular and another with an armoured bust following exactly the proprieties of protocol. The Byzantine outpost in Spain continued to issue its idiosyncratic tremisses undisturbed.

The copper issues of the reign start at Constantinople, Nicomedia, Cyzicus and Antioch with a type showing Phocas and his wife Leontia standing facing and on the reverse an **M** for the follis denomination. Except at Antioch, and at Constantinople where a few examples dated year 2 have survived, this type only lasted until Phocas assumed the consulship in December 603 after which the coinage settles down to a normal consular bust and denominations in Roman numerals, including a revival of the three-quarter follis at Constantinople, Nicomedia and Cyzicus. Exceptionally, Antioch kept the standing figures type until year
3, 194 7 and the **M** denomination throughout the reign, and Ravenna had an armoured bust type for her folles. All Antioch copper down to the dekanummia is remarkably well produced in contrast with Nicomedia or Cyzicus for instance. Catania struck a pentanummia with mint signature *CAT* and Carthage a piece unmistakably from that mint, but the rest of the pentanummia, few and diverse, are usually grouped under Constantinople. Many twelve nummia pieces struck at Alexandria are ascribed to Phocas, without any of them bearing a legend in which his name is recognizable, for that of Justinian seems more likely to be the one aimed at. They are the product of some period of chaos in this reign or the next and merge into copies of the coin in the early Arab period.

There is little silver to be recorded and with one exception the pieces tend to be small, worn and scarce. From Constantinople there is a fine medallion, existing in several strikings from the same pair of dies, with a beardless profile bust right for obverse and a cross between palm branches reverse; this is just four times the weight of a so-called miliaresion (3.45 g.), which in turn has a half-piece, both with the same types. Ravenna has a small coin (0.4 g.) with the same obverse and *ΦK* as reverse, presumably for ' Phocas ', but if read *ΠK* conveying ' 120 ' nummia. From Carthage comes a piece just twice the weight of this with a facing consular bust and a reverse with *AΩ* beneath the arms of a cross, which on this basis can be valued at 240 nummia. There does seem to be a pattern here from *ΦK* (0.4 g.) to the miliaresion (3.45) multiple by eight.

History has little good to say of Phocas except the story of his death. It is not altogether fanciful to look at the man through his coins, for it must surely have been his personal decision to have his portrait put upon them so characteristically and frequently: one recalls too his insistence on his sole right to imperial honours on them. He appears a little old fashioned in his emphasis on the consular office and on Roman numerals for both were on the way out, but was clearly personally proud of himself and of his office; like earlier Roman emperors he too appreciated the importance of coins as propaganda. Fortunately the cruelty that made him abhorred, cannot be seen on his coins.

THE REVOLT OF THE EXARCH HERACLIUS, 608–10: The Exarch and his son, the future Emperor Heraclius, began their revolt in Carthage in the name of the elder Heraclius but putting forward the younger as a candidate for Phocas's throne. A substantial coinage from four mints normally shows two facing consular busts with the younger man in the senior position on the spectator's left, surrounded by a consular legend *δNЄRACLIO CONSVLI*. The work of unravelling the details of the coinage and its peculiar dates has been—like so much work on seventh-century Byzantine coinage—that of Professor Grierson and, as a result, coins provide a substantial part of present day knowledge of the revolt. The dates *IA, IB* and *IΓ*, and *Anno XIII* and *XIV*, all prove to be indictional from *IA* (607-8) to *Anno XIV* (610-11) and the places of mintage give strong leads as to the course of events leading to the attack on Constantinople, traditionally undertaken by land and sea expeditions. A full range of coinage, including copper from forty nummia down to five, with exceptionally the single bust of the elder Heraclius as obverse, comes from Carthage. Alexandria issued some

239*, 240* solidi with an appalling standard of die engraving followed by others of much better style and ALEXAND[RETTA] produced

195, 196 folles and half-folles (years XIII and XIV). Finally Cyprus *(KVΠPOV)* minted a clearly related follis with the strange date *ANNO III*, from which perhaps a *X* is missing. Some of the Alexandretta pieces show bareheaded busts and other busts with crowns on them, presumably after news of Heraclius's success had reached the mint. All the coins are rare, with the exception of the smaller Carthage coppers, and they are seldom found in good condition. The beheading of Phocas in October 610 brought the younger Heraclius to the throne.

HERACLIUS (610-41). The reign is studded with important events and desperate situations which show themselves in the coinage, for instance, in the opening and closing of mints and in the oscillating weight of the copper follis. The coins give portraits of

201 ▶ Heraclius at several stages of his career and

202 ▶ representations of his sons, born in 612 and around 625 respectively, and of his niece and second wife Martina. The members of the family appear in strict seniority on the coins: of two figures the senior is on the spectator's left and of three, the senior is in the middle and the most junior is on the spectator's left. In the early part of his reign Heraclius appears as a figure of heroic proportions when he seemed at long last to have humbled for ever the Persians who had been for centuries the powerful rivals of Rome and Byzantium. Then at the end of his reign a second crisis, created by Arab raiding into religiously dissident provinces, called for similar action again but broken health, including acute dropsy,

203 ▶ rendered him incapable of rising to the occasion. A mass of not very attractive coinage survives from hoards buried in these unquiet times, containing gold, copper and, for the first time, silver (an experiment in bimetallism had introduced a silver coin of real, as against token, value

55, 56 in the hexagram). Of the traditionally important mints, that of Antioch never opened in the reign, nor does it resume

204 ▶ operations later when in turn it fell into the hands of Persians, Byzantines and Arabs. Nicomedia and Cyzicus do not participate in the reformed coinage of 629, thus leaving Constantinople the only eastern mint of consequence. New mints opened

Differences of style at mints

201, 202 Tiberius II *(578–82). Gold solidus.* Obv. *From the mint of Carthage bearing the date AN[NO]H at the end of the legend,* i.e. *regnal year 8 reckoned from his becoming co-emperor in 574. The emperor wears a crown instead of the earlier helmet.* Rev. *The legend ends IЄ (15) which cannot be an officina as there were only ten, but indicates the date—the 15th year of the Indiction beginning 1st September 567: Tiberius died on 14 August 582. The new ' cross on steps ' reverse design is introduced in this reign. Compare the style and particularly the lettering with the Ravenna coin, Nos. 203, 204 below (diam. 20 mm.).*

203, 204 Tiberius II *(578–82). Gold lightweight solidus, from the mint of Ravenna.* Obv. *DM for Dominus takes the place of DominusNoster.* Rev. *The high annular border, characteristic of Ravenna mint coins is more obvious on the reverse. The original die was cut CONOB but has been altered by obliterating the two O's and substituting crosses instead: in fact traces of the second O remain. The alteration showed that the coin was ' lightweight ', i.e. of 22 siliquae instead of 24. It weighs 4.06 g. (diam. 21 mm.).*

and closed in the wake of strategic demands.

In approaching the coinage in more detail, one difficulty lies in the lack of correspondence between the copper and gold types, and it is perhaps best to start at Constantinople and its copper folles on the lines of division made by Grierson in his Dumbarton Oaks Catalogue.

Constantinople Folles. Types (after Dumbarton Oaks)	Dates	Weights (after D. O.)	Other mints issuing similar Follis Types	Constantinople Types of Gold Solidi
1 Heraclius: facing bust.	1–3	10.5 g.	Nicomedia, Cyzicus, Thessalonica, Ravenna.	I Heraclius: facing bust.
2 Heraclius and Heraclius Constantine: standing figures in civilian robes, facing.	3–6	11.1 g.	Nicomedia, Cyzicus, Thessalonica, Seleucia.	II Heraclius and Heraclius Constantine: two facing busts.
3 Heraclius, Heraclius Constantine and Martina: standing figures in civilian robes, facing.	6–13	9.0 g.	Nicomedia, Thessalonica, Cyprus.	
4 Same obverse but with *ANNO* on top of reverse instead of to left.	13–19	5.8 g.	Nicomedia, Cyzicus.	
5 Heraclius in military dress and Heraclius Constantine in civilian dress: standing facing.	a) 20–21	10.6 g.	Thessalonica, Ravenna.	III (year 20) Heraclius with long beard and Heraclius Constantine: two facing busts.
	b) 22–30	5.5 g.		IV (year 22) Heraclius, Heraclius Constantine (r) and Heraclonas (l): three standing figures.
6 Heraclius in military dress, Heraclius Constantine (r) and Heraclonas (l) in civilian robes: standing facing.	30–31	4.4 g.	Ravenna (year 23) and Thessalonica.	

Fig. 3. *Heraclius—Constantinople types for folles and solidi.*

Column 4 in the table only refers to mints issuing types of follis similar to those at Constantinople and does therefore not include either the two bust types of Seleucia or Ravenna or anything from Carthage, which only issued coins of half-follis denomination or less. The weights vary widely for each type and the figures given are those on page 23 of the Dumbarton Oaks Catalogue, vol. II. The dates are also those of the Catalogue, with one change based on new evidence. All mints use Greek numerals except Rome, Carthage and occasionally Ravenna, and when Constantinople and Thessalonica issue a three-quarter follis piece, they mark it with an Λ instead of its original XXX under Tiberius II and again under Phocas. For all the efforts made by Heraclius, especially in Type 5 of his folles which celebrated his victory over the Persians and his recapture 197 of the Holy Cross shown symbolically in his right hand, his folles end the reign at their lowest weight, well under half that at which they started.

The temporary mint at Seleucia is interesting to follow though the coins, folles and half-folles only, are all scarce and some rare. They begin in year 6 and end in year 8, covering a maximum period from 615 to 618 and include a subsidiary mint at Isaura in the last year only. Most of the coinage came from officinae *A* and *B* but *Γ*, *Δ* and *Є* were also in action at Seleucia, while at Isaura only *A* has appeared amongst the handful of known coins. Workmanship and die engraving at both mints were of poor quality and most of the pieces have been struck on previously used flans. The standard type for year 198 6—the two emperors standing—was em-199, 200 ployed and also a two bust type as on the solidi, with Isaura only producing the latter. The modern Silifke on the south-east coast of Turkey may well have seemed to Heraclius well suited for raids on Persian communications as they attacked Constantinople, as well as a good area in which to recruit troops: not far away was a secure base in Cyprus. There is no literary evidence for what was intended or achieved, but Grierson's treatment of the previously mysterious mint marks enables a picture to be built up from the coins themselves. The coins would be needed for the troops and perhaps their re-striking was an attempt to impress the inhabitants with the presence and power of the emperor: today they are found in the area of the mints and in Cyprus to which the expedition may have withdrawn, and not anywhere else. One sees Seleucia as the main beachhead from which a small detachment was sent up country to Isaura (Zengibar Kalesi) even- 208 tually to be withdrawn through Seleucia to Cyprus. It was a barren, mountainous area in which movement was extremely difficult and the expedition was unlikely to have made much impact on the Persians, but it may have helped to raise and train new Byzantine regiments. Ten years later, in the years 17, 18 and 19, there was a mint in Cyprus, probably again in connection with military operations then actively threatening the Persian capital from the north, but its exact purpose is not apparent.

It was Persian pressure in the vicinity of Constantinople that caused the closure of the Cyzicus and Nicomedia mints, and equally the victories of Heraclius in the east, which threatened Ctesiphon, that brought about the Persian withdrawal and their re-opening. The exact dates of closure and re-opening have had to be continually revised in the light of new coins being found but at present they are defined as:

Nicomedia closed 617–18 and re-opened 625-26.

Cyzicus closed 614–15 and re-opened 625–26.

Neither mint was in operation when the reformed folles of 629–30 were issued, and their closure is seen by Hendy as part of a wide administrative change.

The mint of Alexandria experienced a revival after the apparently chaotic years of Phocas and in spite of the town being submerged by the Persian conquest of Khusru II in 618, recaptured by the Byzantines in 628 and finally lost to the Arabs under Amr ibn al-'As in the next reign. It was only then that the dumpy dodekanummia, descendants of the long and not undistinguished series of Alexandrian tetradrachms, came to an end. The independent work of J. R. Phillips and

210 R. Göbl in tying up certain coins with the Persian conquest has enabled an order for the twelve nummia issues with Alexandrian mint marks to be firmly, if not quite impregnably, established: issues without mint marks of six *(S)* and three *(Γ)* nummia pieces with palm-tree obverse and

212 another six nummia with a cross on steps reverse were also produced in copper. The order is:

213 1) Two facing busts: 613–18.

210 2) Persian conquest—single bust with * and *C* in field: 618–28.

3) Two facing busts divided by a cross on steps: 628–9.

4) Busts of Heraclius with long beard and Heraclius Constantine with cross on steps between: 629–31.

5) Three standing figures facing with Heraclonas on left and on the reverse, cross on pyramid: 631.

6) Three standing figures facing as in 5 above but with reverse, cross over $\overline{M}$: 631–41.

7) Constans II, facing bust with orb cr., in right hand and on the reverse, cross over $\overline{M}$: 641 to 642 Arab conquest.

8) Constans II, standing figure facing: 645 to 646 (temporary Byzantine re-occupation).

9) Arab imitations of 7 and 8 above.

The mint almost certainly produced solidi under Heraclius with *IX*, *III* and possibly other additions to the reverse legend *VICTORIA/AVGU*. A group with busts of Heraclius and Heraclius Constantine and these marks, is strongly differentiated 90, 91 by style from other solidi with *CONOB* in the exergue and is heavily associated with the area on the basis of provenance. A strange transitional coin from the *III* mint carries a single bust Heraclius, where 214, 215 he looks like Phocas, and an angel type reverse, also such as Phocas used.

It has proved more convenient to look at Heraclius's copper before his gold, but the Table on p. 131 has given, in column 5, the types and dates of the major Constantinople issues. Both in this reign and the next there is a wide range of privy marks besides officinae, dates and Heraclius's monogram around the cross potent on three steps which forms the basic reverse type of the solidus. In view of his constant military endeavours it may seem strange that Heraclius, after his first issue, discarded 216, 217 the paludamentum over cuirass uniform and adopted civilian robes, particularly the chlamys with decorative tablion fastened by a jewelled fibula with pendants on the right shoulder, and the jewelled crown 218 which cannot be mistaken for a helmet. In 629 solidi do not follow the silver and copper issues with a military type: instead, the previous two bust type is re-issued for two years showing Heraclius with a patriarchal beard and Heraclius Constantine larger and slightly bearded. For the last ten years of the reign Heraclonas joined his father and step-brother in a type with three standing figures in civilian robes. On the reverse $+$, Λ and T appear in the exergue; the series $\Theta, I, I\Lambda$ and IB (the two last as ligatures) found in the right field of the three standing figure type are probably indictional dates 635 to 638. Heraclius's monogram, either to left or right, may simply make up for there being no room for an obverse legend; but for many other letters ϵ, H, K, N, T and the rare X there is, as yet, no explanation. In addition there is a full range of light-weight issues, for 23 siliquae a star on the reverse or on both obverse and reverse, for 21 siliquae $OB+*$ and for 20 either $OBXX$ or $BOXX$. Semisses and tremisses are rationalized to cross motifs ⳨ and ⳨ instead of retaining a Victory type for the semissis as Maurice and Phocas had done, yet the impersonal profile bust was retained in spite of the tentative change made by Phocas.

Ravenna issued distinctive solidi to match all the type changes made at Constantinople and tremisses but, judging from style, other Italian mints were also issuing gold. In Spain the last tremisses were produced by Heraclius prior to the Byzantine foothold there being engulfed by the Visigoths in the mid-620's. A special word needs to be said on the long series of dated solidi from Carthage which, while retaining their weight and fineness, become smaller in diameter and so thicker as one indiction merges into the next: indeed, dates ap-

pearing to be the same are best decided by the diameters of the coins. The series is remarkably consistent although the legends and dates become harder to read as the engraved area shrinks. At the end of the reign the two bust type was still being used when Heraclius died in indiction $I\Lambda$ and it is issued again in the troubled times of indiction $I\epsilon$ until the series resumes with a beardless bust of Constans II. There is, however, one outstanding anomaly—in 632 Constantinople issued the three standing figure type, putting Heraclonas on the solidi for the first time and Carthage followed suit, even to the detached cross above Heraclonas; only two examples are known from different dies marked ϵ of the indiction beginning in 627. Perhaps it was simply too difficult to engrave on so small an area the required number of dies when, for utilitarian purposes, there was only one effective side to use. In any event the capital continued the three figure type until the end of the reign, while Carthage carried on with her two bust issues.

For the first time a silver issue of this reign, the hexagram, survives in abundant quantity. It appears to have been the product of an experiment in bi-metallism with two hexagrams equal in theoretical and actual value to the half-tremissis. Every reign provided the standard gold solidus, semissis and tremissis but there was also a very thin gold piece of one sixth of a solidus, or half-tremissis. It bore the same types as a tremissis and was indeed often struck from tremissis dies, but was half its weight. The fragility of the half-tremissis put it at serious risk in currency and so few have survived that it was not

205 Tiberius II *(578–82)*. *Gold consular solidus.* Obv. *The emperor wears the plain consular tunic with the richly bordered loros above it, carrying the eagle-headed sceptre with cross above and in his right hand the mappa—all character-istic consular regalia. The legend runs ' May Constantine the Emperor live in prosperity '. The reverse has the cross on four steps usual in this reign and the legend ' Victory to Tiberius Augustus ' (diam. 20 mm.).*

206, 207 Maurice *(582–602)*. *Gold solidus.* Obv. *This emperor returned to the old helmeted and armoured bust but with a paludamentum fastened with a fibula on the right shoulder and thrown back over the left.* Rev. *Again a return to the earlier ' angel facing ' reverse. This is possibly a coin of Antioch mint but the widely different styles of Maurice's solidi have not yet been satisfactorily attributed (diam. 21 mm.).*

noticed until twenty years ago. Examples are known for Justin II, Phocas, Heraclius, Constans II, Justinian II, Philippicus, Anastasius II and Leo III, and two Byzantine glass weights of the standard are known. It was Grierson who first took notice of the denomination in a coin of Phocas and he has also suggested possible quarter-solidi for Justinian II and Philippicus. In Heraclius's reign there were miliaresia and half-miliaresia at two and four to the hexagram but their weights, roughly proportionate, vary sufficiently for Grierson to consider them as ceremonial coins. Even so, real money could be used for a very large number of purchases before the widely varying token coppers had to be called in for day to day purchases of essentials. There is some controversy over the date of the hexagram which a literary source gives firmly as 615. The pouring out of silver church vessels to persuade the emperor not to leave the capital, can be seen by historians today to fit better into a decade later when, from West and East, Avars and Persians besieged the capital. The irregular flans, often rudely sheared and hastily struck, give the impression of a crisis coinage and the Persian war, in which the Holy Cross itself had been lost, may well have sufficed by itself and would certainly justify one of the few dates in the reign clearly based on literary evidence.

There is a similar difficulty over the issue of miliaresia, one of which shows Heraclius with a long beard and in military dress holding a long cross (presumably a reference to the recapture of the Rood), being crowned by a Victoriola and standing beside Heraclius Constantine. This must surely go with the reformed copper folles of 629 having a similar, but not identical, obverse. Yet there exists an exactly similar type, both obverse and reverse (cross between palm branches), except for Heraclius being shown with a short beard. Could this have been to celebrate an earlier victory like Ganzaca or was it an error of the engraver, or changed instructions given to him? The usual hexagrams show Heraclius and Heraclius Constantine seated facing in civilian robes with a variety of letters (*K* and *I* are the most usual), stars and monograms in the reverse field. There was, however, a now rare issue at the end of the reign, with three standing figures of roughly equal height. Ravenna issued hexagrams and some smaller pieces under half a gramme in weight and Carthage produced other small pieces of rather over half a gramme; all are scarce and the weights provide a rough and ready help in distinguishing the two mints.

CONSTANTINE III AND HERACLONAS (641). Heraclius died in January-February 641, by then a very sick man, nor had his children ever been robust. He had designated Heraclius Constantine (aged 29) and Heraclonas (aged 15) as his joint successors but the former, under the imperial name of Constantine III, died in April-May 641, it is thought of consumption. Heraclonas was thus emperor and his mother Martina made the most of the situation for her other sons. She had always been unpopular and she was forced by popular demonstration and the Senate first to make Constans II, the son of Heraclius Constantine aged 10, joint-emperor and ultimately to go into exile with her sons. A confusing situation is made worse by Heraclonas also being called Constantine. In view of the quick action of the Constantinople mint in joint reigns during the sixth century it is surprising that no coins for that of Constantine III and Heraclonas are known. Grierson, however, has advanced strong arguments for allocating certain coins, generally given to Constans II, to each emperor under the name of Constantine. All these coins—gold, silver and copper are

Gold Types for Constantinople, Carthage and Sicily	Type numbers and descriptions for Constantinople	Dates for Constantinople gold	Follis Types at Constantinople		Folles and other copper in Sicily
I Constans II alone (641–54).	1 Beardless bust.	641–7	1	641–3. Emperor standing. *Rev.* *ANA/NEO l.* and *r.* of m with cross above.	1 Beardless bust. *Rev.* has no mint mark. Follis only.
			2	642/3. Emperor standing: *OФA* to l. of m with *ANA/NEO* above and to right.	
			3	643/4. As in 2 above but + 111 + instead of *OФA*.	
	2 Bust with short beard, at first merely dots.	647-51	4	644/5–647/8. Same as 1 above but some have emperor with dotted beard.	2 Half-follis dated year $Z = 647$ has beardless and dotted beard types. Follis and half-follis.
	3 Bust with long beard.	651–4	5a	652–6. Emperor standing with long beard. *Rev.* has M with cross above.	3 Bust with long beard. *Rev.* has *SCL.* Follis, half-follis and dekanummia (650/1).
			5b	655/6–656/7. As 5a above but * above M.	

Fig. 4. *Constans—Constantinople types for solidi and folles.*

			6 655/6–656/7. Emperor standing with long beard *KWN/CTAN l.* and *r.* of *M* with* above.	4 Emperor standing with long beard, with indictional date to *l.* and *r. Rev.* has *SCL.* Follis only. (652/3).
II Constans II with Constantine IV (654–9).	4 Two busts: Constans II with long beard; Constantine IV beardless.	654–9	7 655/6–657/8. Emperor standing with long beard. *Rev. ANNO* to *l.* of *M*, and *K* above.	
			8 655/6–657/8. Two standing figures.	5 Two standing figures. *Rev.* has *SCL* (654–9).
III Constans II with his three sons (659–68).	5 Two busts (Constans II with helmet crest to his crown) and *Rev.* two standing figures with cross on globus between. No crest at Carthage or Sicily.	659–c. 661	9 659–65. Emperor standing with *M* to *r.* and indictional date *l. Rev.* three standing figures.	6 Two standing figures on each side. *Rev.* has *SCL* (659–68): goes with an anomalous half-follis with two busts marked *AN/NO Δ* which has yet to be explained.
	6 As in 5 above but *Rev.* has cross on steps. No crest at Carthage.	c. 661–c. 663	10 665/6. Two standing figures, with date to *r. Rev.* has *M* with figure on each side.	
	7 One bust and three standing figures. This type not at Carthage or Sicily.	c. 663–8	11 No date. Bust with long beard. *Rev.* three busts disposed round *M*.	

The enumeration of all the types above is according to Dumbarton Oaks Catalogue, vol. II, 2, from various parts of which the information has been assembled.

208 Heraclius *(610–41). Copper follis of Isaura mint, reverse. The officina is A, the only one so far recorded, and the year 8 (617–18). It is overstruck on another follis of which part of the reverse is clear at the top. The obverse has busts of Heraclius and Heraclius Constantine (diam. 30 mm.).*

209, 210 Period of Heraclius. *Copper twelve nummia piece of Alexandria mint, obverse and reverse. Struck during the Persian occupation 617–28 with sun and moon symbols on either side of the obverse bust—compare the same symbols on the obverse and reverse of Khusru II's drachms, Nos. 419, 422 (diam. 22 mm.).*

211, 212 Heraclius *(610–41). Copper six nummia of Alexandria mint, obverse and reverse. This corresponds with the twelve nummia piece, No. 213, issued 613–18 (diam. 14 mm.).*

213 Heraclius *(610–41). Copper twelve nummia of Alexandria mint, obverse. Issued 613–18 after the coronation of Heraclius Constantine (diam. 15 mm.).*

214, 215 Heraclius *(610–41). Gold solidus of Alexandria mint, obverse and reverse. This is clearly based on Phocas types and was perhaps produced hastily before the official designs arrived. It was probably officially withdrawn as few examples survive. On the reverse III is a mark associated with Alexandria: compare Nos. 90, 91 (diam. 20 mm.).*

216, 217 Heraclius *(610–41). Gold solidus, obverse and reverse. Early issues up to 613, show the emperor in military uniform with paludamentum over left shoulder (diam. 20 mm.).*

218 Heraclius *(610–41). Gold solidus, obverse. Issued after the coronation of Heraclius Constantine, between 613 and 629. They show Heraclius's son with a bust becoming larger until it is equal to the emperor's, and both in civilian dress (diam. 20 mm.).*

219 Heraclius *(610–41). Gold solidus, obverse. Issued between 629 and 631 with both father and son bearded and corresponding to the heavy copper issues of Heraclius with the cross recaptured from the Persians, No. 197 (diam. 20 mm.).*

220, 221 Heraclius *(610–41). Gold solidus, obverse and reverse. The last issue of the reign made when Heraclonas, his son by Martina, was made Caesar in 632. In the first years of the issue the cross is detached above the crown of a smaller Heraclonas (diam. 18.5 mm.).*

222, 223 Heraclius *(610–41). Silver miliaresion, obverse and reverse. Heraclius is being crowned by a Victoriola and this is likely to celebrate the Victory over Persia in 628–9. Some pieces have Heraclius with a long beard which would fit this date but some, like this, have him still with a short one: the obverse type however corresponds as to dress with the copper issues of 629 (diam. 21 mm.).*

208

209

210

211

212

213

214

215

216

217

220

218

219

221

222

223

224

225

226

227

228

229

230

231

232

233

234

235

224, 225 Constans II *(641–68). Gold solidus, obverse and reverse. A piece typical of the Sicilian mint at Syracuse with at the top the characteristic* ◣. *The emperor is shown with Constantine IV, his eldest son, and is of the period 654–9. The reverse has many Sicilian characteristics such as C (= S) in the field, the ∴ symbol and the letter Θ at the end of the legend (diam. 20 mm.).*

226, 227 Constans II *(641–68). Copper follis, obverse and reverse from different specimens. This issue carried Greek legends for the first time—on the obverse* 'εν τούτῳ νίκα *and* ἀνανέωσις *on the reverse. The date and officina number are in the exergue but are not sufficiently struck up for them to be legible on this specimen (diam. 24 mm.).*

228, 229 Constans II *(641–68). Copper follis of Carthage, obverse and reverse. The emperor is here together with his three sons and the issue dates from 659 to 668. As is almost invariably the case with this issue, this piece is overstruck on an earlier follis (diam. 23 mm.).*

230, 231 Constans II *(641–68). Silver miliaresion, obverse and reverse. Period 654 to 659 with his eldest son Constantine IV (diam. 18 mm.).*

232, 233 Constantine IV *(668–85). Copper follis, obverse and reverse. These large pieces were double the value of previous folles; this one belongs to the period 668 to 673 in Grierson's estimation, and others are dated regnal year 30 (683–4) or 31 (684–5) (diam. 34 mm.).*

234, 235 Constantine IV *(668–85). Copper piece of ten nummia, obverse and reverse. Fractions of the follis, which owing to the doubled value now included five nummia pieces, often included a reminder of their increased value. For instance, this piece carries a K or half-follis mark on the left. It is in fact overstruck on a follis of Constans II with the obverse under the new reverse: it is Constans' last type from 663 to 668, and one of the three small busts of his sons can be seen to the right of Constantine IV's helmet. This brings home the revolutionary nature of this reform, so far as ordinary citizens were concerned (diam. 22 mm.).*

involved—show a beardless bust and it is difficult to see why Heraclius Constantine, who had long been represented as bearded, should change in this way at a critical time. One distinctive type of solidus from Constantinople and Ravenna, with a cross silhouetted against the crest of a helmet 241*, 242* (as in Heraclius's first type) seems undoubtedly attributable to this period, though Heraclonas may be a stronger candidate than his elder stepbrother, and there seems a good case for allocating solidi with 266* *CONOBK* in the exergue to the same emperor. But the evidence of overstrikes is against transferring Constans II's year 3 Constantinople folles to Heraclonas: thus Grierson in putting his formidable authority behind coins for these two reigns, has set numismatists a fascinating problem, and more evidence is likely to emerge from the debate, and more concentrated observation of the coins involved.

CONSTANS II (641–68). Constans was the popular name given to the son of Heraclius Constantine and in a world of Constantines it is wise to stick to it. Anyone confronted with an unsorted bag of the copper coins of his reign would be immediately impressed by the contrast between the miserable quality of the folles which turn out to be from Constantinople, and the larger, better designed and struck coins marked *SCL* for Sicily. The folles of the capital hover round 3 g. in weight, those of Sicily are generally above 5 g. There will be no pentanummia, very few dekanummia and even half-folles will be scarce except for a good sprinkling of thick flans from Carthage marked XX. A harder look at

some unsorted gold would reveal a good number of tremisses in which the emperor's hair and his diadem seem curiously merged into one, along with many solidi on which a much finer engraving line has been used and incorporating in the legends an *A* in 224, the form ◣, though this is not found on copper. These are all signs of Sicilian origin and indeed are continuing features of mint production there. Such an unscientific approach in fact reveals one of the two most important numismatic features of the reign, both of them of great general importance too—the transfer of emphasis from East to West in administration and the increasing use of the Greek language. It is well known that in the last five years of his life Constans II made his base in Syracuse and was murdered there, but the coins show clearly that the shift of emphasis began with the reign itself and may indeed have been inherited from Heraclius in whose mind the idea of moving from Constantinople had long been active. Secondly, Greek legends—in fact two of them and the first to be used on Byzantine coins—were put on the same unattractive folles of the capital referred to above. The first was *ЄNTϒTONIKA*—'by this sign 226 [of the Cross] may you conquer '—which Constantine the Great had seen in his vision before the battle of the Milvian Bridge against Maxentius in 312. On the reverse of the coin was *ANANЄO* with 227 an abbreviation mark, for ἀνανέωσις, or renovation; exactly the same idea as was conveyed by the fourth century *FEL TEMP REPARATIO* legends.

Although the copper folles of the capital are so unattractive, they deserve more careful attention than is generally bestowed on them. As Wroth showed with so much patience, each coin should have the date and officina besides the denomination and *ANANЄOS* inscription. Part of the date or officina is often off the flan, let alone tending to be mixed up with the misleading abbreviation mark of ἀνανέωσις, but the dates are valuable if they can be found and it is from them that the successive gold issues can in turn be dated. On the folles the dates 8–10, 18, 22, 24, 26 and 27 have still to be discovered though the two last are probably covered by an undated type. Figure 4 on p. 138 gives lists of the follis types at Constantinople and in Sicily (columns 4 and 5) compared with the types used for gold solidi. At Constantinople dekanummia were issued for a short period at the end of the reign, otherwise only folles and a much smaller number of half-folles were minted. In Italy and at Carthage dekanummia were still issued but nothing lower than that, and this may reflect a lower price range for essentials in the western provinces.

There is a vast amount of gold to be fitted into the simplified Table on p. 138 and a proportionately large number of folles from the capital, Carthage and Sicily. Carthage produced a singularly uninspired series of designs beginning with folles and halves with a standing figure, changing to a beardless bust in 643 and continuing in various bearded, crowned and helmeted forms until, in 659, a piece with four standing figures was issued. This last was on exactly the same lines as the Type 6 folles of Sicily in the same period. The Carthage solidi are more easily distinguished

than ever in their globularity, and harder to read as legends tend to slide off the narrowing flans. Dates are both harder to read accurately and inconsistently used, while several symbols in the field of the reverse add another complicating unknown. Growing and sometimes devastating Arab pressure, which had wiped out the mint of Alexandria early in the reign, may have been partly responsible for the relaxation of mint discipline.

The complications on Constantinople solidi relate *first* to the unexplained letters and symbols added to *CONOB* in the exergue. These are $S, C, \Theta, I, T, +$ and possibly K; though, as explained above, Grierson has attributed the K pieces to Heraclius's sons. *Secondly*, there are two unexplained symbols used at the end of the reverse legends of some coins of Types 5, 6 and 7; one is a simple $+$, and it occurs in all three types; the other, $\curlyvee$, is only found in Type 6. *Thirdly*, in the field there are numeral letters, E, S, Z and H which represent dates and are important as showing when the transition from beardless to bearded bust took place.

A series of lightweight issues are no complication as *BOXX* and *OBXX* have occurred before, but for 23 siliquae besides a prominent star in the reverse field there is a new type with *BOΓK* (the ligature at the end being of 3 and 20) in the exergue: both these 23 siliquae indications occur only on Type 3. Normal solidi of Type 7 have the curious feature of combining the obverse bust with the reverse legend leaving the three standing emperors on the reverse with *CONOB* and no imperial name in any form on the coin. Semisses,

333°-336°

267°, 268°

47

8, 229

tremisses and half-tremisses (of identical type with tremisses) retain the profile bust to right, in a form becoming something of a caricature and difficult to distinguish (except in degree of caricature) from the fractions of solidi of Constantine IV, which contain no half-tremissis but possibly a quarter-solidus. The symbols on Sicilian issues are if anything more complicated than the Constantinopolitan ones: $\Gamma, C, \Theta,$ 225 I, and 4 are prominent as well as $\cdot\cdot$ and other uses of pellets. Some of these connect with symbols on semisses and tremisses. The weights of these western solidi tend to drop in this reign as though based on a slightly different standard, as Grierson thinks, of around 22 siliquae Constantinopolitan: by Justinian II's time this has become established around 4.10 g. Ravenna produced solidi and it would seem many more tremisses, with her characteristic annular border on the reverse.

A good quantity of silver survives from the reign, hexagrams being fairly common in all types corresponding to those shown for solidi 1 to 5 in the Table on p. 138. Far less common are miliaresia and smaller 230, 231 pieces with a cross potent or a cross with palm branches reverse. Carthage continued her traditional small silver issues, one with cross potent reverse, another with PAX and a third managing to squeeze the emperor and his three sons on to the tiny flan. None of these can be called common and some pieces attributed to Ravenna (all in the Tolstoi Catalogue) seem to be unique. Rome, quite uncharacteristically, issued a small silver piece with $R\varPi$ reverse but some solidi also came from this mint at the end of the reign. The usual coin one finds

marked $RO\varPi$ is the XX but there are some rare dekanummia. Throughout the seventh century the copper coinage from Rome remained strangely undistinguished. Naples ($N\epsilon$) was introduced as a mint in the reign, issuing half-folles of two bust type but its products are rare and the designs might have been modelled on those of Rome. 236 ▸

CONSTANTINE IV (668–85). Singly or in the mass the coins of Constantine IV in all metals are apt to give an impression of confusion. Even the most painstaking analysis such as Grierson has given them, and especially the attractive but difficult large folles, cannot altogether dispel this. 232, 2 But working on his lines there are questions to ask of each coin, to which the answers will go a long way in placing it securely: Is the bust beardless? Is the civilian chlamys being worn? Does the emperor carry a spear? Has he a shield on his left shoulder (a point often difficult to answer)? Are the emperor's brothers represented? With such questions one can dissipate an 237 ▸ uncertainty bound to be present when the coins, as in the case of the copper, are worn, overstrikings and in bad condition as they normally are. Carthaginian solidi come to the rescue with a dated series from the fifth to the tenth indictional years but they do not follow the Constantinople gold categories, and there is a change of type in the ninth not persevered with in the tenth 238 ▸ year: this last, however, may represent very accurately indeed the two stages in the deposition of the emperor's brothers in 680 to 681. Going back to Constantinople copper, the lesser denominations do not

236 Phocas *(602–10). Gold consular solidus.* Obv. *The emperor's short name allows PP to be extended to PERP normally in this reign. This is the second type of consular solidi on which the crown has no pendilia; both are of the year 603. The consular regalia shows one change from that on No. 205 above—the sceptre in the emperor's left hand is here a plain cross. The reverse is similar to No. 238 below (diam. 22 mm.).*

237, 238 Phocas *(602–10). Gold solidus.* Obv. *An early issue (602–3) in which the crown has pendilia. Undoubtedly the effigy with a pointed beard—the beard also appears on tremisses in profile—is a portrait very different from the effigy of Maurice before and of Heraclius after it. Phocas' armour and paludamentum are as in the Maurice solidus (No. 206).* Rev. *Phocas also continued the 'angel facing' type for his reverse but both this and No. 207 above seem to show lack of care and skill when compared with their obverses—possibly due to constant repetition of the type by engravers. Later reverses have the legend VICTORI/AAVGU instead of AVGG as here. The officina is I (10) (diam. 20 mm.).*

marry easily with the five types of heavy folles, as there are but three types of half-follis. In dekanummia there is only a choice between a beardless helmeted bust with orb cruciger in the right hand and a bearded one with the helmet sometimes showing diadem ties, and a spear. The issue of the heavy folles involved a doubling of its value and the pentanummia makes a re-appearance, though it is rare: coins of *K* and *I* denomination bear also a sizeable *M* and *K* respectively to remind users of their earlier values.

The obverse type for the vast majority of all coins in the reign is a three-quarters facing armoured bust with a spear over the right shoulder, or occasionally a facing armoured bust with an orb cruciger in the right hand. It seems a clear invocation of the emperor's great ancestors and especially of Justinian, after whom he named his son, at a time when the greatest qualities of courage and perseverance were needed in the face of the full tide of Arab advance. One can see too the revival in size, as well as type, of the reformed folles of Justinian and of his pre-reform gold solidi with three-quarters facing bust to which much more hair about the neck and long moustaches have had to be added to keep pace with the established standards of portraiture. Constantine IV's solidi of this last type for the reign are often of remarkably fine workmanship both in detail and modelling. When work of such quality was being done it is difficult to understand how the legends, even on gold, came to be engraved with several letters missing or with irrelevant portions of legend included from those of the previous reign. Besides this last, fourth,

type—issued 681 to 685—the Constantinople solidi fall into three clearly marked types: first, in 668, the rare, beardless, facing bust type with civilian chlamys and an orb cruciger; second, from 668 to 673, a three-quarters facing armoured bust, beardless with spear, rather a large head and no diadem ties showing and, thirdly, from 674 to 681, a similar armoured bust but with rather a small head, bearded, with shield over the left shoulder and diadem ties visible. All these have the emperor's two brothers on the reverse, but they do not appear after they had been deprived of their imperial status in a family quarrel over the exercise of power in 680 and 681.

Constantine himself had been made an Augustus in 654 so that dates of up to thirty-two regnal years are possible and in fact thirty and thirty-one are recorded on copper folles though unfortunately only Ravenna has a few folles of earlier date. From Constantinople in this reign came the last of the lightweight solidi which had begun under Justinian I and still elude convincing explanation: they are rare for the reign and are of the second and third gold types. Carthage, as already noted, provides a series of dated solidi from 676/7—680/1 when the brothers again disappear from the reverse, but for the earlier years there are still no dates while at the end Arab copies are sometimes difficult to distinguish from official issues. Sicilian solidi, with the same characteristics as under Constans II, follow Constantinople types except in that of the armoured bust without diadem ties. But the real problem in this reign and the next is to distinguish the products of Rome (and in some cases even of Sicily) from those of some other South Italian mints issuing solidi and tremisses. To define further than ' South Italian ' is as far as most general students of the Byzantine series can go, but Dr Kent of the British Museum may shortly point to paths through the maze, created by a limited number of coins with a large number of type varieties. The position in Italy was one of increasing isolation of the Exarch in Ravenna, although the city did not fall to the Lombards until 751; such power as the Byzantines had in Italy was in the centre and south.

The silver of the reign provides a contrast between the comparatively common Constantinopolitan hexagrams, reproducing all the normal gold solidi types except the last, and the scarce miliaresia with cross between palm branches reverse on the one hand, and a few excessively rare smaller pieces attributed to Carthage, Rome (with certainty), Ravenna and another Italian mint on the other.

A few words must be given to the copper issues of provincial mints. In Sicily there were two follis issues with the type of a standing emperor and three with a single bust type along with some half-folles: these are the only pieces easy to find today. Ravenna had a number of follis issues and a rare half-follis, Rome and Naples produced half-folles and Carthage folles with *M* and *ɱ* and a half-follis exploiting the monogram 𝕭 to the full as it combined Constantine, Carthage and twenty nummia. But none of these is commonly found and, except from Constantinople, there is not much Constantine IV copper available. The reign shows the beginning of the drying up of copper issues, a phenomenon which was to effect the coinage for two centuries and a half to come.

A last warning may be in place against too easily attributing badly worn coppers with a three-quarters facing armoured bust and a spear to Constantine IV. There is Tiberius III to be considered as an alterna- 382· tive, though his spear is always held in front of the body. In this reign as in all since Tiberius II, the use of previously struck flans is often a complicating and sometimes an important factor which is worth working out in detail.

a) 685–717. The reign of Justinian II was interrupted intelligibly but irrelevantly by those of the usurpers Leontius (695-8) and Tiberius III (698-705) and the period 685 to 717 is better taken as an whole. Numismatically it certainly is that, in the high standard of engraving of the dies used for gold and in the dominant place taken by mints in Sicily and South Italy. Ill health and mental instability ran in the family of Heraclius and the latter was seen at its worst in his great-great-grandson Justinian II, the last of his line to rule. Justinian's many qualitites of courage, strength and bubbling resourcefulness were offset by a sadistic cruelty which left him no reliable friends in the face of dangerous Arab thrusts from Armenia, Asia Minor and Africa, as well as subversion at home. The former were a continuous factor of the times, eventually culminating in Leo III facing a year-long siege of the capital by Maslama within a few months of his accession. Leontius had exiled Justinian II to Cherson after taking the capital from the inside and he then raised a fleet to recapture Carthage from the Arabs. He was successful but the Arabs under Hassan recaptured it—this time permanently—in 698.

The troops on the return were persuaded to follow Tiberius Apsimarus in challenging for the throne and he took the place of Leontius. Both were estimable men but Justinian was not idle over plotting his return, first with the help of the Khan of the Khazars whose sister he married, and later with that of the Bulgars. After a series of romantic adventures Justinian entered Constantinople through a watercourse near the Blachernae Palace and simply took it over, as Tiberius III fled. Relentless revenge, similar to that of Hitler after the failure of the July 1944 plot, occupied Justinian's second reign in which his newly born son, Tiberius IV, was associated with him after being brought to the capital in 706. In 711 an Armenian general with strong and heretical religious views, Bardanes (Philippicus), easily ousted Justinian but was himself removed by a military revolt in 713. His secretary, Artemius (Anastasius II), was beginning to achieve order—he was a civil servant—when he was overthrown in 715 by the same military chiefs who has disposed of his predecessor; they declared another civil servant Theodosius III emperor, in spite of his own reluctance. Finally, an able career general born in Syria mounted a revolt, once more easily successful, and became emperor as Leo III in 717.

All these emperors, however transient, produced coinage, though not a great deal, and copper in particular is hard to find. Numismatically Justinian II is of great importance as he revolutionized the form of the solidus by introducing in 692 a bust
25, 26 of Jesus as the obverse and putting a standing figure of himself alongside the traditional cross on steps on the reverse. This was the second of four classes of Justinian II's gold in which for the first time the fractional semisses, tremisses and quarters at Constantinople follow the solidus type, the die for the quarter, only found in Class 4, being a beautiful piece of minuscule engraving. The classes are important and may be briefly distinguished as follows:

243, 244 I 685–92 *Obv.*: Young bust in civilian chlamys, merging into one with lightly hatched beard. *Rev.*: Cross on steps.

25, 26 II 692–5 *Obv.*: Bust of Christ bearded and with long hair and legend ending *Rex Regnantium*. *Rev.*: Emperor standing on right wearing loros, holding cross on steps with his right hand: legend ends *Servus Christi*.

245 III 705–6 *Obv.*: Bust of Christ unbearded with curly hair. *Rev.*: Bust of emperor with cross on steps in right hand and orb inscribed *PAX* and surmounted by patriarchal cross in left. Legend ends *Multus An[nos]*.

IV 706–11 *Obv.*: As in III above. *Rev.*: 246,
Busts of Justinian II bearded on left and Tiberius IV, holding cross on steps between them, each wearing chlamys.

Thus from issuing a traditional type solidus 239 ▶
at the start of his reign, Justinian revolu- 240 ▶
tionized it before his exile both as to types and legends, and continued with his changes on his return. These changes seem to have represented the climate of opinion at the time, deeply interested in religious issues, and particularly they were in tune with the 73rd and 82nd canons of the Council in Trullo (691) which attempted to implement the work of the Sixth Oecumenical Council (681). These were to the effect that the Cross must be given due regard as the instrument of the Incarnation and not be cheapened by casual use, and that Jesus should be represented as a man and not symbolized, as in the primitive church. The Popes did not recognize these canons and of the Italian mints only 241 ▶
Sardinia, which was administratively part of Africa, struck solidi of Class II. Immediately on his return from exile Justinian issued gold with a bust of himself, clothed in the loros, as sole ruler and the *PAX* on his orb may have been intended as a gesture of goodwill to Rome: certainly coins bearing the new types were issued in Italy again. It needs emphasizing that even when the emperor occupied the whole of one 242 ▶
side of these gold coins, that side is still the reverse when Jesus (and later the Virgin or Saints) occupied the other: to avoid confusion, descriptions need to be careful particularly when, as in the reverses

239, 240 Gold solidus of the period of the Revolt *by Heraclius and his father against Phocas.* Obv. *Dated at the end of the legend IΓ, the 13th year of the Indiction, or 609–10, and struck in Alexandria by engravers clearly from Carthage (*cf. *Nos. 240 and 202). Heraclius's father is bearded on the right and the younger Heraclius is in the senior position on the left as he was claiming the throne. Both have consular robes—appearing on coins for the last time—and the legend reads CONSVAI though neither was as yet either consul or emperor.* Rev. *Also dated IΓ at the end of the legend (diam. 16 mm.).*

241, 242 Gold solidus probably of Heraclonas *(641) but variously attributed to Heraclius Constantine and Constans II. The crown appears to have the crest of a helmet above. Like Heraclius before him this emperor wears the civilian chlamys with a prominent fibula on the right shoulder.* Rev. *This follows the type normally used by Heraclius, but CONOB is followed by K as on other solidi attributed to Heraclonas or Constans II (see No. 266 below) (diam. 20 mm.).*

25, 26
of Class II, the legend bears little if any relationship to the type. Justinian II's final Class IV was issued when his wife and son reached the capital and the coins are , 247 surely amongst the best designed and most charming of the whole Byzantine series. Both the usurpers and Justinian's immediate successors all reverted to the cross on steps reverse, perhaps predictably, but in the long run his basic change was to become common form. The new legend, from the acclamation ' May he live for many years ', along with the change, not always easily perceptible, from μάππα *(mappa)* to ἀκακία *(akakia)* were also to have a long life on Byzantine coins.

The *Servus Christi* legend was not repeated for over a century but as this was a title of the Caliph 'Abd al-Malik it raises the question of the relationship of the coinage of the two rulers. Immediately after Justinian II's changes 'Abd al-Malik initiated a series of changes in the Arab coinage which had up to then imitated the Byzantine currency in gold and copper and that of the Sassanian rulers in Persia in silver. In 693/4 he produced gold dinars with a standing figure of the Caliph for one type, clearly 429 inspired by that of Justinian on Class II and the whole possibly designed as a rival to it: this was issued until 696/7 when an aniconic, purely epigraphical, type took its place. Why 'Abd al-Malik took the change to a type for his dinars more in accord with Arab religious beliefs and with the Hadith (Tradition of the Prophet), in two stages is not clear but shortly after, the silver coinage was reformed in the same way. His epigraphical types were soon, in their turn, to influence Byzantine silver coin design.

This period saw the end of the silver hexagram after just a century of existence. The coin was issued by all the emperors until Leo III set the miliaresion on a new career, but pieces are so rare, so variant in weight and so regularly struck from solidus dies that it is difficult to believe that they were in normal use as currency, which they still appear to have been under Constantine IV. Some examples show heavy wear, others none at all, but for better or worse Theodosius III is the last emperor to issue them. Other silver hardly survives at all except for a small piece issued from Rome by Justinian II and Leontius which was at least better produced than the square XXX nummia pieces in copper issued there in successive reigns, so roughly sheared and struck as hardly to inspire confidence even with the magic name of *RO*𝕞 upon them.

Except possibly for the reigns of Justinian II, solidi can be found more easily today than copper, or of course silver, for all the emperors of this period. The solidi too are generally in splendid condition, whereas the copper is in a worse state than usual, more easily identifiable from the imperial type or a monogram than from the legend. The Sicilian folles, with others, occasionally have monograms above the *M*. Leontius usually appears as a broad-faced, 248 lightly bearded man wearing the loros, Tiberius III has an armoured bust with a 382* spear in front of his body and a shield on his left shoulder. Philippicus is bearded and rather triangular in face, wearing the 249, 250 loros and with an eagle-headed sceptre in his left hand. Anastasius II wears a chlamys and has rather full and waved hair 383* on either side of a bearded, triangular face while Theodosius III wears the loros and carries in his right hand an orb surmounted by a patriarchal cross. Some mints continued for copper pieces the standing emperor obverse under Justinian II and the two usurpers but the type was becoming standardized to absurdity and was dropped. There are a few dekanummia pieces from Constantinople but the usual survivors are folles and half-folles from the capital, Syracuse and Carthage, with some from Naples, Ravenna and Sardinia, and the XXX's from Rome.

384*

The finding of a number of gold hoards in Sicily in recent years appears to have made Sicilian solidi of this period more easily obtainable than those of the capital. Their characteristic ⋏ and fine line engraving, particularly obvious in the linear border of the reverses, sets these Sicilian pieces as a class apart though their many privy marks, often involving Θ, Γ and P, are still a mystery. The appearance of the name ' Syracuse ' on a follis of Justinian II makes it probable that this was the mint for all coinage there. Even more complicated symbols are found on coins from as yet unidentified mints in South Italy which have been so allocated on grounds of style and provenance; some, for instance, being clearly related to the coins of the Lombard rulers of Beneventum. The gold from Sardinia is no problem as it continues the thick fabric tradition of Carthage and, additionally, often has an S in the field of the reverse. The mint opens towards the end of Justinian II's first reign before the fall of Carthage to the Arabs and ceases in the reign of Anastasius II when Arab

251, 252

raids were so frequent as to plunge the island into anarchy. A few copper pieces are also attributed to the mint, some on the grounds of an S in the reverse field.

b) 717-867. The most important events numismatically of the period are the impact of Iconoclasm on all types but especially on the gold, the introduction of the new silver miliaresion by Leo III and the passing of the copper follis and its fractions.

Iconoclasm was an official policy from 726 when Leo III ordered the icon of Jesus to be removed from the Chalke Gate of the Imperial Palace and a cross to be substituted, until in 843 a synod re-established the veneration of icons, an action still commemorated annually in the Festival of Orthodoxy. The movement had profound social, religious, artistic and even military causes and effects: on coins the numismatist cannot fail to notice the changes it brought. The bust or figure of Jesus disappears from the obverse and members of the imperial family fill both sides of the gold coins, sometimes seated but generally as facing busts. Amongst other iconoclast emperors Theophilus was accused of replacing the image of Jesus by his own. Naturalistic portraiture disappears too and an impressionist style tends to make everyone look much alike even when the sovereigns were iconodule, as were Eirene and Michael I. It was unnecessary to include *CONOB* as the capital was the only mint in the East for gold and the legends had to be abbreviated to fit into the crowded space. *D* or *DN* for *Dominus Noster* tends to drop out and *Perpetuus Augustus* becomes *PA* with the added acclamation *MVLT[OS ANNOS]* soon rendered *PAMVL*. In 843 the impressionist style does not disappear at once and the first indication of returning 'naturalism' on coins can be seen in the bust of Christ copied, not always accurately, from the obverse of Justinian II's Class II solidus. This takes its place as the obverse again but for a long time the emperors continue on the reverse in impressionist style on gold and copper; right down to Nicephorus II in fact, who issued gold pieces in both styles, with copper and silver bearing only a naturalistic portrait.

271

25

439·
, 295

Leo III's new type miliaresia were to provide silver currency for the Empire for the next three hundred years. They were generally aniconic and epigraphic in their types, broad and thin like the Muslim dirhams on which they were often overstruck. Normally, but not invariably, they have a triple pellet border and even so they invited the attentions of the clipper, as many survivors show. These coins of varying weight around 2 g. must represent official abandonment of the bi-metallic experiment undertaken a century before: Grierson has noted that Theophanes implies that their value was two carats or twelve to the solidus just as was that of the hexagram, but that coin weighed 6 g. All early miliaresia bear the names of two rulers and this has led to much difficulty in separating the coins of Leo III and Constantine V, Leo IV and Constantine VI and Leo V and Constantine —all fathers and sons. Coins of the last pair have an unbroken legend and Grierson has noted an *R* with serif in *XRISTYS* which is used by later emperors only and so puts a group of Leo and Constantine

pieces with a single border in this reign too. The division between Leo III and Leo IV is best made by observing the type of cross, as Veglery and Zacos have pointed out: those of Leo III have a narrower cross-bar placed higher and the steps less angled inwards than those of Leo IV. The type is found on early seals of Leo III but seems inspired by Muslim dirhams.

253, 254

255

Leo III made an heroic effort to reestablish a heavy follis and its related fractions and Constantine V continued to issue these, right down to the pentanummia which does not exist for Leo III but probably was issued. After this there were no more fractions and the follis sign itself disappeared. The last *M* reverse (flanked by three *X*'s on the left and three *N*'s on the right with officina letter *Θ*!) was issued from the capital by Theophilus and in Sicily Michael III prolonged it for a few more years. Subsequently a few pieces, some of them coming from the always exceptional mint of Cherson, seem to indicate a relationship of 1 and 1/2 but are more likely to be due to the wide variations in weight acceptable in token money, as they bear no marks of value. Even so, the last folles of Michael II and of his son Theophilus are fine looking coins, sometimes more than 25 mm. in diameter and 7.5 g. in weight with bold design and lettering.

5, 6

The last copper issue of Michael III is interesting for the reason that it might have been designed by the most iconoclastic of emperors: a well-designed coin of about 7.5 g. weight it has impressionist style busts of Michael III *(obv.)* and Basil I *(rev.)* with no denomination or mint.

256, 257

243, 244 Justinian II *(685–95). Gold solidus, obverse and reverse. First issue of 685 to 692 with beardless bust and the, by then traditional, cross on steps reverse. He was sixteen when he became emperor (diam. 20 mm.).*

245 Justinian II *(705–11). Gold solidus, reverse. The third issue in 705–6, immediately after his return to power. The obverse is occupied by a bust of Christ, while the emperor bearded and wearing the loros holds the cross on steps, symbol of the reverse, in his right hand (diam. 20.5 mm.).*

246, 247 Justinian II *(705–11). Gold solidus, obverse and reverse. The fourth and last issue of the reign beginning when his wife and son (Tiberius IV) reached Constantinople in 706. The bust of Christ with curly hair had been used as the obverse of the third type, No. 245 (diam. 20 mm.).*

248 Leontius *(695–8). Gold solidus, obverse. The usurper has his portrait on the obverse and returned to the cross on steps reverse after the revolutionary changes carried out by Justinian II in his second type, Nos. 25, 26 (diam. 19 mm.).*

249, 250 Philippicus *(711–13). Silver hexagram, obverse and reverse struck with solidus dies. The hexagram reverse traditionally had the legend ' May God help the Romans ', but this has ' Victory of the Emperor ', like a solidus (diam. 21 mm.).*

251, 252 Justinian II *(705–11). Gold solidus, obverse and reverse. This coin corresponds with the fourth type (706–11) in Constantinople but was struck in Sardinia at Cagliari. It looks at first sight like a dumpy solidus from Carthage, but under Arab pressure that mint apparently moved to Sardinia, as is probably indicated by the S in the right field. Carthage fell to the Arabs in 698 (diam. 11.5 mm.).*

253, 254 Leo III *(717–41). Silver miliaresion, obverse and reverse. Pieces issued by Leo III and Constantine V are difficult to distinguish from those of Leo IV and Constantine VI as the reverse legends are identical. The cross on the obverse for Leo III has a narrower cross-bar placed higher on the shaft than the later coins. This larger and thinner coin replaced the old hexagrams and miliaresia with an aniconic and epigraphic type copied from Arab dirhams (diam. 23 mm.).*

243

244

245

246

247

248

249

250

251

252

253

254

255

256

257

258

259

260 261 262 263 264 265

255 Leo IV *(775–80)*. *Silver miliaresion, obverse. Double striking has somewhat confused the legend near the steps of the cross and the coin has been clipped to the inner ring of the triple border, once like that in No. 253. The wider cross-bar and the absence of a pellet at the end of the reverse inscription are indications of the later 'Leo and Constantine' (diam. 20 mm.).*

256, 257 Michael III *(842–67)*. *Copper follis, obverse and reverse. Issued 866–7 after Basil I had been proclaimed co-emperor. Michael is described as 'Imperator' and Basil as 'Rex'. It is a remarkably iconoclastic piece in style and type, considering its date (diam. 23 mm.).*

258, 259 Leo III *(717–41)*. *Gold solidus, obverse and reverse. A coin of the beginning of the reign in traditional style. It should be compared with Nos. 11, 12 in which the typically iconoclastic style and type appear on a solidus to be dated* c. *730 (diam. 19 mm.).*

260, 261 Leo III *(717–41)*. *Copper follis, obverse and reverse. The XXX-NNN of the reverse is a meaningless survival of Constantine IV's ANNO XXX. Leo and his son each carry the akakia in the right hand—the last copper issue of the reign (diam. 21 mm.).*

262, 263 Leo IV *(775–80)*. *Gold solidus, obverse and reverse. A complicated 'family' coin of the iconoclastic period. On the obverse, Leo IV on the left is described as 'son and grandson', and his son Constantine VI on the right as 'the younger': the reverse has, on the left, Leo III 'grandfather' and his son Constantine V 'the father'—in each case referring to Leo IV (diam. 20 mm.).*

264 Leo V *(813–20)*. *Copper follis of Sicily, obverse. The emperor's son Constantine is on the reverse (diam. 18 mm.).*

265 Theophilus *(829–42)*. *Copper follis, reverse. From this reign the epigraphic reverse for folles becomes standard. All copper pieces had been folles for some time and there was no need for a denominational sign. It reads 'Theophilus Augustus, may you be victorious' (diam. 28 mm.).*

The Empire had shrunk under Arab onslaughts and, although the reconquest of Asia Minor was being slowly undertaken by Constantine V, large regular issues are only recognizable from Constantinople and Sicily. But Rome and other mints in South Italy play an increasing part in providing solidi and tremisses there, some of them debased into electrum or even billon. The political situation was, however, in continual flux—there was an Arab emirate based on Bari from 847–71, let alone the quarrelsome Lombardic principalities—so that the sources of currency and the pressures on them are not easy to evaluate.

LEO III (717–41). The first gold issue of the reign follows the cross on steps reverse of his predecessors, with perhaps an obverse portrait, though there is a clear falling off in the effectiveness of the engraving. The next issue has the Emperor's son Constantine V occupying the reverse and the tendency towards impressionist portraiture is pronounced. There are semisses and tremisses for both classes. The legends on solidi read variously *DLEON/PEAV*, *DLEOPPA*, *DLEOPA* and *DLEO-PAMYL* showing the evolution of the abbreviated standard form. It is still necessary to state that the British Museum Catalogue is now seriously misleading for this reign, and not only in its inclusion of coins of Leontius as Laffranchi pointed out in 1938. Leo III's 'heavy' copper series—it was struck in three modules with a top weight for folles at *c.* 10 g.—has a reverse divided into two by an ornamental line, with a bust of his son in the top half and the denomination between *ANN* and

XXX below: *M* and *K* have an officina, generally *A*, below, but *I* has not. Already Anno has been left in the air and the *XXX* has become mere decoration: the type is on its way to meaninglessness and immobilization. The 'light' series has two facing busts and no legend on the obverse, and the denomination as the type for the reverse, between *NNN* and *XXX* with officinae *A* and *B*. Probably the last class of copper in the reign has the same reverse but shows the two emperors each holding an akakia in the right hand, with the legend *LEON S CON* with many varieties in its spacing. These coins were ascribed to Leo III by Grierson and differentiated from similar coins of Leo V which lack the akakia detail.

CONSTANTINE V (741–75), continued the 'heavy' series of copper and, like his father, in several modules: busts of Constantine and Leo IV appear on the obverse and Leo III was given Constantine's own previous place on the reverse. He issued another class showing himself and Leo IV enthroned without legend and with a reverse similar to the last. Both these were preceded by a class in which Constantine V occupied the obverse alone carrying either an orb cruciger or a cross potent in the right hand and with the reverse showing the denomination from follis to pentanummia: both the earlier mentioned classes have only folles and half-folles. On his gold, Constantine V occupies the obverse and his father the reverse, but they hold a cross potent instead of the orb found on similar coins of Leo III's reign. Later he joins his son Leo IV with him and the two

258, 259

11, 12

260,

408*

busts have the legend *CONSTANTI-NOSSLϵONONϵOS* (*i.e.* the younger): Leo III occupies the reverse, but wearing the loros. Sicily produced gold of this last class and masses of copper of both earlier and later classes. Other Italian mints produced some very debased ' gold '. The miliaresia of the reign are all issued with Leo IV.

ARTAVASDES (742–4), the iconodule usurper, issued solidi with his son Nicephorus on the reverse and also joint miliaresia. Paris has a solidus from Rome showing Artavasdes and Constantine V—an impossible combination due, Wroth considered, to an engraver's mistake.

LEO IV (775–80) with his son, Constantine VI, issued two classes of solidi, one with four busts; two of themselves wearing the chlamys and on the reverse Leo III and Constantine V wearing the loros; the other has them enthroned on the obverse and has the same reverse as before. The legends have been satisfactorily interpreted by Veglery and Zacos in 1955 as *LϵON/ VS/S/ϵGGON/CONSTANTINOS/O/ NϵOS*—' Leo son and grandson, Constantine the younger '; (reverse), *LϵON/ PAP / CONSTANTOS / PATHR*— ' Leo grandfather, Constantine father '. The key words on the obverse are υἱός and ἔγγονος, and on the reverse πάππος and πατήρ; S is the equivalent of κάι. There are folles corresponding to both classes, and the difficulties over the miliaresia have been discussed above. In this reign a new crown appears with a cross rising straight from the circlet that does not

have any circular or semi-circular feature below it.

CONSTANTINE VI (780–97) and EIRENE (797–802). The ' family ' coins of the iconoclast emperors reach their furthest expansion in the first solidi of the reign showing busts of Constantine VI on left and Eirene *(obv.)*, with seated figures of Leo III, Constantine V and Leo IV *(rev.)*. The legends are difficult to read and vary in detail: obverse, *CONSTANTINOS/ ЬASI[ΛϵVS] / Δ[ϵSПOTHS]*; reverse, *SVN/IPHNI/AГ[IA] MIT[PA] AV [ГVSTH]*, the latter meaning ' with Eirene revered mother and empress '. Eirene can be spelt *HPHNI, IPINI, EIPINH*, etc. A second class of solidus has Constantine on the obverse and Eirene on the reverse and both classes have folles corresponding. On miliaresia the two names are included and none have yet been published for Eirene alone. Eirene's solidi in her sole reign show her on both sides with identical bust and legend *EIRINH ЬASILISSH*. 410* There are folles to match but with *M* for the reverse type. A solidus in the Ashmolean Museum, Oxford, perhaps Sicilian, shows her with a cross potent on the reverse and Ricotti Prina illustrates another of anomalous type with her in a chlamys on one side and in a loros holding a cross potent on the other.

NICEPHORUS (802–11) and his son, STAURACIUS (from 803). There are solidi both for Nicephorus alone with cross on steps reverse and for him with Stauracius who 434*, 435* takes over the reverse. There are also folles for both, those with Stauracius having an obverse with two busts and no legend. No miliaresia are known. Sicily issued a full range of gold and folles with Nicephorus exceptionally wearing the loros. Both emperors are shown normally wearing the chlamys. South Italian mints issued solidi for the dual reign, which are debased in every sense.

MICHAEL I and his son, THEOPHYLACT (811–13). In spite of his iconodule leanings Michael produced coinage similar to that of his predecessor. Folles survive both with his bust alone and with his son's added, though these have been challenged by Dr Metcalf. There are miliaresia for the dual reign and from Sicily a full range of gold and copper issues.

LEO V and his son, CONSTANTINE (813–20). There are solidi with a bust on each side and miliaresia distinguished by an unbroken legend or by a single border. Folles have the two busts on the obverse with no hands showing and the legend *LEON S CONST*, which are amongst the commoner coins in this sparsely provided period. Sicily issued solidi and fractions and characteristic folles with a bust on each side of the coin briefly labelled *Λ-ЄO* and *K-ONCT*.

264

MICHAEL II (820–9) with his son, THEOPHILUS (829–42). Solidi from Constantinople and from Sicily (which also issued fractions) show Michael in a chlamys on the obverse and Theophilus in a loros on the reverse. There are also epigraphic miliaresia. Folles, larger and heavier than their predecessors, show the two emperors robed as above but side by side: the reverse was given over to the denomination with officina *A* on some early examples dropping out in favour of *Θ*. Theophilus carried on these large folles, first of all alone, and then—they are rare—with his son Constantine. Finally he drops the *M* reverse and substitutes a four line epigraphic one, 265 with himself on the obverse. This last prolific class of folles have been examined in detail by Dr Metcalf and attributed to a 266 ▶ variety of provincial mints, constituting a comprehensive reform of the whole monetary system. However, with the exception of one type, thought by Wroth to be a half-follis principally owing to its weight, which might be from Thessalonica, the case for a variety of provincial mints must be regarded as non proven for the present. There are four classes of miliaresia, including Constantine, and another Michael III. His solidi have Theophilus in a chlamys on the obverse, and his father and son on the reverse. 436*, ◀ Another solidus has a patriarchal cross on the reverse instead, and refers to the 267 ▶ emperor as the 'slave of Christ'—the term Justinian II had used—as does one class of his miliaresia. This last solidus looks a fine example of Italian work and was certainly copied there less successfully.

Issues in gold and copper from the Sicilian mint both for Michael II and Theophilus were prolific and some are now common. Where there is more than one emperor the senior wears either chlamys or 268 ▶ loros, it would appear, indiscriminately but a single emperor *generally* has a chlamys on obverse and a loros on reverse. There are solidi with fractions and folles for Michael II alone and with Theophilus, and for Theophilus alone and with Constantine (832–9): on these last, whether in gold or

266 Gold solidus of Constans II or Heraclonas.
Obv. *A very early issue of Constans II, or
possibly of Heraclonas: the reverse has
CONOBK as on No. 242 above (diam.
20 mm.).*

267, 268 Constans II *(641–68). Gold solidus.*
Obv. *Solidi like this with a short beard
followed others with the beard represented by a
row of pellets. This piece is dated on the reverse
and in the same year there are dotted beard coins,
indicating that the change took place in this year.*
Rev. *The S in the field right indicates the date
647–8 (i.e. the sixth Indictional year) or
646/7 (sixth regnal year). The officina is H
(diam. 19 mm.).*

copper, Theophilus occupies the obverse and his father Michael II and son Constantine are alongside on the reverse.

MICHAEL III (842–67). There are three classes of solidi in the reign, all important in relation to the end of iconoclasm. (1) Michael III (left) and his elder sister Thecla, and on reverse his mother the Regent Theodora. (2) c. 852. Bust of Jesus copied from Justinian II Class II and on reverse Michael (left and beardless) and Theodora. (3) 856–66. Bust of Jesus as in (2) above and on the reverse a bearded Michael III. The first and third have epigraphic miliaresia corresponding but the only copper folles from the capital come in 866–7 with Michael on the obverse and Basil I on the reverse. The change from iconoclasm came slowly as a glance at the last follis will make clear. Sicily issued some base solidi, semisses and tremisses in the reign and folles with Michael on obverse and reverse or with M (officina Θ) for the last time on reverse. There is also a rare copper piece for Michael and Basil from Cherson foreshadowing much activity in the mint in the next reigns.

9, 270
1, 272
273
256, 257

X. THE MACEDONIANS AND COMNENI, 867-1204

This period, in which there are many more coins available for study than in the last, covers the post-iconoclastic artistic revival, continuing virtually uninterrupted by the internal and external disasters of the eleventh century. The Empire's resources had been overstretched by Basil II's successful campaigns. When his singularly popular dynasty failed, the Empire suffered from disputes between the military and civil servants at the top and in 1071 had experienced the defeats at Bari, by the Normans, and at Manzikert, by the Selçuk Turks. The former eagerly followed into the Balkans through Epirus and the latter slowly infiltrated into the highlands of Anatolia virtually unopposed. Numismatically much of importance was taking place—the debasement of the gold coinage from the reign of Michael IV until the reforms of Alexius I in 1092; the introduction of a new gold coin, the tetarteron, by Nicephorus II and of the so-called 'Anonymous Bronze' series lasting from John Zimisces to Alexius I; and the revival and steady activity of the mint of Cherson. Finally, after the remarkable continuance of iconoclastic principles in coin design for a century after 843 there was, under the Comneni, a production of gold coins rivalling other contemporary arts in reaching a zenith of quality.

The gold coinage underwent a triple change. The standard solidus or nomisma became larger, thinner and eventually cup-shaped (scyphate) and is today called a (nomisma) histamenon or simply stamenon. The process was connected with the introduction of the tetarteron by Nicephorus II, for the new coin was originally indistinguishable from the old solidus except fractionally by weight; it was probably this that brought so much unpopularity to Nicephorus II over its introduction. The word tetarteron indicates a 'quarter' of something and probably means a solidus diminished by a quarter of a tremissis in weight (not alloy). They had to be distinguished and it was the new coin which retained the old solidus form, while the 'standard' piece became the larger, scyphate nomisma 'histamenon' (i. e. standard). This last is the term which Grierson advocates being used in the period from 963 until 1092 when the tetarteron became something different altogether. Also in 1092 Alexius I introduced a new standard gold coin of 21 carats fine (though nominally 24) called the hyperper. Hyperper is the term now normally used for standard nomismata from Alexius' reform until the end of the gold coinage altogether. There are still doubts over why the tetarteron was introduced; later chroniclers assert a patent deception on the part of Nicephorus II, which is unlikely in view of the great difficulty in distinguishing the new coin from the old; but Grierson has urged the need for a coin roughly equal to the Arab dinar in weight and gold value for use in the provinces recently reconquered from the Muslims. The tetarteron weighed 4.00 g. to 4.10 and the fatimid dinar 4.05 g. to 4.15.

Fig. 5. *Byzantine Empire A.D. 1000–1200*
Fineness of gold in histamena and hyperpers.

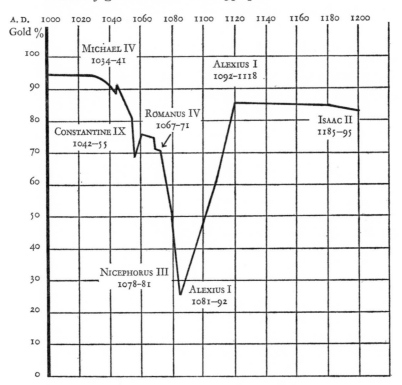

Alongside this must be put the debasement of the fineness of gold used in the coinage, which began in the reign of Michael IV and was ended by the reforms of Alexius I. In this half-century the nomisma histamenon declined to a gold content of 6.5 carats or 26 % as can be seen in Figure 5. Debasement meant that Byzantine gold was no longer a stable currency for international trade, but it is surprising how long it was before Italian trading cities took advantage of the situation to provide such a currency with the Florentine *fiorino* (1252) and the Venetian *ducat* (1284), preceded by Frederic II's experimental *augustale* of 1231. The stabilization of Byzantine currency achieved by the Comneni was ruined by the Latin Conquest of 1204 otherwise Byzantine gold might have regained its old place in international markets.

Alexius I's reform of 1092 has already been mentioned several times as a turning point and it is due to the brilliantly successful research of Michael Hendy that students of the Byzantine series have now a firm foothold in the coinage of the Comneni. Hendy's work, published in 1969, is entitled *Coinage and Money in the Byzantine Empire 1081–261*. By tackling the problems on such a wide front and by studying a large number of Balkan hoards he has been able to find an ordered plan which others, looking at shorter periods and perhaps too much at coins in cabinets, were unable to do. Briefly, the reform of Alexius was effective up to the Latin Conquest and in a disintegrating form beyond it. It was based on a gold *hyperper* 21 carats fine (but theoretically 24 carats) with its two fractions of one third—the *electrum aspron trachy* containing 24 % gold or 6 carats—and of one forty-eighth, the *billon aspron trachy* containing at first about 6 % silver. Copper coinage was provided by the tetarteron and its half, bearing no relation to its gold predecessor which in the early years of Alexius' reign had been debased into virtually a silver piece: the tetartera in the new system provided nothing more than small change. As Hendy shows, the system did not remain entirely stable but it

269, 270 Michael III *(842–67)*. *Gold solidus, obverse and reverse. First issue of the reign showing him with his elder sister Thecla on the obverse, and his mother Theodora the Regent on the reverse (diam. 21 mm.).*

271, 272 Michael III *(842–67)*. *Gold solidus, obverse and reverse. Second issue c. 852. The bust of Jesus is copied from the obverse of Justinian II's second issue of 160 years before (obverse), with Michael and Theodora on the reverse. The change from iconoclasm begins to show on the coinage (diam. 20 mm.).*

273 Michael III *(842–67)*. *Gold solidus, reverse. The obverse of this piece is similar to No. 271 and Michael is bearded on the reverse. The third and last issue of the reign from 856 (diam. 20 mm.).*

274, 275 John I Zimisces *(969–76)*. *Copper follis, obverse and reverse. The first of the Anonymous issues usually referred to as Class A (i), struck on small flans and generally showing traces of earlier strikings of Romanus I or Nicephorus II (see Nos. 298, 299) (diam. 21 mm.).*

276, 277 Constantine IX *(1042–55)*. *Copper follis, obverse and reverse. An anonymous piece of Class D, and, as is often the case, overstruck on Class C: part of the jewelled cross of the latter can be seen in the middle of the reverse (diam. 29 mm.).*

278, 279 Basil I *(867–86)*. *Copper follis, obverse and reverse. A typical piece of the Cherson mint which was very active from this reign until that of Basil II (diam. 16 mm.).*

269

270

271

272

273

274

275

276

277

278

279

280

281

282

283

284

285

286

287

288

289

280, 281 John II Comnenus *(1118–43). Gold hyperper, obverse and reverse. The reverse showing John crowned by the Virgin is a fine piece of design as might be expected from a period of great artistic achievement. The naturalism of this coin contrasts with the bold impressionism found in the hyperpers of Alexius I (as in No. 14). John is correctly described as 'Born in the Purple' (diam. 31 mm.).*

282, 283 Manuel I Comnenus *(1143–80). Gold hyperper, obverse and reverse. Manuel, like his father, is described as 'Born in the purple' and seen as a remote personality, all robes and regalia, nearer to the hand of God (top right) than to his subjects (diam. 32 mm.).*

284, 285 Leo VI *(886–912). Gold solidus, obverse and reverse. The obverse announces the Virgin in both Latin and Greek. On the reverse Leo wears a chlamys with embroidered tablion (diam. 19 mm.).*

286, 287 Romanus I *(920–44). Copper follis, obverse and reverse. There is no mention of the legitimate co-emperor Constantine VII on this coin issued in the period 921 to 944. Romanus was undoubtedly trying to found a separate dynasty of his own. 'Romanus, by the grace of God, Emperor of the Romans' (diam. 25 mm.).*

288 Romanus I *(920–44). Silver miliaresion, reverse. A coin of 931 when Romanus' eldest son Christopher had died. He had made his other sons, Stephen and Constantine, co-emperors seven years before. Constantine VII here appears second of the four (diam. 24 mm.).*

289 Constantine VII *(913–59). Gold solidus, reverse. Issued in 945 when Constantine, at last free from the Romanus family, was reigning alone. He wears the simplified loros and is described as 'Autocrator' in the legend (diam. 20 mm.).*

was not at all—as it once seemed—anarchic, until the thirteenth century. The main mints were Constantinople and Thessalonica: the officina system was re-introduced—their number increased to cope with emergencies—and marked by differences in decoration on the collar of the emperor's maniakion, on his chlamys, his loros, the pendilia of his crown or on his sceptre. In Manuel I's fourth coinage, for instance, there were four officina for billon trachea distinguished by variations on the loros, and on his third coinage it is a matter of pellets (none, one, two or three) on the shaft of the sceptre. Within each officina a number of styles and individualities of die engraving can be traced.

Prior to Alexius' reform the copper coinage was dominated by the Anonymous (*i.e.* without imperial name) series of twelve different types with massive issues of some of them. First issued by John Zimisces they continued until the pre-reform years of Alexius I adorned solely **274, 275** with religious motifs and inscriptions. The series has been ordered and elucidated mainly by the study of overstrikes which **298, 299** provide strong clues when a 'predominant combination' can be established, for example, of C over B, D over C or J over Nicephorus III, as shown in the sixth column of Figure 6. The coins have no denomination given on them—they were all folles—and no issuer's name, but from Constantine X onwards emperors issued both 'signed' and anonymous copper pieces, thereby making their order of issue easier to establish by observing overstrikes. Their pointedly religious nature makes it possible that they were

Fig. 6. *Types of 'Anonymous Bronze' and their attribution.*

1 *Aes Anonymous Type*	2 *W. Wroth,* *B.M. Catalogue*	3 *A. R. Bellinger,* *Corinth finds*	4 *Miss* *M. Thompson,* *Athens Agora*	5 *If signed* *coinage exists* *or not*	6 *Predominant* *combination*

Bust of Christ
Rev.: 4 lines
  (i) small type ⎫
  (ii) large type ⎭
	I
	
	John I–
	Romanus III
		1
		
		(i) John I
		(ii) Basil II–
		Romanus III
			A
			
			(i) John I
			(ii) Basil II and
			Constan-
			tine VIII
				No
				No
					(i) Nicepho-
					rus II and Con-
					stantine VII.
					No restriking

Bust of Christ *Rev.*: Cross on steps	II Michael IV	2 Michael IV	B Romanus III	No	Over A (ii)
Christ standing *Rev.*: Jewelled Cross	III Theodora	3 Constan- tine IX	C Michael IV	No	Over B
Christ seated on throne with back *Rev.*: 3 lines	V Constantine X	6 Isaac I	D Constan- tine IX	No	Over C
Bust of Christ *Rev.*: 3 lines	VI Isaac I	4 Theodora	E Isaac I	No	Uncommon type, some- times over A (ii)
Christ seated on backless throne *Rev.*: 3 lines, + and +	IV Michael VI	5 Michael VI	F Constan- tine X	Yes: plentiful	Uncommon type, some- times over E
Bust of Christ *Rev.*: Bust of Virgin	VII Constan- tine IX	7 Michael VII	G Romanus IV	Yes: plentiful	Over Constan- tine X and sometimes over Romanus IV

Bust of Christ					
Bust of Christ Rev.: Patriarchal Cross	Crusader issues temp. Alexius I	8 Alexius I	H Michael VII	Yes: but uncommon	Nicephorus III over H
Bust of Christ Rev.: Latin Cross		9 Alexius I	I Nicephorus III	Yes: plentiful	Over Michael VII
Bust of Christ Rev.: Cross over Crescent		10 Alexius I	J Alexius I	Yes	Over Nicephorus III
Bust of Christ Rev.: Virgin standing Pellet borders	VIII Constantine IX	11 Alexius I	K Alexius I	Yes	Over J
Bust of Christ Rev.: Cross pattée, XC below	—	13[1] Alexius I	L Alexius I	Yes	Very uncommon; no overstrike identified

[1] No type 12 quoted here; the original was probably a variant or bad striking of type 9.

originally regarded as a representative piece of Byzantine culture in the provinces recaptured in the later tenth century. Certainly Basil II's coins (Class A [ii]) were fine large pieces and some sixty variations of the type have already been identified. Dr Metcalf has been a protagonist here, as with the billon trachea of the Comneni, for a number of provincial mints, but until some team work is undertaken with the co-operation of the Turkish government on pieces in the Turkish museums, the statistical evidence is bound to be unbalanced; the quantity of surviving coins is great and the condition of many is such that precise identification of details is hardly possible. Figure 6 shows the types and their allocation by different scholars: that of Margaret Thompson arising from her work on the excavations in the Agora at Athens is the latest and most accurate but it is still less known and used than it should be by numismatists.

The mint at Cherson was unusually active under the Macedonian dynasty, a swan-song prior to the transfer of the town to Prince Vladimir of Kiev in 989. All sovereigns from Basil I to Basil II issued the characteristic cast bronzes with a floriated cross on steps as one type and a monogram as the other: Constantine VII is alone in having a facing bust type instead of the cross. In this remote outpost there seems to have been under Romanus I an issue of two distinct modules long after the half-follis had disappeared in the capital.

The Macedonian period was one of great artistic achievement as was that of the

Comneni after it. In a reaction against the work done under the iconoclast regime, there was a classical naturalistic revival as is evident in the mosaic in the Church of the Holy Wisdom (Aya Sophia) in Istanbul showing Leo VI (or possibly his father Basil I) prostrating himself before Christ enthroned. But numismatic conservatism, coupled with the reluctance of the emperors to surrender the publicity which iconoclasm had brought to their own images, preserved iconoclastic portraiture on the coins for over a century. The copper of Basil I shows this clearly and his solidi show that the 'family coins' of the iconoclasts were not discarded either. A century later, in Nicephorus II's reign, **438*, 439*** gold showing the emperor in naturalistic and in impressionistic style was still being issued contemporaneously. There must still have been a considerable following for iconoclasm and the change was not pushed on too hurriedly; even in the pictorial redecoration of the Church of the Holy Wisdom the first mosaic was not unveiled until 867.

During the tenth to twelfth centuries some of the masterly artistic creation so evident, for instance, in enamels, ivories, book bindings and sacred vessels was to be seen also in the design and execution of coins: especially was this so in the days of the Comnenus family all of whose emperors issued coins of outstanding quality. In these coins can be found an interesting contrast in style between the naturalism of **280, 281** the standing figures of John II and the Virgin and the impressionism of the remote **13, 14** figure of his father, or even that of his son **282, 283** Manuel, to take only three hyperpers.

290 Constantine VII *(913–59). Copper follis, obverse. The follis corresponds with the solidus (No. 289) when the emperor reigned alone, before he associated his son Romanus II with him (diam. 22 mm.).*

291, 292 Constantine VII *(913–59). Gold solidus, obverse and reverse. This was the last issue of solidi in the reign, after the coronation of Romanus II in 945. Some remarkably fine dies, often like this one deeply engraved, were made for the obverse. Note the contrast between the 'naturalistic' approach to the bust of Christ, and the impressionist busts of the emperors (diam. 20 mm.).*

293 Romanus II *(959–63). Gold solidus, reverse. A rare piece of this emperor, maintaining the impressive line of portrait busts (diam. 21 mm.).*

294 Nicephorus II *(963–9). Copper follis, obverse. This has a portrait of Nicephorus II which may be compared with that on his gold and silver pieces (diam. 22 mm.).*

295, 296 Nicephorus II *(963–9). Silver miliaresion, obverse and reverse. The obverse has a naturalistic bust of the emperor at the crossing of the cross, in the position which would be given to a revered relic, compare obverse of No. 294 (diam. 23 mm.).*

297 John I Zimisces *(969–76). Gold tetarteron, reverse. Indistinguishable from the histamenon except by weight: this specimen weighs 4.00 g. as against a similar histamenon of 4.46 g. (diam. 21 mm.).*

298, 299 John I Zimisces *(969–76). Copper follis, obverse and reverse. An anonymous piece (Class A (i)) struck on a flan previously used by Nicephorus II (3 lines of his reverse legend are visible bottom and left of the bust of Christ) and by Romanus I (+RΩ m at bottom edge of the reverse) (diam. 25 mm.).*

290

291

292

293

294

295

296

297

298

299

300

301

302

303

304

305

306

307

308

300 Basil II *(976–1025). Gold histamenon, reverse. This coin, the successor to the solidus, is now differentiated from the lighter weight tetarteron by its thinner, broader flan as well as by details of the types used. On the right is Basil's brother Constantine VIII (diam. 26 mm.).*

301 Basil II *(976–1025). Gold tetarteron, reverse. A smaller, thicker and lighter coin than the histamenon (diam. 19 mm.).*

302 Basil II *(976–1025). Silver miliaresion, obverse. An impressive coin when unclipped (diam. 30 mm.).*

303, 304 Constantine VIII *(1025–8). Gold histamenon, obverse and reverse. The emperor wears the maniakion and simplified loros, and holds a sceptre in the form of a labarum, and in his left hand the akakia (diam. 27 mm.).*

305 Constantine VIII *(1025–8). Gold tetarteron, reverse. Compare the histamenon*

(No. 304) for the differentiation of the coins by means of their types (diam. 19 mm.).

306 Romanus III *(1028–34). Gold histamenon, reverse. This type of the Virgin crowning the emperor was used in several reigns and seems to have brought out the best in designers and engravers (diam. 24 mm.).*

307 Romanus III *(1028–34). Silver miliaresion, obverse. The Virgin is of the type 'Hodegetria' —She who points the Way, i.e. to Christ on her left arm. This is the only use of this type, so far known, on Byzantine coins. The coin has previously been attributed to Romanus IV (diam. 23 mm.).*

308 Michael IV *(1034–41). Gold histamenon, reverse. A very rare piece, probably of Thessalonica, showing St Michael handing the labarum to the emperor. Hendy has recently shown that it was imitated in Sweden in the 1040's and made the attribution to Michael IV (diam. 25 mm.).*

Artists were making more of the details of robes and their folds, and representing full- and three-quarter-length figures as against the facing busts in formalized paludamentum, chlamys or loros normal heretofore. Some of their beautifully engraved dies stand in stark contrast against the disastrous political, military and social background.

THE MACEDONIAN DYNASTY

BASIL I (867–86) introduced on his solidi the new type of Christ seated on a lyre-backed throne as obverse for the rare (and sometimes forged) class with a standing figure of the emperor facing, robed in the loros, and also for the common class with half-length figures of himself and his son Constantine (died 879) holding a patriarchal cross between them. It has been suggested that the obverse is a numismatic representation of the enthroned Christ over the western door into the Church of the Holy Wisdom and consequently that the emperor prostrating himself is Basil I and not his son Leo VI: on balance the latter is more likely but the possible use of coins in deciding such matters is important. There are two rare solidi of the iconoclastic family type both showing a bust of Basil on the obverse with respectively busts of Constantine and his mother, and of Leo VI and Alexander as the reverses; there is a tremissis also, similar to the latter.

The miliaresia of the reign, all issued in the name of Basil and Constantine, show an increase in weight to around 3 g. and this was to be maintained by subsequent emperors. There seems to have been dif-

ficulty in relating silver to gold with a short period of 14 miliaresia to the solidus, but reverting to twelve, as Grierson has shown, with the follis valued at 24 to the miliaresion. Copper issues have Basil enthroned alone on a lyre-backed throne, and with his son Constantine, while a later one shows him standing three-quarter-length between Leo VI and Constantine. Less common types are one with busts of Basil and Constantine holding a labarum between them and another with busts of Basil on the obverse and of Leo VI and Alexander on the reverse: all but this last have epigraphic reverses.

The mint of Sicily issued gold semisses in unchanged iconoclastic style, though some were so debased as to look like copper.

LEO VI (886–912) was more probably the son of Michael III than of Basil I and had been kept in the background while Constantine was alive; this may have sharpened his independence when he became emperor. His first class of solidi, at the age of twenty, shows him with long hair and beard on the reverse and the Virgin orans, for the first time, on the obverse. On a later and beautiful solidus he is standing with the young Constantine on the right, holding a cross crosslet between them. There are miliaresia corresponding epigraphically with both these classes. On copper Leo appears seated alone, like Basil, on a lyre-backed throne, and with his brother Alexander, each having as reverse a four-line inscription. Less common than these are pieces with busts of Leo and Alexander holding a labarum between them and another with the busts of Leo and of Alexander on the obverse and reverse respectively. The former may have had a half-follis—the weights are 7.8 g. and 1.7 g.—with a much smaller obverse but with a follis die used for the reverse.

ALEXANDER (May 912–June 913) succeeded in thwarting his brother's plan to hand over to his son (by an uncanonical fourth marriage) Constantine VII, but only a copper piece from Cherson, a miliaresion and a solidus are known of the reign. On the last the emperor is shown standing on the left, crowned by Saint Alexander (presumably) on the right: the obverse is Basil I's type of Christ enthroned.

CONSTANTINE VII (913–59) came to the throne at the age of six and proved to be a scholarly figure to whom the world owes much of its knowledge of Byzantium. The first period of his reign was dominated by his mother Zoe and busts of the two appear side by side with Constantine to the left on a rare gold solidus and on a common follis. Another early follis has the beardless Constantine half-length, in the loros. Next came a period, 920 to 945, in which the family of the able Armenian admiral Romanus I Lecapenus took control and the coinage reflects the changes of power from the legitimate dynasty to the usurping one until the Lecapenus family brought destruction on itself. On the solidi first the small figure of Constantine stands on the left beside Romanus, with Christ enthroned on the obverse, while another has their two busts in the same order with the same obverse. On the folles Romanus appears alone with a fine portrait bust and inscrip-

tional reverse. In 921, on solidi, busts of Romanus and his son Christopher occupy the reverse and Christ enthroned the obverse, but soon after Romanus takes over the obverse standing on the left being crowned by Jesus while on the reverse are busts of Constantine (left) and Christopher. On yet another solidus with the same obverse as the last the order of the two busts is reversed and both these issues have corresponding miliaresia with the same message as to status spelt out in their inscriptions. In 924 two more of Romanus' sons—Stephen and Constantine—were made co-emperors but do not appear on the coinage until after the death of Christopher in 931: then it was on a miliaresion on which the head of Romanus I appears at the intersection of the cross on the obverse, as though it were a relic. It was these two sons who turned on their father in 944 and exiled him, but popular support rallied behind the legitimate emperor, Constantine VII, and they themselves were exiled six months later. Thus in the last period, 945 to 959, Constantine VII ruled alone and with his son Romanus II. He issued a fine (and scarce) solidus with a bearded portrait of himself with a bust of Christ on the obverse and also a very common follis with his bearded bust on the obverse. Together with Romanus II he issued a common solidus shewing their two busts, the obverse of which was a bust of Christ; some examples have a fine deeply engraved naturalistic bust in remarkable contrast to the impressionist style of the reverse. There were miliaresia and folles of the joint reign, the former reverting to a plain cross without the intrusive portrait.

ROMANUS II (959–63). Only a rare solidus is known in gold, having a finely executed bust of the emperor with an orb surmounted by a tall cross in his left hand and wearing a robe of unusual pattern; the obverse is a bust of Christ and the whole coin appears to be modelled on his father's last portrait piece. The only copper comes from Cherson and no silver is known. Romanus' two sons, Basil II and Constantine VIII, were both under three years old when he died and their mother married Nicephorus II, a successful general from the nobility of Asia Minor who had been acclaimed emperor by his troops. At this time, when the frontiers of the Empire were being expanded in the east and south-east, the army and its generals play an increasing part in politics at the capital.

NICEPHORUS II (963–9). There are two types of solidi (now more correctly called histamena) both having a naturalistic bust of Christ as obverse but with startlingly different reverses. On one, busts of Nicephorus and of Basil II (beardless on the right) are portrayed in impressionist iconoclastic style while the other has the Virgin crowning Nicephorus (on the right) rendered naturalistically. Indeed, the portrait on this solidus agrees with that on his folles and miliaresia where it was placed at the intersection of the cross, as Romanus I's had been. Nicephorus' introduction of the tetarteron and the difficulty of identifying it have been referred to on p. 172.

JOHN I ZIMISCES (969–76), was an Armenian nobleman and successful general who, with the connivance of Nicephorus' wife, mur-

309, 310 Zoe and Theodora. *Gold histamenon, obverse and reverse. From this short reign of the two sisters (April to June 1042) prior to Zoe's third marriage, this time to Constantine IX, a very small number of histamena have survived (diam. 21 mm.).*

311, 312 Constantine IX *(1042–55). Gold histamena, reverses. That on the left showing the emperor holding a sceptre with tendril ornament is of 21 1/2 carats and that showing him with a labarum-headed sceptre is of 20 carats. Grierson has shown that there was a progressive debasement in four stages—each differentiated by reverse type—during the reign (diam. both 28 mm.).*

313, 314 Constantine IX *(1042–55). Gold tetartera, reverses. The debasement is also to be reckoned with in the two tetartera of the reign from 21 carats (trefoil sceptre) to 17 1/2 (labarum) (diam. both 17 mm.).*

315, 316 Theodora *(1055–6). Gold histamenon, obverse and reverse. After the death of Constantine IX in 1055, Theodora returned to the throne for eighteen months. Compare No. 306 for a similar reverse type on Romanus III's histamena (diam. 22 mm.).*

317, 318 Theodora *(1055–6). Silver half-miliaresion, obverse and reverse. A rare piece similar in types to the half-miliaresion of Constantine IX; compare Nos. 59, 60 for Constantine's scyphate miliaresion (diam. 21 mm.).*

319, 320 Isaac I *(1057–9). Gold histamena, reverses. The reign produced two different histamena. The first showed the emperor—a general—with drawn sword and was received with hostility because it shewed his reliance on his own strength rather than that of God. In the second the sword was sheathed and he holds the labarum in his right hand. In both the emperor appears in military uniform with the short military cloak or 'sagion', thrown back over the shoulders (diam. 23 and 27 mm.).*

309

310

311

312

313

314

315

316

317

318

319

320

321

322

323

324

325

326

327

328

329

330

331

332

321 Constantine X *(1059–67). Gold scyphate histamenon, reverse. Constantine was a noble of the important Dukas family supported by the Church and civil service. His standing figure in maniakion, divitision and simplified loros should be contrasted with that of his military predecessor, Isaac I (diam. 21 mm.).*

322, 323 Constantine X *(1059–67). Copper follis, obverse and reverse. This piece, showing the emperor and his wife Eudocia (on the left), is the first copper coin to bear an emperor's name since the anonymous series began a century before (diam. 28 mm.).*

324 Constantine X *(1059–67). Copper follis, reverse. Another ' signed ' follis of Constantine which is sometimes found struck over the piece illustrated above, Nos. 322, 323. His family name Dukas appears on both. Besides ' signed ' pieces Constantine X was equally responsible for Anonymous Class F (diam. 26 mm.).*

325, 326 Romanus IV *(1067–71). Gold scyphate histamenon, obverse and reverse. All six figures have their names given: on the obverse Christ blesses Romanus (left) and Eudocia his wife, and on the reverse Eudocia's eldest son (by Constantine X) stands in the middle between his brothers Constantine and Andronicus (diam. 27 mm.).*

327 Romanus IV *(1067–71). Copper follis, reverse. A ' signed ' piece reading ' May the Cross help Romanus Diogenes ', in addition to the Anonymous Class G put out in this reign (diam. 27 mm.).*

328 Michael VII *(1071–8). Gold scyphate histamenon, reverse. This is found with two obverses, a bust of Christ and Christ seated on a high-backed throne (diam. 27 mm.).*

329 Alexius I *(1081–1118). Pre-reform electrum trachy, reverse. The gold histamenon reached its lowest point of debasement in this reign, and this was its representative in the first coinage from Constantinople (diam. 33 mm.).*

330, 331 Alexius I *(1081–1118). Pre-reform electrum tetarteron, obverse and reverse. It was as debased as No. 329, and formed part of the first coinage from Constantinople. The reform can be dated to 1092 (diam. 19 mm.).*

332 Alexius I *(1081–1118). Post-reform electrum trachy of Constantinople, obverse (the reverse is No. 337). This coin was valued at 1/3 of the gold hyperper (diam. 30 mm.).*

dered the emperor and took his place. His histamena and tetartera continue the bust of Christ on the obverse and show him on the reverse crowned by the Virgin, sometimes he holds a patriarchal cross in his left hand and sometimes an orb surmounted by a trefoil. True to the tradition of usurpers his portrait appears at the intersection of the cross on his miliaresia: this is one of the commonest silver coins of the Byzantine series today and must have been issued in large numbers. The folles of the reign are the first of the Anonymous series, the rather small A(i) coins often found struck over folles of Nicephorus II. Tetartera were minted but were still only distinguishable by weight from histamena.

274, 275 298, 299 297

BASIL II with CONSTANTINE VIII (976–1025). All gold coins of the reign are of the same basic type with a bust of Christ as obverse, and facing busts of Basil on the left in the loros and Constantine in a chlamys holding a cross of varying type between them as reverse. In the course of the reign the histamenon became much broader, ending with three borders of pellets around the type and a substantial plain surround beyond them. Meanwhile the tetarteron remained unchanged in size but developed varieties of type which by the end of the reign also distinguished it. The gold, like the silver and copper, shows a vast variety of sigla and small differences in the types. The miliaresia begin with a type, now very rare, similar to that of Constantine VII, but they soon assumed the form most associated with the reign having small busts of the two emperors below the arms of the cross—not at the

300

301

intersection, Grierson thinks because there was no room for two. Another miliaresion, rare like the first, has a bust of the Virgin holding a medallion of Jesus with an invocation to aid the emperors: this was attributed by Wroth to John Zimisces. Of the middle type, bearing the emperors' busts there is a strange difference between two varieties in that one, the commonest, is almost invariably clipped and the other never. Taking two specimens at random one measures 20 mm. in diameter and the other 29 mm., but the weights are not the same or apparently even related. Grierson thought that the ' silver famine ' which so affected the contemporary Muslim world was being also felt at Byzantium at the end of Basil II's reign. This may therefore account for the vast amount of copper coined (Anonymous A(ii) with its sixty varieties) and also for its dramatic increase in weight from 5 g. or less to 18 g. or more: was it taking the place of silver?

302

15, 16

CONSTANTINE VIII (1025–8). Gold histamena have what has become the standard obverse, a bust of Christ and a portrait bust reverse of which certain details can be checked from literary sources. There are two types of tetartera—they have become smaller and thicker—of which one shows the emperor carrying the labarum in his right hand (as on the histamenon), while in the other he has an orb cruciger. No silver for the reign is known.

303, 3

305

ROMANUS III (1028–34), married Constantine's daughter Zoe: his histamenon—a beautiful coin but much forged—shows him standing on the left being crowned by

306

the Virgin. Some of these pieces are slightly scyphate. There is a tetarteron with a facing bust reverse—once attributed to Romanus IV—and an obverse bust of the Virgin holding a medallion of Jesus before her breast.

307 There is also a miliaresion which was once attributed to Romanus IV, with an obverse of the 'Virgin who shows the Way' (*i.e.* standing full-length and pointing to the Christ child on her left arm); on the reverse Romanus III stands facing with a patriarchal cross in his right hand and an orb cruciger in his left. It is one of the most beautiful of Byzantine coins.

MICHAEL IV (1034–41), the second husband of Zoe was married to her the same day that Romanus died. A rare histamenon struck at Thessalonica portrays him standing on the right receiving from the Archangel Michael the labarum—a design 308 which Hendy has shown was imitated by Sven Estrithson in Sweden in the 1040's. The usual histamena of Michael IV have 455* the bust of the emperor facing, carrying the labarum in his right hand and an orb cruciger in his left. The debasement of the histamenon began in this reign which has no tetartera and no silver. No coins are known of his nephew and successor Michael V (December 1041–April 1042).

ZOE and THEODORA (April to June 1042). A rare (and also forged) histamenon shows), 310 small, facing, half-length figures of the sister-empresses.

CONSTANTINE IX MONOMACHUS (1042–55), was Zoe's third husband and he outlived

her. His four slightly varied classes of histamena, with a facing bust and a portrait 311, 312 that can be compared with one on a mosaic in the gallery of the Church of the Holy Wisdom, represent stages of progressive debasement: his two classes of tetartera showing the emperor with a 313, 314 triple-topped sceptre and the labarum do the same. The increasingly scyphate form of the histamena is plain to see and silver re-appears in a new pattern with a miliaresion (to judge by its weight) in scyphate form also, and a half-piece small and flat. It looks as if the silver pieces reflect the histamenon/tetarteron relationship. The miliaresion has a standing Virgin orans as 59, 60 obverse and as reverse the emperor standing in military dress with a cross in his right hand and a sword in his left. The half-piece has a bust of the Virgin but an cf. 317 inscription on its reverse.

THEODORA (1055–6), daughter of Constantine VIII and the last of the Macedonian house to reign, issued a fine histamenon 315, 316 showing herself standing on the left being crowned by the Virgin, and on the obverse a figure of Christ standing on a dais. On her tetartera a bust of Theodora balances the obverse bust of Christ. A rare half-miliaresion follows the pattern set by 317, 318 Constantine IX.

MICHAEL VI (1056–7), issued histamena showing himself three-quarter-length, on the left being crowned by the Virgin and a bust of Christ for obverse. This piece was once given to Michael V but has been 29, 30 re-attributed by Grierson on the grounds of fineness of metal and its legend including the title *AUTOCRATOR*, which is also found on Michael VI's tetartera: these have a Virgin orans and a reverse of the emperor standing full-length with a long cross in his right hand and the akakia in his left.

ISAAC I COMNENOS (1057–9). The emperor's original issue of histamena showing him standing in military dress with a drawn sword in his right hand and its scabbard in his left, was so unpopular in seeming to show reliance on his own strength rather than that of God, that he had to issue another. This put the labarum in his right hand and a sheathed sword in his left: both have Christ enthroned as the obverse. On a tetarteron the emperor has an orb cruciger instead of the labarum and the obverse is a bust of Christ. There is a very rare half-miliaresion with a bust of Christ and an inscriptional reverse.

CONSTANTINE X DUKAS (1059–67). The succession of a civilian noble reflects the struggle between the military aristocracy of Asia Minor (like the Comneni) and the civilian bureaucracy of the capital, against a background of mounting danger from Turks and Normans. Constantine issued two classes of histamena, on one of which he stands in the loros on a dais holding the labarum in his right hand, and on the other he is standing on the left being crowned by the Virgin. On the obverse of the first Christ is seated on a throne with a straight back, and on the second his throne has a curved back. The tetarteron has a bust of the emperor with a bust of the Virgin orans on the obverse. The same Virgin, but at full-length, appears on a half-miliaresion with inscriptional reverse. For the first time since Nicephorus II there are signed folles in this reign as well as anonymous ones. One shows Constantine and his wife Eudocia standing facing, holding a labarum between them, and another has a bust of the emperor: the obverses are Christ standing and a bust of Christ respectively. A great amount of copper survives from the reign and the type of Constantine and Eudocia was extensively copied by Turkish tribesmen nearly a century later.

ROMANUS IV (1067–71). An histamenon is attributed to Eudocia as regent standing between her sons, Michael (VII) and Constantine, prior to her marriage with the general Romanus Diogenes. After this, histamena show Christ crowning the new emperor and his wife, with a reverse of Michael VII standing between his younger brothers Constantine and Andronicus. Tetartera have a bust of the Virgin holding a medallion of Jesus before her, with a reverse of either the bust of Romanus alone or alongside that of Eudocia. A number of silver pieces—half-miliaresia or less—come from this reign, and there are signed folles with *C R P Δ* disposed round a cross, meaning 'May the Cross *(C)* help *(R)* Romanus *(P)* the Emperor *(Δ)*.'

MICHAEL VII (1071–8). Histamena have a bust of Michael carrying the labarum and an orb cruciger, with as obverse either a bust of Christ or, rather scarcer, Christ enthroned. Tetartera continue the bust of the Virgin holding a medallion of Jesus type as obverse and have busts of Michael

27, 28 — 319 — 320 — 321 — 334 — 322, — 324 — 442, — 333 — 325, — 336 — 327 — 335 — 328 — 456*,

198

333, 334 Constans II *(641–68)*. *Gold solidus.*
Obv. *The emperor is shown with a short beard,*
but this time there is no date. Rev. *The cross*
following CONOB is one of many symbols, as
yet unexplained, used in this reign. Constans
first appears with a long beard in 651 (diam.
20 mm.).

335, 336 Constans II *(641–68)*. *Gold solidus.*
Obv. *The emperor associated his eldest son*
Constantine IV as co-emperor with himself in
654, and his two younger sons in 659. Constan-
tine IV is in the junior position on the right.
Both emperors wear the civilian chlamys
fastened by a fibula on the right shoulder. The
crown of Constans II is similar to that worn
in No. 241. Rev. *A cross on steps divides the*
two younger sons Heraclius on the left and,
slightly smaller, Tiberius on the right. Below is
another symbol T and the legend, still unchanged,
invokes 'Victory of the Emperor'. The
officina is Θ (9) (diam. 18 mm.).

and his wife Maria on the reverse. Michael issued a miliaresion with the same types as that of Constantine IX showing the emperor standing in armour, and a large variety of half-miliaresia (all rare) with inscriptional reverses. All silver tends to be found in a very worn state, and it is difficult to appraise its weight, though it appears to be falling. There are signed folles with the emperor's bust and possibly some half-folles.

NICEPHORUS III BOTANIATES (1078–81). Another member of the military aristocracy emerged from a chaos of pretenders to marry Maria, while her husband was still living, and to seize the throne with the support of the Turks. His histamena, which can look like anything from good gold to what appears pure silver are of two classes —either having the emperor's bust or his
43, 44 standing figure: the obverse of the former is a bust of Christ, and of the latter Christ seated on a throne sometimes with and sometimes without a back. The tetarteron
41, 42 has the emperor standing and, on the obverse, a bust of Christ. Two very rare half-miliaresia are recorded and some common signed folles with *CΦNΔ* displayed round a cross—' May the Cross *(C)* protect *(Φ)* Nicephorus *(N)* the Emperor *(Δ)* '. A contemporary pretender, Nicephorus Melissenus, issued silver and another, Nicephorus Basilacius, probably some copper.

THE COMNENUS DYNASTY

ALEXIUS I (1081–1118). The debasement reached its nadir in the years before 1092 and the essential thing is to distinguish the pre-reform coins of the two mints at Constantinople and Thessalonica from those of the new system established at the reform. In the early period there are two classes of electrum scyphate histamena, the first having an enthroned Christ as obverse and the second a bust of Christ. The reverse of the first has a half-length figure of the emperor wearing a chlamys and carrying in his left hand an orb cruciger and in his 329 right a sceptre ending in a star of pellets; the second has the same figure but for the sceptre, which ends in a cross with leaves below—there are silver and billon issues of this second class also. From Thessalonica there are also two classes, generally in silver but occasionally in electrum and billon, with a bust of Christ and on the reverse St Demetrius standing on the left and handing either the labarum or a patriarchal cross (both of which have steps below) to the emperor attired in the loros on the right. Each mint has two classes of tetartera in electrum or silver often 330, 331 thick and roughly shaped coins. There is a scyphate miliaresion of the emperor standing in armour and some halves with inscriptional reverses though weights appear reduced even allowing for wear. Thessalonica has a half-miliaresion with St Demetrius handing a cross to the emperor, both figures half-length. Constantinople issued three classes of anonymous folles— one extremely rare—which end the series; and of three classes of signed folles, Hendy assigns two to Thessalonica. However debased the metal, Alexius' histamena were struck from well engraved dies and this is characteristic of the subsequent hyperpers and trachea throughout the dynasty.

The reformed series begins with a commemoration piece on the coronation of John II, showing the young co-emperor crowned by Christ standing on the right: the reverse has standing figures of Alexius and his wife Eirene holding a patriarchal cross between them. There were gold hyperpers, electrum trachea and billon trachea of this issue which was probably only for a short period as the coins vary from extreme rarity for hyperpers to scarce for billon pieces. After this the gold hyperpers of Alexius at all mints conform to the same types, of obverse with Christ seated on a backless throne and for reverse, the emperor standing facing holding the labarum and an orb cruciger, and wearing an embroidered chlamys over a divitision; the figure is flanked by columnar inscriptions and a *Manus Dei* appears, above right. Mints are distinguishable on style and from varieties in the inscriptions. Electrum trachea at Constantinople have the Virgin enthroned and a reverse of the emperor standing facing with a sceptre ending in three jewels, and at Thessalonica Christ seated on a high-backed throne with on the reverse, the Virgin crowning the emperor. Billon trachea have either a bust of Christ or Christ seated on a high-backed throne, combined with a standing figure of the emperor with a long-shafted jewelled sceptre, a bust of the emperor with the labarum or a bust with a cruciform sceptre.

Both Constantinople and Thessalonica issued several classes of copper tetartera, exactly like the earlier electrum coins in form but occupying a completely different place in the system of coinage.

JOHN II (1118–43), had more classes of hyperpera than his father. The reverse types were: first, busts of the emperor and the Virgin holding a patriarchal cross between them; then standing figures of the emperor with a long-shafted labarum crowned by the Virgin, flanked by columnar inscriptions and, finally, standing figures of the emperor with an orb cruciger in his left hand, crowned by the Virgin. These fall into order by the first two overlapping ('muling') with the obverses of Christ seated on a backless throne, and the last having Christ seated on a throne with high back. Exactly the same types were issued from Thessalonica and for electrum trachea both mints issued a type showing the emperor and St George standing with a patriarchal cross (at Thessalonica it was a labarum) between them. For billon trachea both mints used the emperor standing facing (but with different accoutrements) combined with an obverse of the Virgin enthroned. Constantinople also issued a type showing the emperor's bust with a cruciform sceptre that had for obverse a bust of Christ. Tetartera of several classes were issued by both mints and a prolific issue of half-tetartera with St Demetrius as obverse, was brought out by Thessalonica.

MANUEL I (1143–80). Like his grandfather Manuel issued only one class of gold hyperper, its obverse with a bust of the young 'Emmanuel-type' Christ and on the reverse the emperor standing arrayed in a magnificent chlamys with labarum and orb surmounted by a patriarchal cross. There are many varieties but the main types were unchanged and used also by Thessalonica. In contrast there are six classes of electrum trachea with Thessalonica reflecting the first two at the capital and having a type of its own with St Demetrius standing with the emperor. All Thessalonican pieces are deeply scyphate in this reign. At Constantinople the types for each class are: (1) Christ Emmanuel bust/ standing figure of the Virgin crowning the beardless emperor holding labarum and akakia; (2) Christ enthroned/standing figures of the Virgin and emperor (bearded) holding a patriarchal cross between them; (3) Christ standing on a dais/St Theodore and the emperor holding a patriarchal cross between them; (4) Christ Emmanuel bust/ the emperor standing with labarum and akakia (Hendy notes officinae marked by pellets on labarum shaft); and (5) Christ seated on a high-backed throne/Virgin crowning the emperor with labarum and orb cruciger. The billon trachea start with the bust of the young beardless emperor, then his full-length standing figure bearded (first with Christ enthroned on the obverse, then with the Virgin enthroned)—this was probably the point when devaluation to 1/120 from 1/48 occurred as Hendy argues—and finally the Virgin blessing the emperor with the obverse having Christ seated on a throne without back. Hendy has not identified any billon trachea from Thessalonica. Constantinople issued copper tetartera and Thessalonica tetartera and halves; both Hendy and Metcalf agree, on hoard evidence, that another Greek mint was issuing half-tetartera.

ANDRONICUS I (1183–5). There is only one class of gold hyperper in the reign,

having the Virgin seated on a throne with high back on the obverse and, as reverse, the standing figure of the emperor with his well-known forked beard being crowned by Christ. The electrum trachy has a similar, but not identical, reverse and on its obverse a most successfully designed standing Virgin orans. Billon trachea broadly repeat the same reverse but as obverse have the Virgin standing, holding a medallion of Jesus before her breast. Constantinople issued a copper tetarteron, Thessalonica two others and the new Greek mint a half-tetarteron.

THE ANGELUS DYNASTY

ISAAC II (1185–95), an easy-going member of the nobility who had opposed the vigorous but despotic rule of Andronicus, took his place as the Normans advanced on the capital after capturing Thessalonica. Isaac's hyperpers, electrum and billon trachea all had an obverse of the Virgin seated on a throne with high back and holding a medallion of Jesus before her breast. The reverses for the gold hyperper were the emperor and the Archangel Michael standing and holding a sword between them; for the electrum trachy, the Archangel crowning the emperor, and for the billon trachy, a standing figure of the emperor with cruciform sceptre and in left hand the akakia. Both Constantinople and Thessalonica (recaptured 1185) issued a copper tetarteron.

ALEXIUS III (1195–203), the ambitious elder brother of Isaac, deposed him but had nothing better with which to save the Empire from the increasing pressures from Bulgarians, Normans and Crusaders. In this reign standing figures of the emperor and St Constantine with varieties of regalia occupy the reverse of the main coins but the obverses are, for the gold hyperper, the standing figure of Christ on a dais; for the electrum trachy, Christ enthroned, and for the billon trachy, a bust of the young Christ Emmanuel. The devaluation of the billon trachy to 1/184 took place between 1190 and 1199 and perhaps in connection with this the mint re-issued earlier billon trachea that were neatly clipped down to the edge of the reverse type.

349, 35

337 Alexius I *(1081–1118). Post-reform electrum trachy of Constantinople. The reverse of No. 332 (diam. 30 mm.).*

338 Alexius I *(1081–1118). Post-reform billon trachy of Constantinople, reverse. This was valued at 1/48 of a gold hyperper (diam. 31 mm.).*

339 John II *(1118–43). Gold hyperper, reverse. The first issue of this emperor from Constantinople. The second issue is illustrated above, Nos. 280, 281 (diam. 35 mm.).*

340 John II *(1118–43). Electrum trachy, reverse. The emperor holds a patriarchal cross with St George. This was a Constantinople type; at Thessalonica they hold a labarum between them (diam. 34 mm.).*

341, 342 John II *(1118–43). Copper tetarteron of Thessalonica, obverse and reverse. In the*

reformed coinage of Alexius I the tetarteron became a coin for small change: it has no connection at all with its pre-reform namesake (diam. 22.5 mm.).

343 Manuel I *(1143–80). Electrum trachy of Thessalonica, reverse. St Demetrius, patron saint of the city, is standing on the right (diam. 33 mm.).*

344 Manuel I *(1143–80). Copper tetarteron of Thessalonica, reverse (diam. 21 mm.).*

345, 346 Andronicus I *(1183–5). Electrum trachy of Constantinople, obverse and reverse. The obverse is most successfully designed to fit the scyphate shape and on the reverse the well-known forked beard of Andronicus is prominent. He was the last of the Comnenus family to rule (diam. 31 mm.).*

347, 348 Isaac II Angelus *(1185–95). Electrum trachy of Constantinople, obverse and reverse. The obverse type of the Virgin with a medallion of the infant Christ before her, seated on a throne with high back is common in this reign to hyperpers, electrum trachea and billon trachea. On the reverse the Archangel Michael crowns the emperor (diam. 30 mm.).*

349, 350 Alexius III *(1195–203). Billon trachy of Constantinople, obverse and reverse. Unlike his younger brother Isaac II, Alexius had different obverses for his various denominations, which were also clearly distinguished by their respective metals. The emperor appears with St Constantine, dressed in imperial robes as he had every right to be, on the right (diam. 29 mm.).*

351 Latin Conquest Period *(1204–61). Copper trachy, reverse. An example of Hendy's ' Bulgarian Imitative ' coins issued c. 1195 to c. 1218: they are fairly good copies of imperial*

pieces—this one copying Alexius III and St Constantine *(diam. 24 mm.).*

352, 353 Latin Conquest Period *(1204–61). Copper trachy, obverse and reverse. One of some 20 types identified as Constantinopolitan amongst the ' Latin Imitatives ', not actual copies of earlier issues but similar and using imperial names. This one showing ' Manuel ' with drawn sword is ' Constantinople B ' (diam. 33 mm.).*

354 Latin Conquest Period *(1204–61). Copper trachy, reverse. This piece (Latin Imitative type, Constantinople D) also carries the name of Manuel. The emperor wears maniakion, loros and sagion (diam. 29 mm.).*

355, 356 Latin Conquest Period *(1204–61). Copper trachy, obverse and reverse. Latin Imitative type, Constantinople P; it is anonymous with bust of Christ as obverse and the Archangel Michael as reverse: one of the very common pieces of this period (diam. 25 mm.).*

337

338

339

340

341

342

343

344

345

346

347

348

349

350

351

352

353

354

355

356

The Latin Conquest of 1204 has long presented an awkward problem for numismatists as a contemporary chronicler Nicetas Choniates wrote that bronze statues in the Hippodrome at Constantinople were broken into pieces for coin. There were coins therefore: but which amongst all the hotch-potch of much used, badly struck and often from the start illegible bronze scyphates, found in large numbers from the period around 1200, were the Latin ones? The unsatisfactory nature of the suggestions forced Wroth to conclude in 1908 that ' neither Baldwin Count of Flanders, nor any of his successors, who reigned till 1261, appear to have assumed the imperial right of coinage '. The problem was never far from the minds of those interested in Byzantine numismatics but no real progress was made until Michael Hendy published the results of his researches at the end of 1969 in *Coinage and Money in the Byzantine Empire 1081–261*. The second of his two major discoveries reported in this book came as a by-product of the first. By establishing the system inaugurated by Alexius I's reforms and especially the form in which the organization of officinae was re-established, he was able to clear the table, as it were, of a vast amount of regular issues of billon trachea and so take a more precise look at what remained and where exactly it differed from the regular coins.

Hendy found that the irregular issues were distinguished from imperial ones by being:

1) of copper not billon;
2) of smaller and sometimes much smaller size;
3) of irregular shape and fabric;
4) variable in weight;
5) struck from badly engraved dies and often with blundered inscriptions;
6) so badly struck as to leave only part of each type visible;
7) without the distinctive and controlled system of officina marks.

It all adds up to a pretty disreputable and exasperatingly evasive heap of currency! But at least there was less of it and Hendy proceded to do magnificent work in distinguishing, to use his own words, ' several chronological waves of imitative coins overlying the original imperial issues ' of the Comneni and Angeli. These are:

a) An imperial series of neatly executed types which have been clipped down to the engraved part struck by the die, taking the reverse as the part to be preserved as it contained the emperor's name and image. This series Hendy dates from 1195 to 1203 and explains the process as an attempt to keep pace with the declining value of the billon trachy, which was 1/184th part of a gold hyperper after its devaluation in the period 1190 to 1199. They do not appear in hoards after 1204.

b) The Bulgarian coins imitating regular issues of Manuel I crowned by the Virgin, Isaac II standing facing and Alexius III with St Constantine. Both obverse and reverse types of the selected coins are copied though with small inaccuracies and larger mistakes in the legends. These probably belong to the period 1195 to 1218 when Ivan II Asen came to the throne and the regular Bulgarian coinage began: it would perhaps coincide with the Bulgarian offensive into Thrace. The series is naturally well represented in Bulgarian hoards.

c) The series issued by the Latins from Constantinople drawing on a wide selection of imperial types but making an eclectic choice without attempting to copy both the obverse and reverse types of any given coin.

d) A shorter series from Thessalonica similar to c) above but generally omitting the imperial name deliberately. These issues cease in 1224 after the Despot of Epirus had captured the city.

e) A series of small module coins imitating the types in c) and d) above but not constituting fractions of these larger trachea. They include imitations of the large trachea of Theodore Lascaris at Nicaea.

As a result of working on these principles, Hendy has been able to apportion a sizable coinage mainly of copper trachea to the Latin emperors. There are from Constantinople 20 types of trachea (A-T); Thessalonica, 3 types of trachea (A-C); Small module, 7 types copying larger ones (A-G); Constantinople, 1 type of copper tetarteron; Thessalonica, 2 types of copper tetarteron (A and B).

Some of these are common and others exist in single or very few specimens, but once a start has been made collectors can be on the watch for specimens, varieties and even new types. For descriptions of the types, which are not easy to photograph satisfactorily, reference must be made to Hendy's book, but some examples are illustrated here.

The arguments by which this complete change of outlook on the thirteenth century has been effected are naturally complicated. They involve comparison of a large number of hoards, spread over different areas, and highly sophisticated means of dating them. A surprisingly large number of these 'Latin Imitative' coins appear in hoards geographically well spread in the first decades of the thirteenth century. The number is larger than is likely for other possible claimants like Bulgaria or Epirus, and Nicaean coins are in any event identifiable. Overstriking too has its part to play in identification and this is a method easier for the beginner to appreciate. The overstriking of some 'Latin Imitative' types on flans of Isaac II and of Theodore Lascaris is of obvious significance. There is an example of a flan struck with the name of Angelus (the earliest possible emperor would be Isaac II, 1185–95) and overstruck by 'Manuel I'. Besides being clearly impossible, such a piece proclaims as nugatory the attempt to tie in the imperial names or parts of them on these pieces, with the actual emperors. It was these attempts—natural enough as they were— that have ruined many earlier efforts to solve the problem by attributing at least one or more coins with clear authority.

One of Hendy's most surprising conclusions is that the small module pieces are not to be classed with the larger pieces which they imitate, i. e. they are not fractions, being far too irregular in weight. It seems that hoards with the large module coins have few, if any, of the small coins and later hoards show the small coins dominating the decreasing numbers of the larger ones.

One may well ask why these Bulgarian copies and 'Latin Imitatives' were made in preference to newly designed types. It would clearly be of advantage to the Latin conquerors to issue coins acceptable to and understood (as through the imperial names) by the overwhelmingly Greek population. But as Hendy points out the earlier pieces were of some intrinsic value, much more valuable than the new copper pieces (i. e. not billon which involved silver if only in small quantities). Hence this strangely anomalous coinage vaguely looking like the old but with, in fact, distinctive combinations of types of its own. So far no silver or gold coinage for the Latins

has been identified or appears likely to be so. All the coins referred to above are trachea of copper with a sprinkling of tetartera.

THE SUCCESSOR STATES

From the point of view of coinage there were three important states which continued the Byzantine imperial tradition after 1204, two of which could have re-established the Empire if they could reconquer Constantinople. Trebizond, not strictly a successor state in any event, can be considered separately: Epirus and Nicaea were near enough and strong enough to take advantage of obvious Latin weaknesses. Epirus became the protagonist when in 1224 Theodore I (Comnenus Dukas) recaptured Thessalonica from the Latins. But in 1230 Theodore suffered the disastrous defeat of Klokotnitsa at the hands of the Bulgarians. Epirus never fully recovered its position after this, though never willingly conceding premier position as imperial challenger to Nicaea; the Despotate was still a thorn in the side of Michael VIII after 1261. The Nicaeans occupied Thessalonica in 1246 and steadily gained strength from that moment. It is therefore necessary to consider the coinages of Nicaea, and of Thessalonica first under its Epirote dynasty and later under Nicaean rule. Epirus itself only issued an independent coinage from the Despotate capital at Arta, after the loss of Thessalonica.

There is much room for confusion and it is fortunate for all students that Hendy included these coinages in his study. He has laid down a logical system, identifying a remarkable number of variant types from coins often in miserable condition, thereby creating a firm basis for further study. He expects more types to appear and if not everybody will agree in detail with all his attributions, he has established that most valuable thing—a norm from which any deviations may be identified and discussed. For detailed work his book is indispensable, what follows is an indication only of the lines on which he has worked.

A major difficulty lies in there being several Theodores, Michaels and Johns coming from different states, producing the same kind of coinage, at the same time. Occasionally surnames will be added such as Comnenus Dukas (Thessalonica), or Comnenus Dukas Lascaris (Nicaea), but often these were so abbreviated as to leave the issue as open as before. Other criteria have to be used and Hendy makes much of the good style and workmanship of the Thessalonica mint amongst other arguments. The mere presence of St Demetrius on a coin makes Thessalonica a likely place of origin, or of St Tryphon similarly Nicaea, though this can be misleading: and of course there are the hoards—where the coins are found, in what company and in what proportion to others? Hendy writes, ' the general form of the monetary system remains unaltered from the twelfth century ', though as yet the structure of denominations is less clear. There is too a basic difference between the imperial coinage of Nicaea with its small number of issues, each in large quantity, and that of Thessalonica with a large number of different issues, but only a small quantity

of each—so small as for some to have left very few survivors today.

THE EMPIRE OF NICAEA

Gold hyperpers and billon trachea continue to be issued as in earlier days at Constantinople, but silver trachea in large numbers seem to take the place of earlier electrum trachea. The coins come from two mints, Nicaea and Magnesia, the latter being the seat of the Treasury and more important mint because Nicaea was uncomfortably close to the Selçuk frontier, let alone the Latin one.

THEODORE I (crowned in 1208–22). His contemporary, George Acropolites, remarked upon his forked beard and this became characteristic of Nicaean rulers. He used the name of Comnenus with doubtful authority as his wife was a daughter of Alexius III Angelus, and he himself was a Lascaris. Theodore has a gold hyperper somewhat doubtfully ascribed to him and three classes of silver trachea, one of which was copied from John II's electrum trachy showing him holding a cross with St George and with a bust of Christ for the obverse; only the saint is changed to St Theodore. Another is copied from Manuel I's electrum trachy showing him standing with St Theodore (Type 3), and the third has the emperor and St Theodore standing and holding between them a star-topped standard with, for obverse, Christ seated on a throne without a back. Of the five classes of billon trachea as yet identified one is well known and much overstruck by later

357 ▶

358 ▶

362, 3◀

359 ▶

357 Constantine IV *(668–85).* *Gold solidus.*
Obv. *This first issue of 668 only shows the*
emperor beardless and in civilian robes. The
legend runs CONSTANTINUS C CON
in which the C in the middle means ' and ' : thus
two Constantines seem to be referred to—prob-
ably a mistake by engravers in a hurry copying a
legend from pieces showing Constans II and
Constantine IV (diam. 18 mm.).

358, 359 Constantine IV *(668–85).* *Gold solidus.*
Obv. *The emperor is still beardless but the*
bust is armoured and helmeted, with spear over
shoulder echoing (perhaps intentionally) Justin-
ian I and earlier emperors. The fragmentary
legend has at least dropped the second Constan-
tine. The issue was between 668 and 673. Rev.
Heraclius and Tiberius appear again as in
No. 336 above. The officina Γ is in a different
plane from the rest of the legend. VICTOA,
as here, and VICTORA (as in No. 381)
are commonly used for VICTORIA during
the reign (diam. 18 mm.).

classes of the same emperor's trachea. It has on its obverse the Virgin seated with a medallion of the young Christ on her breast and for reverse, the emperor standing with St Theodore, holding between them a patriarchal cross on a long shaft. The saint is in military tunic and cuirass with a spear in his left hand and the emperor wears the stemma, divitision, maniakion and simplified loros with a labarum-headed sceptre in his right hand.

JOHN III DUKAS VATATSES (1222–54). The reign has a complete series of issues from gold hyperpers, silver trachea (9 classes) and billon trachea (12 classes) to tetartera (6 classes). The emperor seems deliberately to copy John II Comnenus to emphasize his legitimate succession, and even includes 'porphyrogenitus' in his title, though he can have had no claim to being 'born in the purple'. There is still something of a problem over attributing gold hyperpers to John II as imperial issues from Thessalonica or to John III from Magnesia. This is a refinement of the difficulty which caused Wroth to change his mind between 1908 and 1911, attributing the same coins first to John II and later to John III. Hendy's solutions, with photographs of all the issues involved illustrated in his book, are convincing even though they have to

364 explain John III appearing with a round-cut beard on gold but elsewhere with a forked one. The first and rarer of the two classes of hyperper has half-length figures of John being crowned by the Virgin, and the other has them at full-length. Both have as obverse Christ seated on a throne without a back, the former with a legend and the

latter without. Both classes give the curious effect of the loros as it crosses the waist being virtually indistinguishable from the divitision and loros underneath.

The silver trachea have some fine designs, in particular:

a) Christ seated on a throne without a back/the emperor and St Constantine full-length, standing facing, holding between them a star-topped shaft.

b) The Virgin seated on a throne with a high back, and a medallion of the young Christ on her breast/the emperor crowned 365, 366 by Christ on the right (named as Chalchites), both full-length, standing facing.

c) Christ seated on a throne without a back/the emperor and St Theodore full-length, standing facing, holding a star-topped shaft between them.

Other classes, perhaps later, are smaller, of poorer style and apparently of debased silver. The billon trachea, in numerous classes, are undistinguished in style, perhaps to some extent due to the poor metal and their much worn condition; there are signs of some of them having once been more attractive and one of these has Christ, again named as Chalchites, crowning the emperor. The tetartera all have a standing figure of the emperor as one type and one, commonly met, has a fine bust of St George as its obverse. After the capture of Thessalonica in 1246 St Demetrius appears on coins of John III, most of them from that city's mint but some, Hendy thinks, from Magnesia.

THEODORE II (1254–8). This emperor often includes the surnames Dukas and Lascaris on his coins. His gold hyperpers are similar in types to those of his father with full-length figures and his silver trachea have two classes, including St Tryphon the saint of Nicaea, and a third showing the emperor with a military saint who is unnamed. There are five classes of billon trachea with obverses showing full-length figures of Christ, St Theodore, St Tryphon and St George, the other having a bust of Christ Emmanuel. Both classes of tetartera have the emperor standing full-length.

No coins are known of Theodore's unfortunate son John IV but Michael VIII Palaeologus, who became guardian and co-ruler after the murder of the Regent only a few days after Theodore's death, issued coins covering the whole range from hyperper to tetarteron. The types he used were similar to those of Theodore II and, with the exception of one class of billon trachy, his family name is clearly displayed on them all. The hyperper as usual at Nicaea shows him full-length crowned by the Virgin with Christ on a throne without a back as the obverse. On silver trachea he is shown full-length standing alone and on the obverse Christ stands on a dais; the tetarteron has a similar combination of types but Michael holds the akakia in his left hand instead of an orb. There are two classes of billon trachea, one with St Tryphon and (reverse), the emperor crowned by the Virgin, the other with Christ seated on a throne without a back and (reverse), the emperor full-length facing.

THE EMPIRE OF THESSALONICA

As a mint Thessalonica was in action from the time of its capture by the Despot of Epirus, Theodore (Comnenus Dukas), until the fall of the Latin regime in 1261: that is, it continued after the Nicaeans occupied the city in 1246. It issued only silver and billon trachea, tetartera and half-tetartera: there were no gold hyperpers. St Demetrius is frequently amongst the types used and Hendy remarks on the continuing good style in the die engraving.

THEODORE (1224–30). There are three classes of fine silver trachea showing:
a) Christ seated on a throne without a back/the emperor and St Demetrius standing full-length, facing and holding between them a shaft headed by a cross within a circle.
b) The Virgin orans facing and full-length/the emperor and St Demetrius full-length with the saint handing over a castle with three towers.
c) The Virgin seated on a throne with a high back, and a medallion of the young Christ on her breast/the emperor crowned by Christ, both standing full-length.

367, 36

There are seven classes of billon trachea on two of which the emperor appears with St Demetrius and the saint, seated with sword in hand, forms the obverse of a third. Likewise, on the tetarteron, the emperor and the saint stand together and on the half-tetartera the saint appears half-length on two classes, and the Virgin orans on the third: the reverse of all three classes is formed by a standing figure of the emperor.

MANUEL (1230–37), was the younger brother of Theodore and used only the title of Despot. He has two classes of silver trachea on one of which he appears standing being crowned by the Virgin; on the other he holds with St Demetrius a labarum surmounted by a triangular ornament. On the eight classes of billon trachea the Archangel Michael appears as the obverse on two and with the emperor he occupies the reverse of two others. On two classes St Constantine appears with the emperor and on one St Demetrius, who also occupies the obverse of another class. One billon piece warrants particular description as the design is unique and unusually ambitious for a billon coin: the obverse has a full-length figure of the Archangel Michael in military dress unsheathing a sword and on the reverse the emperor sits on a throne without a back alongside St Demetrius on the right in military dress; they hold between them a representation of a walled town with three towers, described above as 'City of Thessalonica'. No tetartera are known.

JOHN COMNENUS DUKAS (1237–44), was the eldest son of Theodore but still young at his accession and always represented as beardless. In his short reign there is an obvious decline in the style, module and fabric of the large number of classes issued. Five classes of billon trachea maintain something of the old standards, followed by another four, related to these and of roughly the same weight though smaller

and thicker. Then comes a group of seventeen small module classes several of them repeating the designs used in earlier classes. They may have been issued over a long period and they remain something of a mystery. The only other issue was a half-tetarteron on the reverse of which John includes his full name, Comnenus Dukas.

When John III of Nicaea took over Thessalonica he resumed the issue there of high standard coins such as those for which Theodore and Manuel had been responsible, but only in billon trachea. There were eleven classes of these—again a large number for a period of only eight years. His son Theodore II issued a single denomination only, a billon trachy on which his full name Dukas Lascaris appears: its obverse has a fine floriated cross and on the reverse the emperor and St Demetrius stand holding between them a castle with three towers surmounted by a large star. These three towered representations must be of the city of Thessalonica itself which, from the sea looks exactly like this as its walls straggle up the hill behind. Some of Michael VIII's coins, many of which have St Demetrius on them, are probably attributable to Thessalonica but the coinage of this ruler of Nicaea, Thessalonica and, after 1261, Constantinople itself has still to receive detailed analysis and listing of known specimens.

THE EMPIRE OF TREBIZOND

Trebizond was not, strictly speaking, a successor state as Alexius—the first 'Great Comnenus' of Trebizond—had initiated his revolt against the Angeli before the fall of Constantinople to the Latins in 1204. The two events were so close—only a matter of days between—that it is fair to consider this 'Empire' alongside those of Nicaea, Thessalonica and Epirus.

Trebizond was as famous for its 'aspers' as for the beauty of its princesses and the sophisticated elegance of its Court. Rich silver mines lay within its narrow coastal territory. The asper was not a Byzantine type of coin in style, design, fabric or weight though it was preceded in the reign of Manuel by debased silver scyphate trachea which are clearly and closely copied from Byzantine originals: their obverse shows the Virgin seated on a throne with a high back. What appears strange is the absence of any coins of Trebizond origin prior to the reign of Manuel (1238-63); there is another virtual gap of seventeen years after this reign from which only a little copper survives. The first experimental coinage would appear to be the scyphate trachea. They cannot have been a large issue judging from the scarcity of the survivors, nor a satisfactory one for many are so blurred in striking as to be difficult to interpret without previous knowledge. The specimens illustrated by Wroth from the British Museum give a more favourable impression than is justified. But the style of die cutting on these Byzantine-looking pieces is the same as on the aspers of which vast numbers, with a veritable maze of special signs and symbols on them, were struck. Manuel's is the only reign in which 369 letters abound amongst the special signs, but symbols proliferate too and a remarkable collection they make with a bird's

360, 361 Latin Conquest Period (1204–61). Copper trachy, obverse and reverse. The reverse shows on the left St Helena and on the right St Constantine in the imperial loros and maniakion. It is a Latin Imitative piece of Thessalonica Type C (diam. 35 mm.).

362, 363 Empire of Nicaea—Theodore I Lascaris (1208–22). Silver trachy, obverse and reverse —copied from the electrum trachy of John II with St George (No. 340 above). The military saint here is St Theodore and the mint probably Magnesia (diam. 33 mm.).

364 Empire of Nicaea—John III Vatatses (1222–54). Gold hyperper, reverse. Mint of Magnesia, second coinage. These coins are very like the Thessalonica issues of John II Comnenus and show the emperor with a round-cut beard instead of the forked beard usual in, for instance, his silver trachea. The attribution of these coins has been much debated, and will probably continue to be so (diam. 27 mm.).

365, 366 Empire of Nicaea—John III Vatatses (1222–54). Silver trachy, obverse and reverse. The reverse has the Christ figure named ' Chalchites ', that is a representation of the mosaic icon put up by the Empress Theodora in 843 over the Brazen Door entrance to the Imperial Palace in Constantinople. The destruction of the original image and its replacement by a cross under Leo III had sparked off scenes of popular resentment against the iconoclasts. John Vatatses, as is normal at Nicaea, has a forked beard contrasting with No. 364 (diam. 31 mm.).

367, 368 Empire of Thessalonica—Theodore Comnenus Dukas (1224–30). Silver trachy, obverse and reverse (diam. 29 mm.).

360

361

362

363

364

365

366

367

368

369

370

371

372

373

374

375

376

377

378

369 Empire of Trebizond—Manuel I *(1238–63)*. *Silver asper, obverse. The emperor is shown in a chlamys, touched by the Manus Dei above right. The letter symbol K can be seen between the emperor and the labarum he holds (diam. 23 mm.).*

370, 371 Empire of Trebizond—John II *(1280–97)*. *Silver asper, reverse and obverse. An early coin of the reign with John wearing the chlamys and his name on the left spelt in full. Later in the reign he wears the loros and his name is abbreviated to IW. St Eugenius, as is usual, occupies the reverse (diam. 23 mm.).*

372, 373 Empire of Trebizond—Alexius II *(1297–1330)*. *Silver asper, reverse and obverse. Both the emperor and St Eugenius are mounted, perhaps as a gesture to the Selçuk rulers who appeared on their dirhams in this way. The Selçuks had been acknowledged as a suzerain power by the Empire of Trebizond from the first (diam. 21 mm.).*

374 Manuel II *(1391–1425)*. *Silver half-hyperper, reverse. This bears the legend 'Manuel, in Christ the Lord, faithful' keeping the order of words as engraved. The beauty of Greek letters as seen for instance on eighth and ninth century miliaresia, seems to have been lost (diam. 19 mm.).*

375, 376 Manuel II *(1391–1425)*. *Silver half-hyperper, obverse and reverse. This has the alternative legend 'Manuel, Emperor [ΒΑCΙΛΕVC] the Paleologus '. The emperor is regularly represented with a halo in these later years; the maniakion now has a tri-lobed form (diam. 20 mm.).*

377, 378 Michael VIII *(1259–82)*. *Gold hyperper, obverse and reverse. The six sets of towers on the walls are clear with the exception of one on the right which is obscured by the striking. Double striking has also obscured the head of the Virgin. P-𝕸 may be a magistrate's initials. On the reverse Michael supported by the Archangel Michael kneels before the enthroned Jesus (diam. 24 mm.).*

head, flowers, lis, quatrefoil and star of David alongside the more usual pellets and stars. These last can appear in such numbers on a single coin as to seem decorative in purpose rather than of special significance. Running through the series is the symbol β and also $\vdash\dashv$ which may be a truncated form of Comnenus. Although the suggestion that the letters amongst the symbols may indicate different mints is now discounted, there is as yet no satisfactory explanation of the special signs in whole or in part.

The other Great Comnenus with a large surviving coinage is John II (1280–97). The coins at present attributed to John I in fact fit neatly into the pattern of designs ascribed to John II. They provide a transition from the full name to the abbreviated IΩ and from the chlamys over divitision robes to the loros over divitision. The standing emperor type continued until the reign of Alexius II (1297–330) when it was followed by the sovereign riding to the right very much on the lines of Selçuk coin designs. The Selçuk Turks dominated the interior of Asia Minor and the first Great Comnenus paid tribute to the Sultan of Er-Rum, as the once Byzantine (Roman) part of the Selçuk Empire was called. Throughout its existence the Empire of Trebizond had to fend off Selçuks, Mongols, Danishmenid and Osmanli tribesmen by some means, as well as their own Christian rivals at Nicaea in the early days, along with the Latins. Although forever balanced on a knife edge, their regime was remarkably successful but the horseman type on their coins represents an acknowledgment of the dominant power of the Selçuks (as it did

also in Cilician Armenia) and the weight of the famous asper was that of the dirham—around 2.8 g. The earlier scyphate trachea had tended to be slightly heavier than this and adjustment to the dirham may have been one reason for their discontinuance.

The reverse type of the asper was almost invariably the standing figure of St Eugenius, a third-century martyr of Trebizond birth, and he too changed to become a mounted figure at the same time as the emperor on the obverse. Although a mounted saint is unusual on coins, St Eugenius, as Wroth noted, had been portrayed in this way on frescoes at least going back to the twelfth century.

Before leaving the aspers a comment must be made on their later history, as silver pieces continued to be issued until the 1440's; in 1461 the Empire itself succumbed to Mehmet II. The aspers diminish in size and weight and there is a problem of attribution as between emperors bearing the same name, as well as of decision on whether given pieces are fractions of an asper or simply aspers of reduced weight. That they are all aspers appears the more likely explanation; unfortunately this involves throwing over much of the arrangement of the coins by Wroth whose British Museum Catalogue in 1911 made a brave attempt to put this abundant but patchy series into perspective. Wroth noted that there was some copper and that when the coinage was treated more seriously much more copper would be found. This has been proved true, but as yet little has been published or is available for study in major collections. Copper coins

371

372, 373

370

372

of both large and small module have to be fitted in and are both flat and scyphate in shape. Here is a fine field of study open to serious collectors. The coins are not as abundant as they used to be—this particularly applies to aspers—but the watchful collector can still find them and the traveller too. The series is still crying out for more interest in it, both on the documentary side and on the coins themselves. To ask what the value of the asper was raises a new series of problems for which the documentation—which must be available—has not yet been extracted. Nor is it easy to interpret, once it has been found; for instance, in 1314 it is known that fourteen aspers were equal to one hyperper—but what sort of hyperper of the many then in circulation with different intrinsic values? Many such items are needed before a clear picture can be obtained.

379 ▶

It is difficult to keep the last period of the Byzantine Empire in perspective. It is given a spurious unity by the unbroken rule of the Palaeologus family, albeit at the expense of disastrous civil wars. It meant, in mere area alone, different things at different times as a comparison between the Aegean Empire of Michael VIII and the shattered remnants of it in the 1390's will show. But it lasted nearly two centuries, never fulfilling the hopes of 1261 yet continually disproving the fears of many prophets of doom. Somehow, for all that time, a certain prestige attached to the emperor—heir of St Constantine a millennium ago—for all his enforced political tergiversation, his acceptance of Osmanli suzerainty and his continuous financial embarrassments.

Numismatically there is a break in the midst of the long reign of John V (1341–91) when the Empire ceased to coin scyphate gold and introduced a new series of flat silver coins. The gold solidus, nomisma histamenon, and hyperper tradition which had in the early years meant so much to Byzantine international trading was ended. It was replaced by a western-looking silver currency with variations of a single design stemming from the 'gros tournois' of Louis IX in the mid-thirteenth century with its two lines of circular legend, but here with a bust at the centre instead of a cross. The obverse returned to the bust of Christ 397, 3 which had been seen to perfection on the solidi of Constantine VII but had been 291 discarded by the earlier Palaeologi. There had been an earlier intimation of strong western influence on the coinage under Andronicus II in silver, billon and copper pieces. Indeed, the process was symptomatic of the virtual take-over of Byzantine commerce by the Venetians and the Genoese. These states could provide 380 ▶ warships at critical times and thereby gained such privileges that Byzantine merchants found themselves in a worse position than foreign rivals, even on their own soil. In the civil wars too if one side had the support of Venice, the other could rely on help from Genoa as the states were warring rivals in their own home waters, as 381 ▶ elsewhere.

Throughout the first period when gold was still being coined, a single obverse design was used in which the Virgin orans—or in Byzantine terms, the Panagia Blachernitissa—was shown rising from

A new artist at the mint

379 Constantine IV *(668–85)*. *Gold solidus.*
Obv. *This issue between 674 and 681 carries*
a bearded version of the previous one. The
reverse is the same as that on No. 359 above
(diam. 19 mm.).

380, 381 Constantine IV *(668–85)*. *Gold solidus.*
Obv. *The emperor's last issue 681 to 685.*
A dramatic change in the quality of design and
engraving is evident: an engraver of genius has
appeared at the mint and his influence is
extended over several subsequent reigns. Rev.
Constantine IV deposed his brothers, after
continued family quarrels, in 681, and they are
taken off the reverse (diam. 19 mm.).

the walls and towers of Constantinople, the
377 city which her icon was frequently called
upon to protect. Actually there had been
one earlier type under Michael VIII with
the Virgin seated on a high-backed throne,
but as Pachymeres wrote ' the necessities of
the time brought about debasement, the
older types were replaced by a view of the
city under Michael VIII and a content of
only 15 carats fine gold in 24 '. This was
an ambitious design, like many reverse
designs of this period: it needed both neat
engraving and good technical striking for
it to succeed. The beauty of this ' Virgin
within the walls of Constantinople ' design
is, however, rarely seen, in spite of its use
by successive sovereigns for nearly seventy
years in prolific issues of gold hyperpers.
Faulty technique in making the alloy and
in striking the pieces led to cracks in the
flans which in extreme cases extend to their
very centre, and more than one striking
would appear to have been considered a
necessity. The debased metal, ultimately
reduced to more than 50 % alloy and
containing much copper, may have been
too hard, and unsuitable for scyphate
striking, with the result that this excellent
design is hardly ever properly displayed.
Reverse designs, equally ambitious, have
391 fared better, like that of the proskynesis
of Andronicus II before Christ or the
very complicated one of Michael VIII
kneeling before Christ while supported
378 from behind by the Archangel Michael.
Such types were the work of artists worthy
to be compared with those engaged on the
contemporary mosaics of the Fetiye and
Kariye churches in Constantinople.

Both George Pachymeres (1242–1310) on
the Byzantine side and Francesco Pegolotti
writing a manual for Italian merchants
about 1320–40, broadly agree on the
amount of debasement that was carried out.
It may not have been altogether due to the
exigencies of the emperors as a long term
process was going on by which the western
Mediterranean countries were turning from
silver to gold based currencies, while in the
eastern Mediterranean exactly the opposite
change was in progress. What matters to
the numismatist is what actually happened
and the pattern of debasement may be seen
in the table on p. 232.

The last of the debased gold issues was
made by John VI (1347–54), and there are
not more than a handful of survivors of it
now. Then, though it is very rare, there is
a large silver piece of good metal, style and
weight for Andronicus IV (1376–9) and   402, 403
a number of equally good pieces with
the legend $I\Omega\Delta\epsilon C\Pi OTIC$. These early   397, 398
silver issues are referred to by Bertelè as
' amongst the most splendid of mediaeval
coins '. Lacking a clear lead from the
coins themselves as to which of these two
came first, it seems fair to regard so great a
change as the work of the legitimate
Emperor John V rather than that of his
rebellious eldest son, Andronicus IV.
Such a placing would also fill what would
otherwise be a twenty-two year gap in the
coinage.

This stage in the development of Byzantine coinage has been confused, first, by the
intrusion of some clear forgeries of gold
hyperpers purporting to be of Manuel II.
All three known specimens come from the
same pair of dies and the coin was included
in Wroth's British Museum Catalogue in

	Carats of fine gold in hyperper	
Emperors	*100 % = 24*	*Notes*
1081–1185 Comneni 1185–1204 Angeli	20.5	
1204–61 Latin Emperors	—	No gold known.
1222–54 John III Vatatses	16	At Nicaea.
1261–82 Michael VIII	15	Virgin within Constantinople type.
1282–95 Andronicus II	14	Proskynesis type.
1295–1320 Andronicus II	12	Christ blessing Andronicus and Michael IX kneeling.
1328–41 Andronicus III	11	Pegolotti gives R 6 and Cu 7.

Fig. 7. *Debasement of the hyperper.*

spite of its most unlikely combination of obverse and reverse types, its suspicious lettering, the alloy of its metal and its overheavy weight. Secondly, a pure gold 'medalet'—to use Professor Grierson's 'mot juste'—weighing 1.88 g. was taken by Bertelè to be the unique survivor of an attempted reform of a currency tied to gold. Putting both these ideas aside there is a break in the reign of John V (1341–91) from a currency based on heavily alloyed gold to one based on good silver of 950–1000 fine.

The spelling of the name John on these large flat silver pieces has already been noticed and is of importance as a great number have the alternative spelling in full *IΩANIC*: these last are of less weight and obviously of poorer style and technical craftsmanship than those with the name abbreviated. Coins in this group of large silver pieces with the full name can be placed unequivocally after those with the abbreviated form, but this does not apply to the fractional pieces. Once sufficient coins have been assembled it can be seen that the stylistic change occurs in the course of the reign of Manuel II. One of the peculiar features of these later issues of the large silver pieces, which were still called 'hyperpers' like the scyphate gold they replaced, is the frequency with which the sovereign's name is found to be missing on the flans; it has to be reconstructed from letter stubs and from the disposition of subsequent words. It looks occasionally as though an intentional clipping of the silver has been made, but it may be a matter of chance as the top right section of the legend in the outer circle was vulnerably placed. Possibly the flans were cut down before striking as the poor style ones are a gram or more lighter than the issues produced previously.

411,

The weights of these coins can be misleading owing to this interference with the flans at some stage, irrespective of wear and tear. The order of issues is therefore:

Approx. weight	Emperor	Style	Notes	
8.25–8.67 g.	John V	Good style with *IΩ* legend.	Ratto 2264: VF condition: all those illustrated as John VIII in B.M. Cat.	398
7.85–9.01 g.	Andronicus IV	Good style.	One specimen *F*, the other *EF*: both good flans.	403
7.70–8.50 g.	Manuel II	Good style.	Ratto 2248.	411
± 7.15 g.	Manuel II	Bad style.	B.M. Cat. 2.	412
± 6.95 g.	John VIII	Bad style with *IΩANIC* legend.	Ratto 2267.	415

Fig. 8. *Order of silver hyperper issues.*

These were the 'silver hyperpers' taking the place of the sorely debased gold ones. They had several fractions—a rare 3/4 piece with a double circle of legend and weighing 417 *c.* 6.5 g. in the time of Manuel II and John VIII, a common 1/2 and a common 3, 414 but generally much worn 1/8 which is often unattributable, even between a John or a Manuel. There seems to have been no 1/4. The commonest coins of the group are the half-hyperpers of Manuel II of which vast numbers must have been issued in two classes having the same types but different legends, each with a number of slight variations:

374 a) + *MANOVHΛ|ЄN|XPICTΩ|TΩ| ΘΩ|ΠICTOC*

376 b) + *MANɤHΛ|BACIΛЄVC|O| ΠΑΛЄΟΛΟΓΟC*

Bertelè has calculated that the silver hyperpers were each equal to a quarter of a gold Venetian zecchino or ducat, but it seems strange that there was no coin equivalent to the Venetian grosso, the most popular and widely copied coin in eastern Mediterranean commerce and one already copied by Andronicus II. The quarter silver hyperper would have been near to but rather below the weight of the grosso, and this could be an explanation of its strange omission from the fractions coined.

There were copper issues in this last period but little from them has survived. Some have the same reverse type as the silver hyperper series, showing the emperor in his distinctive tri-lobed maniakion but others are more traditional with the emperor standing. The relationship of the copper to the silver pieces is not known.

MICHAEL VIII (1261–82). The reign begins with a scarce hyperper having as obverse the Virgin seated on a throne with a high back and the standard reverse for this reign of Michael kneeling, supported by the Archangel Michael behind and above him, before Christ seated on the right. This issue was followed by another with the obverse changed to the Virgin rising from the walls and towers of Constantinople about which the phrases of Pachymeres have been quoted already, including its debasement from 16 to 15 carats fine gold. In this reign the view of the City always has six groups of three towers each, disposed round the walls. The issue must have been large as there are many small die variations besides the varying pairs of letters generally but not always on the obverse such as A/Δ, A/K, A/Λ, Δ/K, K/N, P/m, P/Θ; these are not yet satisfactorily explained.

As at Nicaea there were silver trachea which have the same reverse with, as obverse, a bust of Jesus having K/X in the field, or the Virgin holding a medallion of Christ before her and seated on a throne with a richly decorated back. Next come the billon trachea, scyphate like their predecessors, and in rich profusion. Some of these have the standard reverse of the reign with Michael kneeling supported by the Archangel, others a type, also strongly associated with Michael VIII, of the emperor enthroned alone, sometimes with a sword across his knees. There are some fifty different classes of which perhaps twenty may be assigned to Thessalonica or Nicaea: but there are also half as many again which could well prove to be of this period when specimens with readable legends become available. The first issue in the long series is probably one with the standard reverse of Michael supported by the Archangel with its obverse a bust of Christ and K/X in the field. (The author is grateful to Mr S. Bendall for making available his patiently collected card index of these billon pieces which involve 3 figure, 2 figure, and single figure reverses: some types are represented by one or two pieces only, others by a dozen or more: weights vary wildly even within a single type, but broadly between 4.15 g. and 1.15 g. One type with two known specimens shows weights of 3.11 and 2.02 g.). By contrast there are very few copper tetartera for the reign; one such shows the emperor standing full-length on the obverse and his son Andronicus II also full-length on the reverse. Another has St Michael as obverse type and the emperor three-quarter-length on the reverse. This scarcity of copper issues may foreshadow a change which takes place in the reign of Andronicus II.

ANDRONICUS II (1282–328). There is a numismatic confusion in this long reign parallel to the political, religious, economic, administrative, personal, national and international elements of disorder which at the end launched the Empire into a generation of civil war: it was never able to make a lasting recovery from this. Numismatically the reign awaits detailed study and indeed awaits the collection of evidence of which there is much and of varied character. It will not be possible to go into detail as to the types on the coins that are known, but every student needs to be clear as to the periods when Andronicus reigned alone, then reigned with his son Michael IX until

Contrasts in imperial robes

382 Tiberius III *(698–705). Gold solidus.* Obv. *The emperor wears a crown but the rest is military—armour, a shield and a lance carried in front of him (diam. 20 mm.).*

383 Anastasius II *(713–15). Gold solidus.* Obv. *The emperor carries in his left hand the akakia and wears a chlamys fastened with a fibula—he was a civil servant by profession. The legend ends MЧLA for ' multos annos ' or ' Long live the Emperor ' (diam. 19 mm.).*

384 Theodosius III *(715–17). Gold solidus.* Obv. *Also a civil servant, Theodosius wears the loros associated with his religious position. He carries the akakia and in his right hand an orb surmounted by a patriarchal cross. A more elaborate hair style has clearly become fashionable (diam. 19 mm.).*

his death (1295–1320) and finally, after a period of civil war, reigned with his grandson Andronicus III (1325–8). In fact the joint reign was interrupted in 1327 by another civil war with Andronicus so that in effect it lasted for little more than two years. The mass of the coinage comes, as might be expected, from the first joint reign, but in many cases the types used in the two joint reigns were the same, so that there tends to be a good deal of misattribution. The emperors, however, are differentiated, Andronicus II with a forked beard, Michael IX beardless (rarely and at the end of his reign, with moustaches and more rarely still with a short beard), and Andronicus III with a forked or pointed beard. Clearly coins from the joint reign of Andronicus II and III will be comparatively scarce owing to its short duration.

Once clear on these periods a further warning needs to be given. It seems, though no study has yet been made of this, that at some point in the middle of the reign a drastic change was made from the electrum, and billon trachea and the copper tetartera of earlier reigns since Alexius I. Instead of them, or in parallel with them, flat silver coins modelled on the grossi or 61, 62 matapans of Venice for size, weight and to some extent for types also, were minted, along with western-looking billon and 89, 390 copper pieces, also flat and rather smaller; however, some slightly scyphate pieces of the same size continue to be issued.

The gold hyperpers begin with a new reverse design of the emperor making 391 proskynesis (adoration) before Christ standing on the right; this was the same prostration that the emperor's subjects made to himself. There was plenty of room for the inscription in the top left of the field and it is here that a large number of varieties can be noted, both in the words used and in their division into lines. The coin is scarce now but must have been issued in large numbers. One reason for its scarcity may be that, though itself debased by a carat (now 14 fine) from Michael VIII's hyperpers, it was still finer by two carats than those which immediately followed it: the proskynesis type would tend to be melted down in the mint. The obverse of these pieces is always the Virgin rising from the walls of Constantinople shown with six groups of three towers each.

The joint reign with Michael IX necessitated a new design for hyperpers; in this Christ stands in the centre blessing the two kneeling emperors—Andronicus II on his 392, 393 right and Michael on his left. All three figures are facing. Problems of space for fitting in the legend arose and both circular and columnar arrangements were tried. A good engraver could make either clear but less good ones could not and letters were blundered and even their order at times confused. The metal used for this issue was only 50 % gold and striking cracks combined with double striking often make the legends difficult to decipher accurately. At some stage in this period the obverse design was changed from the circuit of walls having six groups each of three towers to four groups of three. One rare group of hyperpers has the circular legend without any names, simply ' Emperors of the Romans ', but Michael IX beardless and moustached shows where they must be placed; they have the four groups of towers on the obverse. More will be included about this legend when silver issues are considered.

394 Exactly the same design of Christ blessing the two kneeling emperors was used for the second joint reign (and later 396 still, for John VI), but in this case the junior is bearded and the obverse always has the four groups of towers design. Legends again are circular and columnar and can be retrograde and generally awkward to decipher. When engraver error is added in there are many combinations to be tried, for pieces exist with the figures and names of Andronicus and Michael transposed, and others with the names transposed but not the figures.

Byzantine silver coins are notoriously scarce and yet in this reign when the whole organization of the coinage seems to be in the melting pot there is comparative abundance for the period 1295–320 and nothing on either side. No doubt some pieces will be found and one can easily imagine a type and legend for the joint reign of Andronicus II and III. A type for Andronicus II alone might help us towards more certain views about the introduction of the 'grosso' type into Byzantine coinage. Coins naming Andronicus and Michael and showing the two emperors standing facing with a labarum-topped standard between them are scarce; they are clearly of the grosso type (for the first time) and have an obverse of Christ seated on a throne first with and later without back. Almost identical with these is a 61, 62 much commoner class with the legend 'Emperors of the Romans' which usually has the co-emperor beardless and so falls

into the joint reign with Michael IX. These coins were formerly attributed to Andronicus II and III but after the analysis of the type recently made by Veglery and Zacos this can no longer be maintained. The very abundance of these pieces points strongly to the earlier of the joint reigns.

The copper or billon of the reign has a multiplicity of designs, many of which are represented by a few pieces only, though a serious study of all the existing material has still to be made. Veglery and Zacos for the 'Emperors of the Romans' type alone (in billon or copper) collected some fifteen varieties. But there are also a great number of types with the names Andronicus and Michael, the latter beardless, competently designed and executed but tending to be badly preserved owing to their thin flans. The dominance of the cross motif and of legends enclosed in borders right round the central type, give a western look to the coins. Amongst these Andronicus and Michael pieces may be noted.

1) The two emperors standing 3/4 length, facing and holding the labarum between them: *reverse*—monogram made up of ΠΑΛΓ.

2) The two emperors standing full-length, facing and holding a long cross between them: *obverse*—small bust of Christ with the legend 'May the Lord help the Emperors' enclosed in borders around it.

3) As above but with labarum instead of cross: *obverse*—cross potent with arms of equal length and a pellet in each angle. A fairly common type found with both circular and vertically disposed legends.

4) Christ blessing the kneeling figures of

238

the emperors (as on the gold hyperpers): *reverse*—Archangel Michael, half-length.

5) The emperors standing half-length, facing and holding a patriarchal cross between them: *obverse*—head of a winged seraph. Another fairly common type.

The size and weight of these coins and other variants are consistent without being at all uniform. A few have diameters of over 23 mm., some as little as 19 mm., with weights from over 2.5 g. to 1.3 g. In this long middle period of the reign there appears to have been a prolific coinage in all metals.

The gold hyperpers of the second joint reign, with Andronicus III, have already been noted. There is at least one silver type on which each emperor occupies one side of the coin and it has many varieties. There are also some copper pieces in the Vienna Cabinet. Even for a short reign there is not much to go on, but for the periods when Andronicus II was reigning alone there is an extensive copper or billon coinage which still needs to be disentangled from the issues of his grandson. Indeed the material needs collecting together so that legends can be built up from similar pieces.

ANDRONICUS III (1328–41). The reign should have been long enough to have produced a substantial coinage in all metals, but in fact little has been identified, particularly in gold. At present the picture is a scrappy and unsatisfactory one. There are scyphate gold hyperpers showing Andronicus kneeling before Christ who stands in front of a throne on the right: on the reverse the Empress Anne of Savoy

stands facing on the left with her son John V on the right. These are scarce coins and the only silver types to be attributed with certainty to Andronicus III are equally scarce. In one the emperor stands full-length on the left greeting St Demetrius, but occasionally the figures are reversed and there are several varieties: the obverse has Christ seated on a throne with a high back and in the field $B/\mathcal{G}$ or K. Another with the same reverse has Christ standing on its obverse, with $B/\mathcal{G}$ in the field with a star and fleur-de-lis. A silver piece has Andronicus and the Virgin (on the right) standing facing and on the reverse St Demetrius with lance and shield. All of these look to be from Thessalonica judged by their style, and indeed for the coins as yet attributed to this reign, that mint seems predominant. In a hoard found at Thessalonica in the 1930's which Dr Longuet recorded, there were some nine different classes of billon or copper which he attributed to Andronicus III and the mint of Thessalonica was a likely one for the whole group. In the reign both flat and scyphate pieces have their place as they do in the Thessalonica hoard; they are smaller, lighter and less competently designed than similar pieces attributed to Andronicus II, and few have any legends at all. It will be seen how much depends on obtaining specimens in good enough condition to show the faces of the emperors depicted and their robes.

JOHN V (1341–54). Dr Longuet remarked on the closely integrated nature of the coins in the hoard from Thessalonica and dated them between the last years of

385 Michael VIII *(1259–82). Silver trachy, obverse. Bust of Christ with K-Ꙗ in the field (diam. 25 mm.).*

386 Michael VIII *(1259–82). Billon trachy, obverse. Head of Christ surrounded by four crosses with stars between them (diam. 23 mm.).*

387, 388 Michael VIII *(1259–61). Billon trachy, reverse and obverse. The Virgin enthroned with a medallion of Christ before her and (reverse) the emperor with St Michael (diam. 27 mm.).*

389, 390 Andronicus II *(1295–1320). A flat billon or copper piece, obverse and reverse. The reverse with its cross surrounded by a legend looks western. The obverse has the emperor and Michael IX. An issue of lower denomination perhaps, corresponding to the silver copies of Venetian grossi, Nos. 61, 62 above (diam. 20 mm.).*

391 Andronicus II *(1282–1328). Gold hyperper, reverse. Proskynesis of the emperor before Christ standing on the right—a type developed from that of Michael VIII, No. 378 (diam. 26 mm.).*

392, 393 Andronicus II *(1282–1328). Gold hyperper, reverse and obverse. Christ standing in the centre blessing the kneeling figures of the emperor, on the left, and his son Michael IX. Period 1295–1320. The obverse has the Virgin rising from the walls of Constantinople with only four sets of towers: this change takes place in the course of the joint reign (diam. 23 mm.).*

394 Andronicus II *(1282–1328). Gold hyperper, reverse. Here Christ is blessing the emperor and his grandson Andronicus III. When the features of Michael IX and Andronicus III are not damaged by wear or faulty striking the difference is clear—compare No. 392. This joint reign was only from 1325 to 1328 and included a civil war between the two emperors (diam. 27 mm.).*

395 Andronicus III *(1328–41). Silver miliaresion, reverse. This reign of more than twenty years has as yet few coins accepted as belonging to it. This piece has St Demetrius standing on the left, but others exist with the figures reversed: it would appear to indicate slack mint discipline at the die engraving stage. The central letters ΓΟΑ stand for Ο ΑΓ[ΙΟΣ], referring to St Demetrius: compare DUX on Venetian grossi (diam. 20 mm.).*

385

386

387

388

389

390

391

392

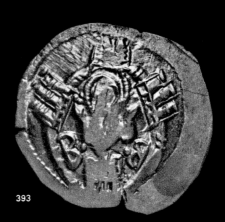

393

392

394　　　　395

396

397

398

399

400

401

402 403

404 405

406 407

396 John VI Cantacusenus *(1347–54). Gold hyperper, reverse. The legitimate emperor, John V, is on the left and the older John VI on the right. Probably the last gold hyperper to be struck. The legend reads forward on the right and retrograde on the left (diam. 23 mm.).*

397, 398 John V *(1341–91). Silver hyperper, obverse and reverse. The curious effect of the bust of Christ moving to the right is unusual (as is the number of stars and pellets round it) and may be due to the engraver copying directly from an icon. The legend begins top right on the reverse IΩΔЄC ... (diam. 27 mm.).*

399 John V *(1341–91). Silver half-hyperper, reverse. Similar to later pieces of Manuel II (No. 376). This piece has the full name IΩANIC (diam. 20 mm.).*

400, 401 John V *(1341–91). Silver one-eighth hyperper, obverse and reverse. The long legend John the Paleolo(gus) distinguishes these from John VIII pieces (diam. 15 mm.).*

402, 403 Andronicus IV *(1376–9). Silver hyperper, obverse and reverse. Only three such hyperpers have as yet been published, and no fractions (diam. 27 mm.).*

404, 405 Period of John V. *Silver piece, obverse and reverse. The obverse shows the walls and towers of a town and the reverse reads, round the central cross ΠΟΛΙΤΙΚΟΝ. Perhaps local currency to maintain trade in a period of civil war. Some have figures of John (V), Andronicus (IV), or Manuel II included on them (diam. 15 mm.).*

406, 407 John VII *(1390). Silver half-hyperper, obverse and reverse. Son of Andronicus IV, John reigned for a few months with Turkish help. The obverse has St Demetrius, sword in hand, riding to the right (diam. 20 mm.).*

Andronicus III and the struggle between his son John V and John VI Cantacusenus, which ended with the latter's retirement to a monastery (but not from politics) in 1354. One class represented by three pieces shows, without legend, an adult emperor in the senior position on the left with a small imperial figure on the right. As Longuet says, this must represent John VI and John V probably just after the agreement at Blachernae in 1347 when the legitimate emperor was aged 15 and a complicated defence of Cantacusenus' right to be senior emperor had been devised before his coronation.

JOHN VI (1347–54). Cantacusenus had been the right-hand-man of Andronicus III and was the wealthy leader of the aristocratic faction. One of the ablest men of his day, he was prepared to commit his personal fortune to the defence of the state; but while he was actually doing this and away campaigning, the Regency for John V rejected him. As a result in 1341 he declared himself co-emperor and a disastrous civil war began. From 1347 he was officially recognized as co-emperor until a coalition of his enemies, including the Genoese, restored John V just after Cantacusenus had abandoned his pretence of ruling as co-emperor with him. Bertelè has established a considerable coinage for John VI with John V in all metals and a single piece for Cantacusenus alone including his family name: on this he stands beside St Demetrius. The joint coinage is of great interest as it is apparently the last before the overall reform which abandoned gold and introduced a large flat silver hyperper with its fractions. All the Cantacusenus pieces are scarce and generally difficult to identify owing to their legends being only partially legible and curiously arranged. Technically their standard is low and the weights of copper pieces vary widely. The scyphate gold hyperpers can easily be confused with those of Andronicus II and III but as usual the beards are helpful if they are still clear: each emperor has the circular legend $I\Omega/\epsilon N/X\Omega$ with that on the left retrograde, the letters are badly formed, such as U for Ω. The flat silver pieces have as obverse a standing or a seated Virgin and as reverse the two emperors standing facing with a long cross between them: the younger emperor is on the left, as he is on the hyperpers. In copper Bertelè distinguishes two scyphate types and three flat for the mint of Constantinople and three flat types for Thessalonica.

JOHN V (period 1354–91). At some point in the period between 1354 and 1379 the decision was taken to adopt silver currency with fractions, helped by some token billon and copper for small change. Previously there had been gold, diminishing in quality and quantity, some silver also scarce, and plentiful billon and copper. The new coins were on flat flans, whereas of the old ones, the gold was scyphate, the silver flat and the rest mixed. The new silver currency continued until the end of the Empire, basically unchanged with the older type billon and copper being replaced, especially in the reign of Manuel II, by flat copper pieces, some of them with similar imperial busts to those used on the

silver. The change was a big one even if the Empire was small and composed of little more than Constantinople itself, Thrace and the flourishing Despotate in the Morea. It must have taken time to plan and execute. Some reasons have been given earlier for attributing the change to John V rather than Andronicus IV, backed respectively by Venice and Genoa. A possible time for the plan to be worked out was during the emperor's long and involuntary stay in Venice in 1370–71 as the whole purpose of his visit was to obtain financial aid. John V had gone there from Rome where he had personally been converted to Roman Catholicism. Bertelè has stressed the strong relationship between the new Byzantine coins and Venetian silver standards but the change may well have been much earlier than the 1370's. Very few Andronicus IV silver hyperpers survive and no fractions at all though these may well appear in time: there is some billon and copper of the old type. Some literary evidence for the change is badly needed so that a firm date can be established.

John V's silver hyperpers are of good metal, style and weight and can easily be distinguished from those of his grandson John VIII on grounds of style: but additionally John V uses the abbreviation $I\Omega$ and John VIII the full name. The legend, beginning on the outside, takes two full circles—' John, Lord, the Palaeologus, by the grace of God, Emperor of the Romans '. This surrounds a facing nimbate bust of the emperor in a helmet-like crown and wearing the tri-lobed maniakion decorated with pellets, which is characteristic of imperial dress in this last period. The obverse is a bust of Christ with his right hand in the act of blessing and his left carrying the Gospels; in the field on either side are $\overline{IC}/\overline{XC}$ generally with a pellet or some other decorative symbol under each, this is surrounded by a single band of, in all, sixteen alternate stars and pellets. One piece has thirty-two alternate stars and pellets and the bust of Christ is off-centre to the right as though moving in that direction; it looks as if it had been copied from an icon direct. A number of these silver hyperpers have the legend beginning inside but this, like one with no nimbus for the emperor, is probably an engraver's mistake as at least three of them are from one die. The suggestion has, however, been made that these very neatly executed coins with the legend beginning on the inside should be placed at the start of the series before it was decided to engrave the legend from the outside inwards, perhaps in the reign of Andronicus IV.

The fractional halves have only a single circle of legend—'John, Lord, the Palaeologus'—with the same designs but for the full name of John in the legend and a varying number of pellets surrounding the obverse bust of Christ. The 1/8th hyperpers have the same legend but with John sometimes abbreviated again and the legend not marked off from the emperor's bust by a border: the obverse has no circle of pellets. Both the fractional pieces are rather scarce and the 1/8th is clearly different from all later ones by reason of its long legend with well cut letters.

For Andronicus IV in this series of coins only the silver hyperper is known and it is in all respects of the same character as similar pieces of John V except that some pieces have the peculiarity of having $\overline{IC}/\overline{XC}$ on the obverse, each enclosed in a small circle, and the obverse type is surrounded by pellets without stars at intervals. Of a number of miscellaneous coins bearing the name of Andronicus or attributed to him, several have the word *ΠΟΛΙΤΙΚΟΝ* (literally, 'something of the citizen') inscribed round the cross or other central type. They are of thin silver and may well have been a product of the civil war between John V and Andronicus IV. They may have been issued by towns as tokens or money of necessity. The names of John (V), Andronicus (IV), and John (V) with Manuel (II) appear on the pieces but there are also anonymous ones with designs such as three keys, a double-headed eagle and the outline of a walled town. Like German bracteates these coins were so thin as to be liable to breaking as well as disintegration and corrosion in normal wear and tear. They are scarce and appear to form a distinct form of currency apart from the silver hyperpers and their fractions.

JOHN VII (1390), the son of Andronicus IV, was in control of the capital for five months, with Turkish help, but his reign was ended abruptly when Manuel (II) recaptured for his father, the city he hoped eventually to inherit himself. Some coins have been attributed to John VII, including a silver half-hyperper with its obverse St Demetrius sword in hand riding to the right; the reverse has the bust of an Emperor John in the familiar tri-lobed maniakion and the legend 'John [abbreviated] Lord, the Palaeologus, [and abbreviated] by the grace of God, Emperor'. Some copper pieces have been attributed to him having one type of SS Helena and Constantine standing on either side of a calvary cross, but specimens with a clearer reverse have the name of Manuel II unequivocally.

MANUEL II (1391–1425)—an able and cultured man is described by Ostrogorsky as 'one of the most sympathetic figures of late Byzantine history'. He had stuck to his father throughout and John V's obvious preference for him over his elder brother, Andronicus IV, with his son John VII, had produced civil war and disruption all through the last part of John V's reign. Manuel II's coinage is a plentiful one with silver hyperpers being amongst the scarcer ones. These coins can be of admirable style but some have so deteriorated in style and technical execution as to be only distinguishable by the name, from those of John VIII. They follow the earlier pattern closely, with sixteen or fewer pellets round the obverse though alternating pellets and stars are found occasionally. The half-hyperpers are abundant and of consistently competent style, with two legends as has been noted above. Both hyperpers and half-hyperpers have a wide variety of letters and symbols on the obverse. Pieces of 1/8th hyperper are common but are often so worn as to be difficult to separate from similar pieces of John VIII: it sounds an easy matter to distinguish *MAN* from *IΩA* but with badly formed and worn letters it does not prove to be so. These small silver pieces must have been greatly in demand as they appear in very worn condition in many little hoards buried in the City at the time of the actual conquest of it by the Turks. There was also a rare three-quarter fraction of poor style to which reference has already been made.

There are a number of small copper coins, some comparatively heavy like the class already mentioned as attributed by some to John VII and another with Demetrius riding to the right: specimens of these are 1.9 g. and 2.2 g. respectively and both have the emperor's bust with the tri-lobed maniakion as reverse. More usually they weigh well under half this and all are small measuring between 16 and 12 mm. in diameter. Many show the emperor standing with a sceptre and on the obverse Christ standing and enclosed in a mandorla. One of this last class has an inscription including the name of John, perhaps issued when his son John VIII was crowned co-emperor in 1421. One of the bust type has a cross potent with arms of equal length and a star in each quarter; another has St Demetrius standing. But there are numerous classes although the coins themselves are scarce, widely scattered and with legends often hardly legible.

JOHN VIII (1425–48) had virtually been in control since his coronation as co-emperor in 1421, as Manuel was worn out and had retired to a monastery. John had been active in the field against the Turks, but he realized, in spite of his father's warning, that there could really be no hope of success unless western powers were interested in helping—and that this meant union between

The style of Iconoclasm

408, 409 Constantine V *(741–75). Gold solidus.* Obv. *The emperor in the civilian chlamys with akakia in his left hand and a cross potent in his right.* Rev. *This shows Leo III, the deceased father of Constantine and founder of the dynasty. He is shown in identical regalia with that of his son. The legend ends Per Annos Multos and sometimes has the letter Θ added, perhaps indicating the officina (diam. 19 mm.).*

410 Eirene *(797–802). Gold solidus.* Obv. *She was sole empress at the time and the reverse is almost identical with the obverse. Though Eirene was opposed to iconoclasm, the style of the coinage is unchanged (diam. 20 mm.).*

the Orthodox and Roman Catholic Churches. It was a most unpopular cause and was never accepted in Constantinople, although John personally pushed it through at the Council of Florence in 1438.

John VIII's silver pieces follow the same pattern as his predecessors but continue the downward trend in style and technical competence already noted under Manuel II, though neither in weight nor fineness of metal was there much decline. Weights are difficult to judge as pieces were sheared off the edges almost promiscuously, in the first place no doubt to trim the flans to a given weight; but this left mis-shapen flans which invited unofficial interference. His pieces are to be distinguished by the use of his unabbreviated name on all the larger ones and even on 1/8th hyperper pieces there is generally something more than $I\Omega$ when they are legible at all. There is again a rare 3/4 fraction and half-hyperpers are much scarcer than those of Manuel and the legends not quite so regular. Legends on half-hyperpers follow the second of those described as Manuel's above, but the title 'Despot' is sometimes substituted for 'Basileus' and the title $\Pi ICTOC$ ('believer') is also occasionally introduced as on Manuel's first type.

The copper issues follow the types used by Manuel and include one with SS Constantine and Helena, one with cross potent and stars and another with Christ in a mandorla. The weights and sizes are similar too but the engraving of the Constantine and Helena type has much deteriorated with the passing of a decade or so.

There are no coins known for Constantine XI though collectors have searched diligently for them. There can have been small need for more coins, and the little hoards buried during the siege of 1453 consistently follow the same pattern of containing many silver hyperpers of John VIII, many half-hyperpers of Manuel II and some worn 1/8th hyperper pieces of Manuel II and of John VIII, a number of which could be attributed to either emperor. There are seldom any copper pieces.

The coin collector generally finds that a glance round the frontiers of the country of his particular interest is rewarding. The very nature of the Byzantine Empire in time and space, not to speak of its important trading position in East/West commerce meant that its influence on coinage both to the east and west of Constantinople was widespread and important. It has been brilliantly sketched in *Introduction à la Numismatique byzantine*, by the late Colonel Longuet in his section entitled ' Influences transmises '. He is particularly interesting on the interaction with Western coinages but in a short space manages to give a comprehensive view all round. Here an attempt is made briefly to look at the subject from the point of view of the eastern frontier of Byzantium and her opponents there—the age-old Persian enemy represented then by the Sassanian dynasty (A.D. 226–651), the Arabs who took their place in the mid-seventh century and the Turkish tribesmen who infiltrated the Abbasid Caliphate and set up a host of small tribal states in Iraq, Palestine and eastern Anatolia from the eleventh century onwards. It includes also the Christian state of Lesser or Cilician Armenia (1080–1375), an enemy of Turk

and Byzantine alike, on the time-honoured road south-east from Constantinople through the pass of the Cilician Gates.

The interaction of the coinage systems and types of these enemies of Byzantium with the Empire is fascinating even at a superficial level and full of complicated problems for those wishing to study them in depth. This is only one aspect of a vast series of questions involved in the influence of Byzantine coinage outside the Empire itself. One might as easily start from the Crusader coinages, that of the Normans in south Italy or those of Bulgaria and Serbia, these last in particular needing some enthusiastic collectors and students. Here some sketchy examples must suffice to point the way.

PERSIA. The rulers of Persia had been enemies of Rome since Republican days and the defeat of Crassus at Carrhae in 53 B.C. by Orodes II (57–38 B.C.) is a salutary reminder that Persia was a power—not to speak of a culture—on equal terms with Rome. So it was to continue. Orodes was of the Parthian dynasty ruling from 247 B.C. to A.D. 226 when it was displaced by the still more nationalist Sassanian rulers.

These were the 'Kings of Kings' with whom the Byzantines had to deal. The Byzantines, like the Romans, were never able to contain the dangers constituted by this vigorous state and its light cavalry of archers. The Persian forces penetrated to the sea of Marmora in Phocas' reign and again, much more dangerously, when Heraclius was emperor.

420 Khusru I (531–79) was the opponent of Justinian I and his continual attacks caused the recall of Belisarius from Italy, an event which had disastrous consequences. The war against the Ostrogoths was thereby probably prolonged by decades and the expenditure on it raised to a figure that Justinian's finances could not stand, if his other projects were to be forwarded with 422 vigour. Khusru II (590–628) owed his throne to the support of the Emperor Maurice and so had a good excuse for attacking his murderer, the usurper Emperor Phocas.

In another successful attack on Heraclius, Khusru was able to co-ordinate with pressure by the Avars on the European side: Khusru gained Egypt and Palestine and swept right across Asia Minor to besiege Constantinople in 626. Heraclius's own expedition against the Sassanian capital at Ctesiphon and his success at the battle of Nineveh caused the retirement of the Persians and the collapse of the whole Sassanian regime. Heraclius supported a puppet king but civil war, following exhaustion from the long struggle against the Byzantines, meant that the Sassanians could do little to oppose the Arabs who swept over their Empire to victory at Niharvand in 641.

The Sassanians had a silver based currency and used few gold pieces, so few that they were probably ceremonial coins rather than currency. There were also only few copper coins if the number of survivors is anything to go by. Silver drachms are found in thousands and new hoards constantly find their way onto the market. The silver flans are broad and thin, and the strikings often show that there was insufficient metal to fill the dies, in spite of, or perhaps, because of, the wide margin outside the engraved types. The design of the types changed little over the centuries. The obverse was provided by a right-facing bust of the King of Kings and the reverse by a fire altar with two priests— one of whom was often the King himself— tending it. From the reign of Firuz (457-84) regnal years begin to appear to the left of the altar and the mint signature was already established on the right of it. Mint signatures number over 270 although several of course are variants referring to the same mint. The religion of Zoroaster was a powerful nationalist unifying force and a rival to Christianity in the whole of this region.

The last King of Kings was Yazdigird III (632–51) through whom the Arab conquerors ruled until his death. He was followed by a series of Arab Governors whose coinage carried on his coin types and more generally those of Khusru II, but with Arabic or part Arabic legends. The Sassanian kings are more easily to be distinguished on their coins by their crowns than by their portraits or names, but those bearing the flamboyant winged crown used by Khusru II—they are the commonest in the whole series—can thus be deceptive.

The Sassanian drachm was, in metal and fabric, the forerunner of the Arabic dirham, which was slightly smaller in size and weight and, after the reforms of 'Abd al-Malik at the end of the seventh century, of course aniconic in types. Kufic script took the place of the king's head and the Zoroastrian fire-altar. There was little interchange of ideas in coinage or types between Sassanians and Byzantines. Anastasius in his reforms did not adopt the addition of the regnal year which had just been made by Firuz and regnal years were not added to Byzantine coins until Justinian's reforms in 539. When Khusru II captured Egypt in 618, presumably to make the transition easier to the inhabitants, he issued from Alexandria a coin of twelve nummia so exactly modelled on Byzantine types that it has long been considered an early coin of Heraclius. Only recently have the difficulties involved in this type been resolved by emphasis on the sun and moon symbols on the obverse: they have been transferred from the reverse of Khusru II's drachms on which they appear very small on either side of the altar flames.

209, 210

THE ARABS. If Persia provided the Arabs with their ideas for a silver coinage, it was Byzantium that produced the early models for their copper and gold pieces. Then what must have been a very disorderly coinage was comprehensively reformed in two stages by 'Abd al-Malik in the 690's. Before the Arabs conquered so much Byzantine and Persian territory they had used gold and silver primarily as bullion,

411, 412 Manuel II *(1391–425)*. *Silver hyperpers, reverses. A deterioration in style and lettering took place in the reign. In No. 412 the first letters of the name are not clear but HΛ at the end leaves no doubt (diam. 26 and 23 mm.).*

413, 414 Manuel II *(1391–425)*. *One-eighth hyperper, obverse and reverse (diam. 13 mm.).*

415 John VIII *(1425–48)*. *Silver hyperper, reverse. The legend begins with the name in full. This was the last reign in which coins were minted (diam. 22 mm.).*

416, 417 John VIII *(1425–48)*. *Silver three-quarter hyperper, reverse and obverse. This denomination has only been found for the reigns of Manuel II and John VIII. The engraved type is slightly smaller than that of the hyperper and the weight c. 6.52 g. (diam. 22 mm.).*

418 John VIII *(1425–48)*. *Silver half-hyperper, reverse. The legend starts with the name in full (diam. 18 mm.).*

419, 420 Khusru I *(531–79)*. *Sassanian silver drachm, obverse and reverse. The reverse shows the regnal year (32) on the left and the mint (AIRAN=Susa) on the right. Note the sun and moon symbols on both obverse and reverse (diam. 30 mm.).*

421, 422 Khusru II *(590–628)*. *Sassanian silver drachm, obverse and reverse. The mint RS is as yet unidentified and the regnal year is 27 (616–7). The sun and moon symbols on either side of the altar flames were transferred to an otherwise very Byzantine looking piece at Alexandria during the Persian occupation of Egypt, Nos. 209 and 210 (diam. 31 mm.).*

411

412

413

414

415

416

417

418

419

420

421

422

423

424

425

426

427

428

429

430

431

432

433

423, 424 Arab-Byzantine *copper follis, obverse and reverse. Before their capture of Syria and Palestine in 638 the Arabs had virtually only used metals for bullion, not as coin. Hence in the early days there were many copies of Byzantine copper and gold pieces until 'Abd al-Malik's reform in 697 set Arab coinage on a new aniconic and purely epigraphic course. This piece is based on a follis of Constans II though it reads Leo in Greek on the right of the obverse. On the reverse in the exergue is Dam(ascus), the mint (diam. 20 mm.).*

425, 426 Arab-Byzantine *copper follis, obverse and reverse. Another type much copied by early Arab mints was that of Heraclius and his two sons. On the reverse this reads* THBЄPIAΔ[OC] *and from top right in Arabic 'good', i.e. current. The follis became 'falus' to the Arabs (diam. 23 mm.).*

427, 428 Arab-Byzantine *gold dinar, obverse and reverse. This piece followed a series of copies of Byzantine solidi with their Greek legends, and used instead an Arabic legend. It can be dated c. 691–3 just before the 'standing Caliph' type (No. 429 shows a copper specimen of this type) which itself preceded the purely epigraphical types of 697 onwards (diam. 19 mm.).*

429, 430 Arab-Byzantine *copper follis, obverse and reverse. The obverse has the 'standing Caliph'*

type closely connected with Justinian II's solidi with the 'Emperor standing' on the reverse (692–5): the legend reads 'Caliph and Ruler of the Faithful'. The reverse has an adaptation of the 'cross on steps' type found on Byzantine solidi in the seventh century with the mint Manbij: the legend reads 'God is One, Muhammad (the Prophet of God)'. Some folles with this obverse have the Byzantine M instead of the adapted cross (diam. 20 mm.).

431 Selçuk Turks—Suleyman II. *Large copper piece dated* A.H. *595 or* A.D. *1198–9. The Turkish tribesmen who controlled the Caliphate from the mid-eleventh century in the name of Muslim Orthodoxy, tended to disregard the Hadith over the representation of living things. The Selçuks in particular liked to represent their rulers, as here, mace in hand and riding to the right (diam. 33 mm.).*

432, 433 Artukid Turks of Keyfa. *Two obverses of copper pieces copied directly from Byzantine Anonymous Class A and Class D with (No. 432) a bust of Christ and (No. 433) Christ seated facing. These were originally issued* C.A.D. *1000 and* A.D. *1050 but copied by Fakhr üddin Kara Arslan between* A.D. *1144 and* A.D. *1174. In these border areas Turks and Crusaders tended to issue near copies of each others coins—perhaps to ease trade (diam. 25 and 28 mm.).*

but from scanty literary references some coins seem to have been used for small payments; none appear to have survived. The Arabic word 'falus' used for a copper coin was simply 'follis' and early copper pieces were based on the Byzantine folles that the Arabs met at the time of their victorious surge at the end of Heraclius's reign. Indeed, one falus showing Justin II and Sophia is so absolutely true to its original that the legend 'Skythopolis' (= Baisan) generally makes no impact on the viewer as something rather odd. The reverse of this piece bearing the original mint mark *NIKO* can be as good a reproduction as the obverse but, of the many dies known, several have obvious copyist's errors such as letters in reverse.

423, 424 The commonest Arab-Byzantine folles show a standing figure copied from that of Constans II, two standing figures from Heraclius and Heraclius Constantine but much smaller, and three standing figures 425, 426 copied also from Heraclius, this time with his two sons. There is another common type with the bust of an emperor wearing a crown with cross and a chlamys probably taken from one of the figures of Heraclius and Heraclius Constantine on the very common gold solidi issued between 612 and 630. Mint names often appear in Greek as well as Arabic, especially Emesa (Homs), Aleppo, Damascus, Heliopolis (Baalbek) and Tiberias. All these types tend to occur in the many small finds of copper coins made in Palestine, mixed with earlier Byzantine ones and, of course, looking very much like them.

The transition from a Byzantine based currency to a purely Arabic one is to be traced more clearly in the gold issues and is tied up with important changes in Byzantine types introduced by Justinian II. At the start there are close copies of solidi of Phocas (only one known), of Heraclius and Heraclius Constantine and of Heraclius with his two sons. All have part of the cross removed, leaving $\mathcal{I}$ or $\mathcal{I}$ as the reverse type, with copies of the original Greek legends. On the last of the three types noted above, however, an Arabic 427, 4 legend is introduced. 'Abd al-Malik (Caliph 685–705) may have been responsible for this change and was certainly responsible for the new 'standing Caliph' type with a cf. 429 bearded figure facing, right hand on his sword. A series of gold dinars, with this obverse and dated on the reverse, exists from A.H. 74 to A.H. 77 (*i.e.* A.D. 693-96/7) when the purely aniconic dinar series begins. The copper pieces with the standing Caliph obverse still have $\mathcal{M}$ on the reverse but some follow the symbol $\mathcal{I}$ used on the 429, 4 reverse of the gold.

This figure of the standing Caliph is not unlike that of Justinian II standing by the 26 cross in his second type (692–5) and could have been inspired by it, as it had been issued just a year before and represented a revolutionary change in Byzantine coin types owing to the obverse being devoted to the newly adopted bust of Christ. This bust could have been an additional inducement for 'Abd al-Malik to make the change, but to the Byzantines the important thing was that the new gold dinar was based on the Arabic weight of one mithqal equal to 4.25 g. *i.e.* less than the solidus.

In the tenth century when the Byzantines launched a counter-offensive which recaptured much territory to the east and south-east previously under the control of the Caliphate, Nicephorus Phocas introduced a new gold coin—the tetarteron—which was lighter than the solidus and roughly the same as the then popular Fatimite dinar, weighing just over 4 g. The reason for introducing the new coin is not yet clear but it may well have been an attempt to provide the inhabitants of the recaptured provinces with a coin to the value of which they were accustomed under their previous rulers, the Abbasid Caliphs of Baghdad.

Many writers have noticed the abrupt change that comes over the Byzantine silver miliaresion when it was re-issued by Leo III; the weight, fabric, types and, above all, the style is completely different. It is aniconic with an obverse type of a cross on steps and the legend ' May Jesus Christ Conquer '. The reverse is purely epigraphic making good use of the decorative Greek capital letters in what is usually a five-line inscription: both types are surrounded by a triple circle of pellets. The coin seems clearly derived from the Arab silver dirham with its purely epigraphical kufic types surrounded by a triple border and of the same thin fabric. The dirham is a little broader by 3 mm. and considerably heavier at around 3 g. compared with the miliaresion's under 2 g. The miliaresia sometimes occur struck over dirhams that have been clipped down to the right size, and there are probably more which have been so effectively restruck as not to show any of the understriking. Arab pieces of dates from 705 to 772 have been identified by Dr George Miles and the overstriking occurs from the reign of Constantine V to that of Michael III. This is a strange phenomenon and it has been suggested that a silver treasure captured in one of Leo III's later victories over the Arabs may have contained a large quantity of dirhams and that Leo III decided that there was now a sufficiency of silver to launch the new type miliaresion, not only modelled on the Arab coins but actually overstruck on some of them.

TURKISH TRIBES. When the Abbasid Caliphate at Baghdad declined in power Turkish tribesmen pressed over its eastern frontiers. In 1055 one of these tribes, the Selçuks, captured Baghdad and ' liberated ' the Caliph from his heretical Shiite advisers: they went on to propagate the orthodox Sunni form of Islam in his name. In their wake came other small tribes, Artukids and Zangids, who set up principalities in the area of south-east Asia Minor and Syria. Some of these principalities were to have very remarkable coinages from the twelfth to the fourteenth centuries—especially in copper—until they were swept away by Saladin and his Ayyubid successors in Egypt or by the Mongols who captured Baghdad in 1258.

The Selçuks themselves succumbed to the Mongols, but from the time of Alp Arslan (1063–72) and Malik Shah (1072–92) they increased their hold over all but the west coast area of Asia Minor and particularly over the central highlands after their victory over the Byzantines at Manzikert in 1071. Their Sultanate of Rum (' Rome ' because the territory had belonged to the Byzantines who referred to themselves as 'Romans') had its capital at Konya which became a great cultural centre, still remarkable for its Selçuk architecture. From the first it was the suzerain power acknowledged by the Empire of Trebizond and later similarly acknowledged by the Armenian Kingdom of Cilicia. Selçuk coins are well 431 known for the type of their ruler riding on horseback to the right, a type wisely adopted by the later rulers of Trebizond and by the Armenian kings whose silver trams of around 1240 had bilingual inscriptions and the names of both the Armenian and Selçuk rulers.

Though they are perhaps less important the Artukids produced more interesting and eclectic coins of which the main copper series still present major problems to the numismatist. One branch of the Artukids ruled from Keyfa and there Fakhr üddin Kara Arslan (1144–74) produced a virtual copy of the Byzantine Anonymous Bronze 432 Type A with its bust of Christ obverse, and another copying the seated Christ of 15 Anonymous Class D, a century or more 433 after the original issues. Another branch 276 of the Artukids, at Mardin, produced copies of the upward looking bust of 440 Constantine I, and of Heraclius and Hera- 33 clius Constantine, much enlarged from their solidus for this big copper coin. This last coin was made for Kutb üddin il-Ghazi (1176–84) and his predecessor, Necm üddin Alpi (1152–76), issued a large copper 441 copy of John II's gold hyperper showing 281 the emperor crowned by the Virgin. The interest of this piece, in contrast to most of

the others, lies in its being nearly contemporaneous with the original: John II died in 1143. An electrum trachy of John II showing him with St George holding a cross on steps between them was also copied in Erzerum about thirty years after 435 ▶ his death. One of the commonest types to be found in mixed hoards in Syria is a close copy of a copper coin, both obverse and reverse, with Constantine X and Eudocia 442, ◀ standing facing with a labarum between 322, � them: this was made by the Aleppo Zangid ruler Nur üddin Mahmud (1146–73) under whom Saladin began his career. 434 ▶

In northern Asia Minor the Danishmenid tribe produced coins with the type of Christ crowning the emperor and others with the legend 'The Great Amir Zulkarneyn' in Greek, and the Zangids based on Mosul had double-headed eagles and thunderbolts of Zeus. There are Roman imperial busts and Greek goddesses, men ride lions and dragons and the wise men adore the Virgin and Child—there is seemingly no 444 end to the anomalous types on these Turkish medieval coins of which many types are commonly found in great numbers. Coming from people professing to be Sunni Muslims these figured coins are the more surprising and suggest that their conversion to Islam as they crossed Persia had been over-hasty. These copper types are often 436 ▶ crudely cut on the dies, generally interesting 437 ▶ in character but hardly skilful in their execution: they went hand-in-hand with well-designed and executed traditional type gold dinars and silver dirhams. Their purpose, which is generally assumed to be an attempt to ease trade with Christian

Iconoclast 'family coins'

434, 435 Nicephorus I *(802–11)*. *Gold solidus*.
Rev. *This shows his son and co-emperor*
Stauracius described as Despot. Obv. *The*
emperor is entitled Basileus as distinct from
Despot—a distinction often reinforced by the
wearing of the loros as against the chlamys
(diam. 22 mm.).

436, 437 Theophilus *(829–42)*. *Gold solidus*.
Obv. *The emperor styled Basileus.* Rev. *On*
the left is the bearded effigy of the emperor's
deceased father Michael II, and Constantine,
the emperor's son, is on the right. The usual
additional letter is on the obverse on this coin
where the space is less cramped (diam. 20 mm.).

neighbours, is still a mystery. But the coins are impressive and have long been so, for many are gilded or silvered and pierced to be worn as talismans.

ARMENIA. The new state of Lesser Armenia in Cilicia was consolidated in its independence by the First Crusade, and its first king, Levon I (1187–1219), acknowledged the western Holy Roman Emperor Henry VI as his suzerain. He was of the Roupenian family, claiming relationship with the Bagratids who had ruled from their capital at Ani until the Selçuks had swept the Byzantines out of this area at the battle of Manzikert (1071). Escaping from the Selçuks to the south the Armenians made their capital at Sis; they had no wish to live under the Byzantines who regarded them as heretical and despised them in spite of their great services to Byzantium as soldiers, sailors, architects and emperors. Byzantine emperors looked on the new state as another crusading Kingdom which had no business to be there. Thus, though the Armenians were culturally in a Byzantine milieu, the coins of their kings show a stout, western-oriented independence. They will adopt Turkish types and show the king seated cross-legged as Saladin had been represented, or riding to the right as the Selçuks so often portrayed him but they would not use Byzantine designs. Their coinage was of silver 'trams' (drachms), debased silver 'takvorins' and billon pieces but in earlier years there were some fine large copper 'Tanks' and 'Kardez'; later some smaller copper 'Poghs' were issued. There are a very few gold pieces, so few as to be a prey to forgery, but the coinage was based on the silver 'tram', which again distinguished it from Byzantium with her gold based system. The major mint was at Sis from which almost all the coins were issued, though Tarsus was used occasionally, and the early technical standards were high; but as silver became debased, the coins wore easily and the takvorins were hastily struck. Many hoards of these coins in bad condition have been found and a number contain southern French pieces pointing to trade and pilgrim connections.

THE CRUSADER STATES. One other enemy to the south-east provides an interesting field of study in relation to Byzantine coin types—the Crusader States in Syria and Palestine. In Antioch the Normans were installed and both there and in their south Italian base the Byzantines had very lately been the ruling power. In spite of their dedicated opposition to Byzantium, the Norman princes adopted many coin types for their copper pieces from their enemy, especially borrowing from the Byzantine Anonymous series. The Crusaders in Edessa did the same, to such an extent that for a long time some Anonymous coins (Types H, I and J) were considered to be Edessan issues by the Crusaders: they are thus attributed as late as Ratto's Catalogue of 1930.

In the Sicilian kingdom of the Normans occasionally elaborate copies of Byzantine coins were brought out, including debased silver scyphates of Roger II with his son and of William I with his son, both closely copying a billon trachy of Alexius I on

265

which St Demetrius is shown handing the emperor a patriarchal cross. But the coinage of Norman Sicily is of such interest in having pieces with Greek, Latin or Kufic legends that it is unfair to stress its Byzantine imitations. The coins there reflect the religious tolerance that was so distinguishing a characteristic of the state amongst its Latin and Orthodox Christian neighbours.

For much too long coins have been practically the preserve of collectors regarding the whole business as an enjoyable hobby for moments of relaxation, and even then only when the spirit moves them to have a look at their trays. The coins recall here and there strange or happy circumstances under which they were acquired, the general admiration for this piece or the surprising interest of a friend in another. Any individual is entitled to look at his coins in this way, but one of the purposes of a book such as this is to suggest that there are other considerations too, and that if regarded in one such additional way the collection, however small, can become more significant: enjoyment can be greatly enhanced by the new friends with common interests brought by it. Coins are belatedly becoming important subjects of study by economists, historians, metallurgists, designers and art historians, to mention the more interested parties. In view of this the mere possession of coins becomes something of a trust, something that should not be kept at the mercy of the collector's whim alone. This applies with even more force in the case of the investor who may not be interested in the coins, as coins, at

all. In this chapter suggestions are made on the lines of an approach from the point of view of art, gathering material scattered over earlier pages. It is of course only one aspect of many that could be chosen as being of general interest.

The approach to coins as examples of contemporary art is an easy one to start upon as we all have our likes and dislikes in this respect and it brings immediately a certain channelling of interest to a collection; the collector will no longer acquire coins indiscriminately. Subjective as our opinions may be, a nucleus for thought about the series as well as a guideline in collecting will have been established. Early in my own collecting days when I was full of the interest and qualities of Anastasius' and Justinian I's reformed folles, I recall a young acquaintance saying that what *he* wanted to do was to make a serious study of the so-called 'provincial' copper issues of the Iconoclast emperors: these can now be shown to be Sicilian. It was a most intelligent choice, though at first I found it astonishing as the coins were a scruffy lot, small and apparently negligible from an artistic point of view. But of course the choice was right: this was a neglected spot:

the coins were then plentiful, cheap to acquire, difficult to read and badly needing the tender care of an enthusiast. The 'Anonymous Bronze' series with its high proportion of overstruck pieces, the, at first sight, dull and lifeless twelve nummia pieces of Alexandria or the Antioch folles in the reigns of Tiberius II and Maurice are examples of other patches where the patient skill of individual collectors has been needed to resolve small problems with by no means unimportant results. There are many such uncared for patches remaining, but if they seem to require too much detailed specialization—and they often do require this—then the studying of coins as examples of art and particularly as showing imperial portraiture, is a good substitute. It can be carried out perhaps better with gold coins than others as so much more care was expended on their production.

In the Later Roman Empire a 'type' of imperial profile the embodiment of stern unwavering justice and integrity was developed with individual variations. A comparison between the bust on Constantine's solidus of Ticinum in 315 with the head on a Nicomedia specimen twenty years later will show the difference between the 'type' and the portrait, for comparison with a bronze bust of Constantine confirms the latter as a portrait: the upward look on his coins was even made into a sermon by his contemporary and biographer Eusebius. His successors developed another 'type' of the Christian warrior, which had a facing bust in helmet and cuirass with head turned three-quarters right, right hand holding a lance over his shoulder and the

left supporting a shield. This type was to dominate the gold solidi until Justinian I's changes in 539 brought in the facing bust in helmet and cuirass; in its turn this became the standard pose for a long time, though in the seventh century civilian robes were adopted. But one may well ask how far the coin representation of Justinian can claim to be a portrait. He faces us on literally thousands of gold and copper coins and there are at least two mosaic pictures for comparison, but one of these at its last restoration was so 'restored' as to leave no single tessera in its earlier place, besides having been clearly 'restored' before that. This must be ruled out but the originally contemporary picture in S. Vitale, Ravenna, has also been restored many times; if it represents the original outline it hardly shows the same full-faced characteristics of the coin bust. What perhaps weighs more heavily is that Justinian's portrait on coins does not substantially vary in its twenty-six years occupation of so many obverses. There was no dramatic transition from 'young head' to 'veiled head' such as there was with Victoria—only it is true, after fifty-eight years! It is curious too that the 'portrait' of Maurice on coins can vary so widely, sometimes looking very like that of Justinian himself, in his twenty-year reign. The coins *could* provide a contemporary portrait, but it is very doubtful whether they did.

Professor Grierson maintains that it was Phocas who introduced portraiture on Byzantine coins and there can be little doubt that his coins, so different from those of Maurice before him and of Heraclius after him, are portraits. Phocas was proud

The survival of Iconoclastic style

438 Nicephorus II *(963–9). Gold histamenon. Rev. The Virgin on the left and with her hand above that of Nicephorus (both indications of superiority), holds a patriarchal cross with the emperor on the right. The emperor's portrait is naturalistic and comparable to many others on his silver and copper coins* (cf. *Nos. 294–6). The obverse has a ' naturalistic ' bust of Christ (diam. 21 mm.).*

439 Nicephorus II *(963–9). Gold histamenon. Rev. The bearded emperor wearing the loros is on the left and holds a patriarchal cross with his hand above that of Basil II on the right, beardless and wearing a chlamys. Both are portrayed in the impressionist style typical of Iconoclasm, which had officially come to an end over a century before in 843, and in spite of its contrast with the ' naturalistic ' bust of Christ on the obverse as in No. 438 above (diam. 22 mm.).*

of his personal achievement in becoming emperor from being a junior officer and he may have been personally interested in seeing that a real representation of himself was made. His head even appears on the profile bust of tremisses which had remained virtually unchanged from the very beginning of the Byzantine Empire. It may be that people generally were beginning to think that the emperor's picture should accompany his name on coins, as even in the reign of Justin II one class of solidi has the emperor with a stubby beard.

The fact of the busts of Heraclius changing on successive issues in his reign of thirty years leads to the presumption that they show the man as he was, beginning with a short beard which by 630 had grown to patriarchal proportions. The type changes were radical in dress and number of figures represented, as well as in the actual features of the emperors. But if looked at from the point of view of artistic achievement, Heraclius's coins cannot rank very high; only the long bearded type of 630 is more than of average competence. The type changes nevertheless merit careful study in the light of some slight literary evidence and of the ages of the characters represented.

At the end of the seventh century there was an inspired period of artistic portraiture from the end of the reign of Constantine IV —his last gold issue shows a new and gifted engraver at work—to that of Theodosius III. The break between the sub-standard solidi of Constantine IV's second and third issues and his fourth and last is startlingly dramatic and shows what an artist of first-rate ability can do on the confined space allotted to him. The new design seems a purposeful evocation of Justinian I, after whom Constantine had named his son, but the facial details are plainly individual. It looks as if there was a conscious effort to improve the standards of design and execution at the mint as successive sovereigns are represented by confidently and carefully engraved solidi.

This brilliant period with portraits of Leontius, Tiberius III, Anastasius II and Theodosius III, and also some pieces made for Justinian II, particularly the obverse and reverse of his last issue with his son Tiberius IV, changed abruptly on the accession of the iconoclast emperors. The period 726 to 843 produced coins which perhaps better than anything else bring home to later generations the deep-seated nature of the changes involved in Iconoclasm—the concentration, both in design and legends, on the imperial family, the elimination of Christ as an obverse type. The change in style to impressionist design and linear engraving brought about so great a change as to cause many later critics to write off the products as incompetent. Coins of the Iconoclast emperors are unmistakable, with a new approach to art. In spite of the widespread destruction of holy paintings and mosaics there were clear ideas as to how these should be replaced: it is far from an inartistic or uncultured time.

Indeed, iconoclasm made a lasting impact on coins, especially in the artistic use of lettering as an important component in design. Similar ideas had had much the same effect in Muslim lands but the Greek capital letters, beautiful in themselves, had no need for the fantastic elaboration turning Arabic, which had no capitals, into hardly intelligible Kufic lettering. Even the impressionist rendering of the imperial figures continued long past the victory of the Iconodules in 843—for over a century in fact, down to the reign of Nicephorus II who appears on his solidi in both impressionist and naturalistic style. Nicephorus' bust appears on copper and on silver (in minute form), both in a naturalistic way, so that a check can be made and the reality of the portraiture established. Historians may here also find backing for the view that iconoclasm had a popular support much larger than contemporary iconodule chroniclers would have people believe. The coins show a speedy reintroduction of the 'naturalistic' bust of Christ as an obverse type but not of naturalistic representation of the emperors. For a long time the two contrasting styles ran in parallel. When a single coin has an obverse in one style and its reverse in another, it becomes glaringly obvious—as in the British 'Churchill Crown' of 1965—and the piece fails to achieve credibility as an artistic unity. Such was one issue of gold histamena by Nicephorus II, and there were many earlier ones.

After Iconoclasm, the Macedonian dynasty established itself in popular favour and occupied the throne from 867 to 1056. It was a period of many changes numismatically—a new gold coin (the tetarteron), the enlarging of the old solidus into a thinner but much broader piece of the same weight (the histamenon), and the adoption of the scyphate shape to distinguish the broader and heavier piece even

further. Engravers had more opportunity on the larger flans and one or more standing figures appear as regular types, thus reducing the part played by portraiture but increasing the opportunities for effective design. Once the scyphate shape had been adopted, technical difficulties in striking flans between the dies occurred if a second hammer blow was needed; some slight movement of the dies was all but inevitable. When a large quantity of copper was introduced into the alloy for gold hyperpers in the late thirteenth century, necessitating several hammer blows for a single striking, this problem assumed serious proportions. It does not appear from the coins that it was solved.

During the Macedonian period, however, a good standard both of design and technical execution was maintained, including some coins that remain attractive today. Such are Theodora crowned by the Virgin and a similar design for Romanus III. Romanus also issued a miliaresion with a full-length representation of the Virgin Hodegetria pointing to the Christ child on her arm as the way of life. The Virgin Blachernitissa, with arms held up in the 'orans' position, fills the circular space of the scyphate histamena or trachea well; a particularly successful example was issued for Andronicus I as an electrum trachy. There are several successful portrait coins too amongst which the three bearded busts of Leo VI, his son Constantine VII and grandson Romanus II on solidi are outstanding, fine looking coins with impressive detail. But the best portrait is probably that of Constantine VIII on the wider histamenon flan. Zoe and Theodora in a

438*, 439*
294, 295
271
272, 273
291, 292
316
306
307
345
289
293
304

reign of nine weeks issued an effective gold histamenon with their two busts on the reverse; it was a remarkable achievement considering the haste with which it must have been prepared.

An attractive introduction into designs of this period was the so-called 'lyre-backed' throne on which Christ can be seen seated in the mosaic over the main entrance door to the Church of the Holy Wisdom in Constantinople. The mosaic shows the Emperor Leo VI in an attitude of proskynesis or adoration before Christ and the lyre-backed throne appears on the same emperor's coins; the artist clearly appreciated that here was something worth detailed emphasis. On both gold and copper coins of the previous emperor, Basil I, the same throne appears but it did not catch the imagination of the designer and it is clumsily and ineffectively portrayed. This throne was to become a part of one of the standard obverse types, along with a rectilinear one with high back and another without any back at all.

From this period in which good things continually appear from a steadily competent background, coin design takes a clear step forward under the Comneni (1081-1185), as did so many of the arts at that time. All the gold hyperpers issued in the century are well designed and some reach a very high level indeed. This may well have been one of the objectives of Alexius I's reform of the whole currency in 1092. Certainly Alexius' own hyperpers are a challenging example of Byzantine art in which the emperor is viewed from close up and below, at full-length and crowned by a *Manus Dei*. Viewed thus, the body

becomes longer than natural, the head smaller, while the chlamys thrust forward on one side and held back on the other is represented by the circlets of different sizes on its lining; those near the eye are of exaggerated size and those further away much smaller. In contrast two hyperpers of his son John II, showing the emperor crowned by the Virgin, have a quiet naturalism more characteristic of the age. Alexius' grandson Manuel I appears as a standing figure overwhelmed by the imperial garments and regalia about him, more in touch with the *Manus Dei* above than with his subjects below—as was no doubt intended. The Virgin Blachernitissa on Andronicus I's electrum trachy has already been referred to as a finely spaced design peculiarly suitable to the convex surface. The more difficult task of designing the concave side of the flan is achieved on an electrum trachy with John II and St George holding a cross on steps between them. Even some of the billon pieces of this period are worthy of careful attention, if they can be found in sufficiently good condition.

The Latin Conquest disintegrated the mint organization at the capital and the series of copper types A to T which Hendy has convincingly associated with the period, have few which can even be claimed as competent in design and technical production, let alone deserving praise as works of art. As is to be expected the coins reflect the steady pressure on the regime by its many enemies after so astonishing a success, and also the failure of the then distracted West to give it support. At Nicaea the Lascaris family maintained

273

440 Artukid Turks of Mardin. *Copy in copper of a solidus of Heraclius (No. 218) and Heraclius Constantine by Kutb üddin il-Ghazi (1176–84) (diam. 32 mm.).*

441 Artukid Turks of Mardin. *Copy in copper of a gold hyperper of John II blessed by the Virgin, by Necm üddin Alpi (1152–76). John II died in 1143 so that this hyperper would be current when copied (Nos. 280, 281): many other pieces copied were not so (diam. 30.5 mm.).*

442, 443 Zangid Turks of Aleppo. *A copy by Nur üddin Mahmud (1146-73) in copper, both obverse and reverse, of a follis of Constantine X and Eudocia (Nos. 322, 323), the standing Christ as obverse (diam. 22 mm.).*

444 Artukid Turks of Mardin. *Copper piece representing the three wise men adoring the Virgin and Child—perhaps copied from a manuscript—by Husam üddin Yoluk Arslan (1184–1200). This ruler—called the Bald Lion—was proud of having fought at the Horns of Hattin defeat of the Crusaders in 1187 (diam. 31 mm.).*

445 Cilician Armenia—Levon I *(1187–1219). Silver tram, obverse. His coinage is of western type as befits a prince who owed his crown to the help of Frederick Barbarossa and the Emperor Henry VI (diam. 21 mm.).*

446 Cilician Armenia—Levon III *(1301–7). Copper Kardez, obverse. The kings of Armenia had constantly to preserve their independence against the Byzantines in their early years. Later, with the Byzantine frontier far away, they had to preserve themselves amidst rival Muslim princes. Levon III appears seated in oriental fashion (diam. 20 mm.).*

447, 448 Kingdom of Sicily—Roger II *(1130-54). Silver scyphate ducat, obverse and reverse. A close copy of Byzantine trachea, in particular, as Hendy has shown, that of St Demetrius handing the labarum to Alexius I. The king in imperial Byzantine robes here holds a patriarchal cross with his son Roger of Apulia in military dress standing on the left (diam. 25 mm.).*

440   441

442   443

444

445

446

447

448

449 Chlamys, tablion and fibula. *The normal civilian dress of Byzantine sovereigns as seen on coins from the reign of Heraclius onwards is composed of the long purple cloak or chlamys, decorated on both sides of its opening by an embroidered tablion and fastened on the right shoulder by a fibula or brooch, generally with a triple pendant. The assumption of the chlamys formed an important part of the coronation ceremony. All these articles of clothing are to be seen in the mosaic in San Vitale at Ravenna showing Justinian I entering the church. Particularly the fact of the tablion extending on both sides of the opening of the cloak is shown clearly. The church was consecrated in 547 and the mosaic probably made shortly before: Theodora died in 548.*
The two white pearls on either side of the cheeks are the ends of the pendilia hanging from the crown.

450 The simplified loros. *This ivory in the Paris Cabinet des Médailles shows Christ crowning the Emperor Romanus II on the left and his wife Eudocia. It is a work of the mid-tenth century. Romanus II wears the simplified loros fitting over the head with the back portion drawn across his right hip and draped over his left arm. It will be seen that the chlamys worn by Eudocia has an embroidered tablion of which virtually only one side is visible.*

reasonable standards of coinage and in silver produced some really effective pieces based on traditional designs. Trebizond, with much good silver at her disposal, produced little more than an idiosyncratic style prior to accepting the Selçuk horseman 369-373 as an obverse type, representing the Great Comnenus. The halcyon days of the twelfth century must have seemed far away to those who looked at their money.

Two chances, in fact, of reversing the trend remained and one of them was nearly taken to the full. The coinage of the earlier Palaeologan emperors employed a number of ambitious designs especially for gold hyperpers, but in other metals too, which have only failed to impress by reason of atrocious technical imperfections. The shaping of the flans, the inadequate mixing of the alloy and faulty double striking between the scyphate dies all play their part. The flans are often crudely sheared and the alloy may have been in any event too hard to suit the striking techniques used, but the result was unattractive. Deep cracks running far into ill-shaped flans and double striking make calm artistic assessment of the designers and engravers work a matter of real difficulty. One of the most often used and finest designs of all, the Virgin Blachernitissa rising from the walls and 377 towers of Constantinople, has been the greatest sufferer. Other designs have been mentioned above which justify the view that it was not only in mosaic and fresco work that Byzantine artists had much to give the world in this period of political impotence but of great artistic achievement.

In the mid-fourteenth century another chance occurred of rescuing the coinage when the use of gold was terminated and a new silver currency had to be designed. Western ideas of coin design had already been tried for both silver and copper coins in the reign of Andronicus II and under John V a good design was adopted based, for its reverse, on the popular gros tournois of Louis IX, which had also been the model for the English groat. There was an outer and an inner circle of legend round the 397, 398 imperial bust and there were great possibilities of exploiting the beauty of Greek capital letters. The obverse was a bust of Christ of traditional type and the early issues justify Bertelè's description of them as 'amongst the most splendid of medieval coins'. But these issues were consistently copied for the worse and the whole series, covering just under a century, forms a good example of the dangers involved in copying. Amongst many casualties were the Greek capitals of the legend which became, under John VIII, a travesty of scratchings as 415 compared with the bold letters of the 412 original. But perhaps people's minds had other things to worry about.

The Byzantine series of coins, taken as a whole, is not one in which good design and craftsmanship can be confidently expected, as it can be for instance in the currencies of the ancient Greek city states, or in that of fourteenth-century France and Flanders. Nevertheless it contains many highlights, possibilities of development and much interest in spite of our present knowledge of mint organization being so small. In the last resort our judgment is subjective; every collector will have his special favorites and can develop strong reasons for his choice and it is by such challenge of opinions that knowledge and appreciation grows.

XV. LOOKING AHEAD

It will be clear to the reader that the whole period after the return of the Byzantine emperors to Constantinople in 1261 is not yet adequately explained or recorded numismatically. Large or small fields of study are open to anyone interested, for the period is full of major and minor difficulties. What exactly were the principles upon which the change to a silver based currency was made? Had there been some partial realignment of the currency earlier, to a western system? How can the lack of coins in a reign like that of Andronicus III be explained? Above all the relationship of the coins in various metals to each other needs clarification and particularly the relationship of flat and scyphate copper pieces of approximately equal weight.

Over the last thirty years, work on Byzantine coinage has made such progress that there are several centuries over which the general position is clear enough with only some detailed problems here and there to be solved, and of course newly discovered coins to be fitted in. Once the general pattern is broadly understood a watch can be kept for coins which *ought* apparently to be there but have not so far been recorded, or for coins of a crucial reign, year or type upon which more information is needed. As the area of intensive search is narrowed, the chances of success are increased; all collectors can take part in this search but in the course of it they would be well advised to discuss their finds with other workers in the field before publishing anything. People with experience are ready to advise and if a new coin of importance turns up there are several journals ready to publish something about it. By contrast, in the Palaeologan period there is as yet insufficient published evidence to enable a pattern to be built up; concentrated work such as Hendy has recently done on the Comneni, Angeli and Latins is badly needed. It is still for the Palaeologi a matter of collecting information as to specimens and their whereabouts and of establishing as much hoard evidence as possible. One wonders whether the dozens of hoards, previously unpublished, such as Hendy found, may have their counterparts somewhere for the later period. The restricted size of the Empire and the absence of interest in the matter by Turkish governments of the past render unlikely a rediscovery of many Palaeologan hoards in museums or elsewhere—but it is still possible. A steady erosion of hoard evidence by piecemeal sale has been taking place over the years, along with the deliberate falsification of details to cover illegalities. Also, the coins which may give valuable clues—like those described by Dr Longuet in the Thessalonica hoard—have not been in themselves of the kind to attract the dealer or collector. They are difficult to interpret and have little or no value either intrinsically or as works of art. Indeed, some of these coins, seen in their natural state with dirt adhering and corrosion active, can be positively off-putting!

It has, however, been established that coins can generally be expected to give something approaching a portrait of the emperor or emperors involved. This has been noted earlier, for instance in dealing with the beards, or lack of them, in the cases of Andronicus II, Michael IX, Andronicus III and John VI. The positioning of the younger man in the senior position on the left when two emperors are involved is always worth examining as Professor Grierson showed when dealing with the ' consular ' coins of Heraclius and his father. Grierson has recently stressed the care shown by the Byzantines in observing protocol on their coins. The distinction between the robes worn by the two emperors or the indication of their relative ages can both be important. Once such points have been observed, knowledge of the background history comes into play as a valuable asset providing information, for instance, that coins of John V with John VI are likely to be found and that some of John VI alone, are possible.

It is still a matter of difficulty to know what the exact metal composition of coins may be and to obtain this knowledge requires scientific co-operation involving high levels of skill and patience. The progress of scientists in achieving minute accuracy in non-destructive methods of metal analysis is of the greatest significance to numismatists, and it is equally important 451 ▶ that those who possess coins should be prepared to submit them to such scientists experimentally as well as seeking aid from them. It must not be forgotten that numismatists are asking for a difficult job to be done and that it can only be done accurately with the fullest co-operation. The numismatist must be able to state how much damage (if any) to a given coin is permissible, and what precisely he wants to 452 ▶ establish; what he knows already about the coin, what he expects may be found and what elements, and in what concentration, he is interested in; finally what degree of accuracy is required. The processes of thermo-neutron activation and X-ray fluorescence provide attractive means of weight measurement, particularly as they include minor components and the very small ' trace elements '; but their accuracy has limitations which have not always been appreciated by numismatists and, notably, the problem of surface enrichment, affecting one component of the alloy, has to be 453 ▶ discounted.

The older specific gravity techniques, the efficiency of which has been considerably sharpened in recent years, can give very accurate figures for binary alloys, but unless this can be presumed the results are bound to be misleading. Once again the numismatist is asking his scientific colleague

451 Basil I *(867–86). Gold solidus. Obv. Christ enthroned on the so-called 'lyre-backed' imperial throne which can be seen in the narthex mosaic of Leo VI in the Church of the Holy Wisdom in Istanbul. The engraver works in impressionist style and the throne does not seem to have caught his imagination (diam. 19 mm.).*

452 Constantine VII and Romanus I *(920–44). Gold solidus. Obv. A naturalistic view of the same type as in No. 451 above, but one in which the artist seems to have been impressed by the beauty of the throne (diam 21 mm.).*

453 Alexander *(912–13). Gold solidus. Rev. The emperor is blessed by St Alexander. The obverse is similar to No. 451 above. Note the full extent of the loros here ending (unusually and unnaturally) over the right forearm (diam. 21 mm.).*

to do something requiring extreme care and patience. There are other methods, but unfortunately the laborious and totally destructive one of wet chemical analysis is still the best of all. Even so, there are coins which are expendable owing to their being extremely common, or in badly damaged condition; in the scientist's hands, such pieces might become of great use. There may be great developments in this field of metal analysis from which numismatists will benefit, but always with the statistical warning that the analysis, however accurate and by whatever method, of a *single* coin can be misleading; useful as it is, it needs corroboration. Nevertheless it is now becoming possible to link the ores from particular mines with those used in coins, and it may be possible to track the use of silver from the great Gümüşane mine in the Empire of Trebizond, for instance.

It is difficult to distinguish billon from copper by eye and the *amount* of silver contained in the former can be important even when very small, as Hendy found in his researches. Analysis of Palaeologan billon and copper will have to be undertaken in due course. Some of these coins are clearly billon but many more may well prove to be so. The importance of analysing the content of gold coins has long been recognized both in measuring the exact nature of any debasement and in establishing the order of types within a reign. While engaged on this Grierson found that a coin of Constantine IX had been wrongly attributed by Wroth to Constantine VIII, that is before any debasement had been undertaken. Accurate measurement of weights and analysis of content is now seen

to be of importance for coins of all metals even if only a negative result, that there is no consistency in weight or content, is arrived at. Looking back to the origin of the coins and the action taken by the actual craftsmen employed in the mint, we have to recognize that their orders must have involved the making of so many coins out of so much metal: the average weight of a large number of coins therefore becomes in some cases more important than a few individual weights. Equally, the average content of particular metals may mean more than an individual analysis, if the mix of the alloy is not consistent.

Accurate observation of detail of design and especially the variations in specific details can be important, for instance, in defining officina differences and even those of mints, but can easily be exaggerated in order to establish a ' new variety ' not in some authoritative catalogue. What matters is the frequency of the variations and their purpose.

The current emphasis upon hoard evidence—for such good reasons and with such good results—makes it imperative for coin buyers at all levels to do their best to find the provenance of anything they are buying. One cannot put it more precisely than this, as it is generally no easy matter. But continued questioning on provenance will make everyone in the coin trade more careful themselves on the matter, though some of them need no prompting on it. Skill in probing the defensive screen put up by those with Byzantine material to sell is necessary if the coins involved are to be used scientifically to their full potential. Again, the mere fact that several pieces of similar type, or with similar patination, appear on the market at the same time may be significant in unmasking a forgery or in ' reconstructing ' a hoard. Where information as to place, date and content is clear, the use of hoard evidence needs little emphasis, except perhaps to remark on the importance occasionally of the *absence* of certain coins that might have been expected, as well as those actually there. Such absence may indicate, for instance, the withdrawal officially of heavier pieces to bring in a lighter or at least a different type of coin. Grierson has noted the absence of post-reform Justinian I folles in Asia Minor hoards in connection with the first Sicilian countermark series of Heraclius. In the flans for the Sicilian series there is a great predominance in the use of early folles up to 539 as against the heavier facing bust Justinian pieces. The currency of much lighter folles in the seventh century must at some time have made it worth while melting heavier coins, and Grierson suggests that this may have begun to occur in Heraclius's reign. All collectors now need to know more about hoards and what can be learned from them. For those prepared to take trouble over detail there exists in Hendy's *Coinage and Money in the Byzantine Empire 1081–1261* a practical textbook of the greatest value in this respect. He shows how sophisticated the techniques can become from the basic facts of find-spot, content, estimated date of concealment and possible reasons for it.

The student and collector of coins have many paths open to them, requiring more or less time and energy in their pursuit. What is perhaps most important of all is the sharing of experience with others, comparing and discussing pieces and so establishing their interest outside personal associations and pride of possession. Coin collectors need to ask questions and work towards the answering of them. In the Byzantine series, there is immense scope 455 ▶ for such questions and good returns for accurate knowledge of detail and a sharp eye when buying coins, even in the highly competitive market of today. Travellers without knowledge will be lucky if they pick up worthwhile, or even genuine coins on their wanderings, but knowledgeable ones can still do so; it is a source to keep in mind when one's journeys reach the end of well beaten tracks. It is jokingly said that peasants in some Byzantine lands go about 454 ▶ with the latest priced sale catalogues in their pockets and it is in fact unlikely that attractive bargains in gold solidi or hyperpers will be met; but little hoards of billon or copper pieces can still be found by the cognoscenti, and the value of such to the numismatist and historian can be greater than gold.

The traveller will now meet forgeries on quite a big scale. At one time the Byzantine series was comparatively free from modern forgeries as so few people were interested in it and the effort of forgery was not worth while. This is not the situation today. There are some excellent forgeries of gold 456 ▶ solidi in particular but of quite common 457 ▶▶ copper pieces too, made by 'pressure casting '. They are difficult to identify quickly as forgeries unless a number of pieces all from the same pair of dies happen to be presented at once; the writer once was handed a bag containing seventy-two pieces

Histamenon and tetarteron

454, 455 Michael IV *(1034–41). Gold hista-menon.* Obv. *The piece is thin and broad to make clear the distinction between it and the smaller, thicker and lighter tetarteron. It was in this reign that the debasement of the hista-menon began from 24 carats to eventually about five carats under Alexius I.* Rev. *The emperor wears the simplified loros fitting over the head, with a maniakion covering neck and shoulders. In his right hand is the labarum and a Manus Dei above blesses the representative of Christ on earth (diam. 31 mm.).*

456, 457 Michael VII and Maria *(1071–8). Gold tetarteron.* Obv. *The Virgin with plain nimbus holds a medallion with a bust of Christ before her breast—a representation called by the Byzantines ' Nikopea ', or Victory-maker.* Rev. *The emperor wears the simplified loros. The decorations on the cross, which vary, give an indication of the debasement: this piece being of eleven carats, which is much lower than the histamena of the reign (diam. 19 mm.).*

of this kind! Byzantine collectors today must know something of forgery—what pieces are likely to be found, where they are made and how disposed of. This is yet another reason for meeting others interested in the series, for this kind of information is not readily obtainable. There is too little publicity given to forgeries which generally start their career plausibly, if a little ingenuously, as 'imitations' or 'replicas'. Everyone can help in exposing them, but it must be remembered that they require as careful photography and descriptive recording as genuine coins. There is already room for a manual on and a catalogue of Byzantine forgeries, such as exists in the ancient Greek series for the work of Becker and Christodoulou. Fortunately at the moment it would be shorter.

It may be fitting to end this book with its justification in the words of Cosmas Indicopleustes, an Egyptian merchant of the time of Justinian I who ended his life as a monk:

'...and there is yet another sign of the power which God has accorded to the Romans, to wit, that it is with their coinage that all nations do their trade: it is received everywhere from one end of the earth to the other: it is admired by all men and every kingdom, for no other kingdom hath its like'.

APPENDICES

I. COMMON COIN AND WEIGHT NAMES

ASPER(S)
Greek: Τὸ ἄσπρον; Latin: *asperon*. Literally 'white'. The basic silver coin of the Empire of Trebizond, founded in 1204, weighing originally *c.* 2.9 g.

AUREUS
English plural: aurei. Literally: gold. A gold coin similar to a solidus but struck on the pre-Constantinian standard of 60 to the pound weight.

CARAT(S)
Latin: *siliqua(e)*; Greek: Τὸ κεράτιον(ια). A measure of weight in the Mediterranean area based on the carob seed of which 1728 went to the Roman pound *i.e.* 0.189 g. From this to a measure of purity in metals: a solidus was 24 carats in weight (4.5 g.) and a coin could be, like the hyperpers of the Comneni, 24 carats in weight but only 21 carats fine (*i.e.* 3 carats weight of alloy).

DUCAT(S) or ZECCHINO
A gold coin of Venice introduced in 1284 and weighing 3.59 g. Its name derived from the Latin word ducatus (= duchy) in the legend.

FOLLIS
Greek: ὁ φόλλις. The English plural generally used is folles but sometimes the more accurate folleis is found. A basic copper coin of 40 (Greek numeral *M*) nummia.

GROSSO
English plural: grossi. Venetian silver coin first issued in 1192 and weighing *c.* 2.2 g. Commonly called a 'matapan'. Much copied in standard of metal, weight and types by Mediterranean rulers.

HEXAGRAM(S)
Greek: ἡ ἑξάγραμμα. A silver coin weighing six scruples issued first in the reign of Heraclius, in value 1/12 of a solidus. Not issued by the Isaurian dynasty or later.

HISTAMENON
Greek: Τὸ νόμισμα ἱστάμενον. The English plural used is either histamena or stamena. Literally 'standard' as against the substandard tetarteron from the time of Nicephorus II onwards. The histamenon took the place of the solidus as the standard gold coin in the reign of Nicephorus II

and remained so until the reforms of Alexius I. It soon became larger and thinner (' spread fabric ') and then scyphate.

HYPERPER(S)
Greek: Τὸ νόμισμα ὑπέρπυρον. The English plural can be hyperpera following the Greek form. This was the standard gold coin of Alexius I's reform in 1092 at 21 carats fine, taking the place of the histamenon and earlier solidus.

LIGHTWEIGHT SOLIDUS
(Plural: *solidi*.) A series of gold coins issued in the reigns from Justinian I to Constantine IV, lighter than standard by 4, 2 or 1 carat and usually clearly marked as such *e.g. OBXX* standard of 20 carats (or 4 carats light).

LITRA
Latin: *libra*; Greek: λίτρα. A pound weight composed of 12 ounces, each of 24 scruples, and equal to 327.45 g. Constantine the Great's standard was 72 solidi to be struck from a pound of gold, each *c.* 4.5 g.

MILIARESION
Greek: Τὸ μιλλιαρήσιον. English plural: miliaresia. The basic silver coin varying in number to the gold nomisma in accord with the current gold/silver ratio: under Justinian I, 12 to the solidus or nomisma. The name possibly comes from 1000 silver pieces to a pound of gold in the third century. As a coin it disappears in the eleventh century but remains as money of account.

NUMMUS
Greek: Τὸ νουμμίον (νουμμία) = little. In English either nummion (nummia) or nummus (nummi). A small copper piece, 1/40th part of a follis.

OUNCE
Latin: *uncia*; Greek: ἡ γουγκία (or οὐγκία). The twelfth part of a litra or 27.28 g. and itself divided into 24 scruples.

SCRUPLE(S)
Latin: *scripulum*; Greek: ἡ γράμμα. A weight of which 24 went to an ounce *e.g.* a weight of 1/2 ounce would be marked *IB* = 12 and a hexagram means 6 scruples weight or 1/4 ounce. 1 scruple = 6 carats = 1.135 g.

SCYPHATE(S)
Greek: τραχύ. The word means ' cup-shaped ' and the Greek word ' rough '. See under *Trachy*.

SEMISSIS
Greek: Τὸ σημίσσιον. English plural: semisses. Gold coin half a solidus in weight and value.

SILIQUA(E)
Greek: Τὸ κεράτιον. A weight of 1/24 of a solidus—see under *Carat* and *Scruple*. Used of small silver coins, especially as issued at Ravenna and Carthage.

SOLIDUS
Greek: Τὸ νόμισμα. English plural: solidi. Basic gold coin of 23–24 carats fine and struck from the time of Constantine the Great at 72 to the pound of gold: weight therefore 24 carats or *c.* 4.5 g.

TETARTERON

Greek: *Τὸ νόμισμα τεταρτηρόν*. English plural: tetartera. New gold coin introduced *c.* 963, lighter in weight by a quarter of a tremissis or 2 carats weight. After the reform by Alexius I it became a small change copper coin.

TRACHY

Greek: *Τὸ νόμισμα τραχύ*. English plural: trachea. The word means 'rough' and it is used for 'scyphate' as it has been customary to call coins of this 'cupped' shape. Generally associated with stamena but to quote Hendy, 'it means quite simply "scyphate" in opposition to the smooth flat fabric of the tetarteron', *i.e.* by itself not a coin.

TRACHY ASPRON

Greek: *Τὸ τραχύ ἄσπρον, i.e.* the white scyphate piece. This can be either the electrum trachy (1/3 of an hyperper) or the billon trachy (1/48 of an hyperper and later less) according to context, as both were 'white' at the time of issue, the billon piece being blanched in manufacture and seldom appearing white now. Both coins were introduced by Alexius I in 1092.

TREMISSIS

Greek: *Τὸ τριμίσσιον*. English plural: tremisses. Gold coin of one third the weight and value of a solidus.

II. ROBES AND REGALIA

AKAKIA (ἀκακία), ANEXIKAKIA (ἀνεξικακία).
A bag of purple silk (βλαττίον) tied in the centre with a white handkerchief (μανδήλιον) and containing dust as a symbol of mortality. It looks on coins very like a parchment roll and is sometimes referred to as such (volumen). It is not always easy to distinguish it from the less stiff mappa and the change from mappa to akakia comes at the end of the seventh century after the termination of the consulate.

CHI-RHO SYMBOL
The first two letters in Greek of Χριστός (the Anointed One), formed into the monogram ☧ which Constantine saw in his dream and made part of the labarum. The monogram is, however, known in pre-Christian times. Sometimes referred to as a ' chrismon ' or ' christogram '.

CHLAMYS (χλαμύς).
A long purple cloak, the assumption of which was a key part of the imperial coronation ceremony: generally fastened on the wearer's right shoulder with a fibula and adorned with tablia. It was a civil garment symbolizing the emperor's political authority to rule the world in the place of Jesus and to be worshipped. When the emperor blessed the people, he did so, according to Constantine VII, with the edge of his chlamys not, as one might have expected, with his hand.

COLOBION (κολόβιον).
A sleeveless outer tunic.

DIADEM (διάδημα).
A piece of material, pearl-edged with a central jewel and others disposed around it, tied at the back of the head: the ties are often shown fluttering or hanging down behind the head.

DIVITISION (διβητήσιον).
A white or purple ankle length and wide-sleeved robe generally to be seen under the chlamys, especially at the wrists. Much the same as the skaramangion (σκαραμάγγιον) which was a military version slit at the bottom to make riding easy, and used in more diverse colours.

FIBULA (φίβουλα, φίβλα).
A brooch for fastening the paludamentum

or chlamys on the wearer's right shoulder: generally a roundel with three ornamented pendents.

HIMATION *(ἱμάτιον)*.
An outer garment, or cloak.

LABARUM *(λάβαρον)*.
Originally a Roman military standard to which Constantine added the Chi-Rho symbol, as seen by him before the battle of the Milvian Bridge. This was also associated with the words seen by Constantine 'Conquer, by this sign' *(ἐν τούτῳ νίκα)* as on the early folles of Constans II. Usually it is on a long shaft but sometimes it forms the head of a sceptre.

LOROS *(λῶρος)*.
A consular robe originally called a toga picta or trabea triumphalis from its coloured edge. Eventually it was narrowed down to a long scarf richly embroidered on both sides (*i.e.* only the edge remained). It symbolized the winding sheet of Jesus and, in its brilliant decoration, his resurrection. From being consular it became associated with the emperor's religious authority. While still a scarf it can be traced from ankle level in front of the body, up to the wearer's right shoulder, over it and under his right arm; then diagonally across the front of the body and over the left shoulder: next diagonally across the back and under the right arm at waist level: then across the waist to the left and loosely draped over left forearm: see Fig. 9 which shows the garment in an early stage. Illustration 450 shows the simplified loros which appears first in the ninth century and became standard in the late tenth. This was a broad embroidered strip going up the front of the body, going over both shoulders (presumably with an aperture for the head), then brought across the back and under the wearer's right arm, across the waist and over the left arm.

Fig. 9. *Early loros and mappa.*

MANIAKION *(μανιάκιον)*.
A collar and shoulder piece used with the later 'simplified loros'. This, on coins, can be mistaken for the embroidered border of the chlamys.

MAPHORION *(μαφόριον)*.
A long veil used as a hood.

MAPPA (μάππα).

Fig. 9 The linen handkerchief dropped by a consul to signify the beginning of the games. Difficult to distinguish from the later akakia except in being less stiff and straight-sided. The handkerchief binding the akakia in the middle may be a survival of the consular mappa.

ORB or GLOBUS CRUCIGER (σφαῖρα).

Originally an orb or globus alone, which represented the world. The cross was added to the orb held by Constantinopolis on solidi of Theodosius II. Justinian I was the first emperor to be shown holding it. Symbolic of the emperor's authority over the whole world as the representative of Jesus who held sway over it or would eventually do so. Grierson, surveying the evidence, thinks it was not a piece of regalia but merely symbolic.

PALUDAMENTUM (παλυδαμέντον).

A plain, long, purple coloured military cloak which the emperor normally wears prior to the reign of Heraclius who adopted the civil chlamys. Generally worn over a cuirass as is obvious when Maurice introduced the type showing the paludamentum thrown back over his left shoulder. Fastened on the wearer's right by a fibula.

PATRIARCHAL CROSS

A normal western or 'Latin' cross + with a shorter transverse limb added above the existing one ‡.

PENDILIA, PREPENDOVLIA (πρεπενδούλια).

The invented shortened form is generally used and sometimes the term kataseista (κατασεωστά). These 'hanging pieces', falling over the ears could be attached to the diadem or crown differentiating it clearly from the helmet as, for instance, under Justinian I. They fell out of use under Heraclius for some 300 years, except for empresses.

PTERYGES (πτερύγες).

Literally, feathers; part of the Roman military equipment, being strips of leather with metal plates attached to give protection (but also free movement) to shoulders and thighs. Short strips often appear at the right shoulder under the paludamentum: those over the thighs were much longer and can be seen on folles of Heraclius.

SACCOS (σάκκος).

A later name for the divitision used in fourteenth and fifteenth centuries.

SAGION (σαγίον).

A short type of cloak associated usually with military uniform, seen on coins of the twelfth century onwards. Fastened centrally under the chin by a fibula, it is often shown thrown back over both shoulders.

SCEPTRE

An eagle-headed sceptre (scipio) was part of the consular regalia. Later a cross took the place of the eagle as can be seen under Phocas. Sceptres later still tend to be either cruciform or labarum-headed, but occasionally have simply jewels at the top end of the shaft.

STEMMA (στέμμα).

A crown formed of a metal circlet with a

cloth covering within the framework and forming, with the chlamys, a key part of the coronation regalia. The kamelaukion (καμελαύκιον) was similar but with semi-circular ribs from front to back and from right side to left, making the whole stand higher. The term stemma seems to cover both types but the crowns of Byzantine workmanship still existing all have the additional ribs.

STOLE *(στολή)*.
A long upper garment.

TABLION *(ταβλίον)*.
Plural: tablia. A square of richly embroidered material attached to the two edges of the chlamys about chest to waist high, when it is closed. Normally only one is seen but both are clear on the mosaic at S. Vitale, Ravenna which shows Justinian I entering his church: this also shows tablia of other colours worn by courtiers. 449

TOUFA *(τοῦφα)*.
A ceremonial and triumphal crown with peacocks-feather crest as seen clearly on folles of Theophilus and, best of all, on a silk at Bamberg Cathedral Treasury where a city personified presents a toufa to an emperor. Sometimes difficult to distinguish from a helmet, as on Justinian I's 36-solidi medallion.

TUNIC *(χιτών, tunica)*.
A close-fitting under garment.

III.   SOME GREEK NUMERALS, LETTERS AND WORDS

Numerals	English Equivalent	Greek name	English phonetic rendering
1) A, *A*, Λ	1	εἱς	(h)ees
B, *B*	2	δύο	theeo
Γ	3	τρεῖς	trees
Δ	4	τέσσαρες	tessares
Є, E	5	πέντε	pende
S, ϛ	6	ἔξι	(h)exi
Z, Z	7	ἑπτά	(h)epta
H	8	ὀκτώ	okto
Θ	9	ἐννέα	enneha
I	10	δέκα	theka
IA	11	ἔνδεκα	(h)entheka
IB	12	δώδεκα	thotheka
K	20	εἴκοσι	eekosi
Λ	30	τριάκοντα	triakonda
M, m	40	τεσσαράκοντα	tessarakonda
N	50	πεντήκοντα	pendeekonda
P	100	ἔκατον	(h)ekaton
C, Σ	200	διακόσιοι	theeakosiee

2) Letters: Γ = G   P = R

Δ = D   C, S = S : C (or CЄ) is used for καὶ (and) and instead of K

H = Long E   Ч = U or V, also used for numeral ϛ

Θ = TH   Φ = PH, sometimes F

Λ = L   Ω = Long O, sometimes ω

Ƶ = X   Ȣ = OU

Π = P

Several letters are found combined in ligatures as *MP* = MP or *MNH* = MNH.

3) ΘΚΕ (or CVRIE) ΡΟΗΘΕΙ ΤΩ CΩ ΔΟΥΛΩ: Θεοτόκε (or Κύριε) βοήθει τῷ σῷ δούλῳ = 'May the Mother of God (or the Lord God) help your servant'. Note βοήθει spelt with R or B.

ΔΕCΠΟΤΗC, ΔΕC, ΔΕCΠ: δεσπότης = 'Lord, Emperor'. Feminine ΔΕCΠΟΙΝΑ as in ΔΕCΠΟΙΝΑ CΩΖΟΙC ΕΥCΕΒΗ ΜΟΝΟΜΑΧΟΝ = 'May Our Lady save the pious Monomach'.

ĪC X̄C NIKA: Ιησοῦς Χριστός νικᾷ = 'May Jesus Christ conquer'. Also ΘΕΟFILE AVGOVSTE SV NICAS = 'Theophilus Augustus may you conquer'.

MP ΘV: μήτηρ Θεοῦ = 'Mother of God'.

C R: Σταυρὲ βοήθει = 'May the Cross help'. Also C Φ (φύλαττε) = 'May the Cross guard'.

ΕΝ ΘΕΩ ЬASILEVS ΡΩΜΑΙΩΝ: ἐν θεῶ βασιλεύς Ρωμάιων (or ΘV XAPITI: Θεοῦ χάριτη) = 'By the grace of God Emperor of the Romans'.

Emperors are described as ΕΥCΕΒΗC ('pious'), ΠΙCΤΟC ('faithful believer'), ΠΟΡΦV-ΡΟΓΕΝΝΗΤΟS ('born in the purple'), ΔЧLOS XPISTЧ ('the servant of Christ'), AVTOCRAT' (αὐτοκράτωρ = 'Roman Imperator' which itself appears as IMΠΕRAT').

ЬASILEЧ ЬASILE: βασιλεύς βασιλέων = 'King of those who rule'. Sometimes in latin REX REGNANTIUM.

ΕΝ ΤΟVΤΩ NICAT: ἐν τούτῳ νικᾶτε (plural) and ΕΝ ΤЧΤΟ NIKA (νικᾷ singular) = 'By this sign [—the Christogram—] may you conquer'.

⊙ = ὁ ἅγιος ('the Saint') sometimes extended Ο ΑΓΙΟC. Also Ὁ ΑΡ Χ = 'The Archangel'.

ΑΝΑΝΕΟS (also ΑΝΑΝΕ and ΑΝΑ): ἀνανέωσις = 'Renewal, renovation'.

IV. BYZANTINE EMPERORS AND DYNASTIES

Dynasty of Constantine

324–37   Constantine I
337–61   Constantius II
361–3   Julian
363–4 Jovian
364–78 Valens

Dynasty of Theodosius

379–95   Theodosius I
395–408   Arcadius
408–50   Theodosius II
450–7   Marcian

Dynasty of Leo the Great

457–74   Leo I
474   Leo II
474–5   Zeno
475–6   Basiliscus
476–91   Zeno (again)
491–518 Anastasius I

Dynasty of Justin

518–27   Justin I
527–65   Justinian I
565–78   Justin II
578–82   Tiberius II Constantine
582–602   Maurice (Tiberius)
602–10   Phocas

Dynasty of Heraclius

610–41   Heraclius
641   (Jan.–?April) Heraclius Constantine (III)
641   (?April–?Dec.) Heraclonas (Constantine)
641–68   Constans II
668–85   Constantine IV
685–95   Justinian II
695–8   Leontius
698–705 Tiberius III
705–11   Justinian II (again)
706–11   Tiberius IV
711–13   Philippicus (Bardanes)
713–15   Anastasius II (Artemius)
715–17   Theodosius III

Dynasty of Leo the ' Isaurian '

717–41   Leo III
741–75   Constantine V
775–80   Leo IV
780–97   Constantine VI
797–802   Eirene
802–11   Nicephorus I
811   Stauracius
811–13   Michael I (Rangabe)
813–20   Leo V (the Armenian)

Dynasty of the Amorians

820–9	Michael II
829–42	Theophilus
842–67	Michael III

Dynasty of the Macedonians

867–86	Basil I
886–912	Leo VI
912–13	Alexander
913–59	Constantine VII
920–44	Romanus I (Lecapenus)
959–63	Romanus II
963–69	Nicephorus II (Phocas)
969–76	John I (Zimisces)
976–1025	Basil II
1025–8	Constantine VIII
1028–50	Zoe with:
1028–34	Romanus III (1)
1034–41	Michael IV (2)
1041–2	Michael V (adopted)
1042	(April to June) Theodora (her sister)
1042–55	Constantine IX Monomachus (3)
1055–6	Theodora alone
1056–7	Michael VI
1057–9	Isaac I (Comnenus)
1059–67	Constantine X (Dukas)
1067–71	Romanus IV (Diogenes)
1071–8	Michael VII (Dukas)
1078–81	Nicephorus III (Botaneiates)

Dynasty of the Comneni

1081–1118	Alexius I
1118–43	John II
1143–80	Manuel I
1180–3	Alexius II
1183–5	Andronicus I

Dynasty of the Angeli

1185–95	Isaac II
1195–1203	Alexius III
1203–4	Isaac II and Alexius IV
1204	Alexius V (Murtzuphlus)
1204–61	The Latin Emperors

Emperors of Nicaea

1208–22	Theodore I (Lascaris)
1222–54	John III (Dukas Vatatses)
1254–8	Theodore II (Lascaris)
1258–61	John IV (Lascaris)
1259–61	Michael VIII (Palaeologus)

Dynasty of the Palaeologi

(1259)–82	Michael VIII
1282–1328	Andronicus II with Michael IX 1295–1320
1328–41	Andronicus III
1341–91	John V
1347–54	John VI (Cantacusenus)
1376–9	Andronicus IV (Palaeologus)
1390	John VII (Palaeologus)
1391–1425	Manuel II
1425–48	John VIII
1448–53	Constantine XI

INDEX

The text of this book and the four-colour offset illustrations were printed by the Imprimeries Réunies S.A., Lausanne.—The heliogravure reproductions were executed by Roto-Sadag S.A., Geneva.—Photolithos by Atesa, Geneva.—The binding is by Clerc & Cie S. A., Lausanne.—Layout and design by André Rosselet.—Editorial: Suzanne Meister.

Printed in Switzerland